"A compelling, well-researched exploration of *cholent*, a huge fan favorite! Haber is both knowledgeable and entertaining as he uses the Shabbat stew to follow Jewish migrations throughout the world."

**Jamie Geller**: Best-selling author of *Quick & Kosher*, *Joy of Kosher*, and *Jewlish by Jamie*

"*Cholent* isn't just a dish—it's a story, a memory, a passport, and somehow also your entire family arguing in one pot. This book takes what we all thought we knew about *cholent* and blows it wide open, tracing every slow-simmered bite across continents, cultures, and centuries. It's smart, soulful, and deeply delicious—exactly what Jewish food writing should be. You'll never look at your Shabbos pot the same way again."

**Chanie Apfelbaum**: Creator of "Busy in Brooklyn," author of *Millennial Kosher* and *Totally Kosher*

"In this rich and flavorful journey, Joel Haber uncovers the remarkable history of *cholent*, the Sabbath stew, that has been quietly bubbling through Jewish history for centuries. With the warmth of a seasoned storyteller and the curiosity of a culinary detective, Haber explores the traditions, migrations, and innovations that shaped this beloved dish.

"Part history, part cookbook, and entirely delicious, this book reveals why *cholent* is far more than a stew, it's a story."

**Susie Fishbein**: Best-selling author of the *Kosher by Design* series

"At ten years old I snuck out of Hebrew school to watch Meyer, a fat old one-toothed cook at the synagogue, make *cholent*. Little did I realize the history of Jewish cuisine was bubbling away in that pot. This enthralling account of *cholent* and its many relatives around the world is as deep, rich, and satisfying as the dish itself. Zey gezunt!"

**Ken Albala**: Tully Knoles Professor of History, University of the Pacific

"Joel Haber's *Cholent: The Most Jewish Food on Earth* takes you on a culinary and historical adventure like no other. Using religious and cultural analysis, Joel shows how the Shabbat stew blends many aspects of Jewish and food history. After Shabbat laws shaped the dish, it continually adapted to encompass local ingredients and societal tastes. Truly the *most* Jewish food there is!"

**Naomi Nachman**: Author of *Perfect for Pesach* and *Perfect Flavors*

"*Cholent: The Most Jewish Food On Earth* by Joel Haber is a fascinating and deeply researched look at the Sabbath stew that has been at the heart of Jewish life since antiquity, tracing its ingenious overnight cooking method developed so Jews could enjoy a hot meal without cooking on Shabbat. Blending history with recipes, Haber shows how the ingredients of *cholent* evolved across the Jewish diaspora—from adding whole eggs in Spain to cardamom in India and paprika in Hungary—revealing how a single pot of stew tells the story of a people spread across the world."

**Jennifer Abadi**: Author of *A Fistful of Lentils* and *Too Good To Passover*

"Over millennia of exile and migration, Jews have made homes in just about every corner of the globe. Wherever they landed, they carried their *cholent* pots with them. In his new book, *Cholent: The Most Jewish Food on Earth*, Joel Haber leads us on a whirlwind journey in search of *cholent*'s many incarnations. Along the way, this long-cooking stew emerges as an emblem of both Jewish resilience and resourcefulness. Complete with recipes, Haber's book will have you reaching for your own *cholent* pot."

**Jane Ziegelman**: Author of *Once There Was a Town: The Memory Books of a Lost Jewish World* and *97 Orchard: An Edible History of Five Immigrant Families in One New York Tenement*

"*Cholent* is Jewish food history at its finest, a delicious journey into how Shabbat cookery has shaped our collective experiences in the diaspora. Haber seamlessly stews Jewish tradition, law, history and recipes into one fabulous read. A rich, culinary journey of Shabbat through the ages and into the future."

**Naomi Ross**: Author of *The Giving Table* and culinary instructor

"This is a fascinating book. Joel Haber has taken on the most Jewish of Jewish foods, *cholent*, and traced the story of its dispersion through the different countries of the diaspora. This is a digestible history, and there are traditional recipes as well, both well-known and exotic. I can't wait to try them."

**Susan Weingarten**: Food historian and author of *Haroset: A Taste of Jewish History*

# CHOLENT

## THE MOST JEWISH FOOD ON EARTH

Joel Haber

Foreword by
Adeena Sussman

Green Bean Books

***For Mom***
Who Inspired My Love of Food

***For Dad***
Who Inspired Much of My Personality

*and*

***For Gil Marks***
Who Inspired My Passion for Food History

*Cholent: The Most Jewish Food on Earth*

First published in 2026 by
Green Bean Books,
c/o Pen & Sword Books Ltd,
George House, Units 12 & 13
Beevor Street, Off Pontefract Road,
Barnsley, S. Yorkshire S71 1HN

www.greenbeanbooks.com
michael@greenhillbooks.com

ISBN: 978-1-80500-241-3



The Publisher's authorised representative in the EU
for product safety is Authorised Rep Compliance Ltd.,
Ground Floor, 71 Lower Baggot Street, Dublin D02 P593, Ireland.
www.arccompliance.com

CIP data records for this title are available from the British Library

Printed and bound in the UK by
CPI Group (UK) Ltd, Croydon, CR0 4YY

Typeset in 11/13.5 pt Minion Pro and 9.5/12.5 Myriad Pro

# Contents



## Recipe List

# Illustrations

# Acknowledgements

You wouldn't be able to engage with this book if not for these awesome people.

Obviously most important of all, thanks to Mom and Dad for your undying support, love, and enthusiasm. You have helped in more ways than I can possibly enumerate, and contributed so much to turning me into who I am today. Further, thanks to my entire extended family for your constant curiosity, assistance, and love.

Thanks as well:

. . . to Gil Marks, of blessed memory, who was such an inspiration to me. He was always ready to answer questions I had, and was the first person I ever met who "did food" professionally, in this way.

. . . to Gila Fine, my wonderful accountability partner, for your incredible friendship, invaluable advice, and for reading this entire book in process. I still believe it was my idea to check in with each other, but I'll let you have it, if you insist!

. . . to David Brummer, who also read nearly the entire manuscript, and gave me wonderfully helpful feedback.

. . . to Adeena Sussman, for including me in *Shabbat*, and for writing this book's Foreword. You unfailingly champion so many others around you, showing how boundless your kindness is.

. . . to Yael Unterman, who unwittingly started me on this food studies journey.

. . . to Shannon Sarna, for giving me my first real food writing job, freelancing for *The Nosher*.

. . . to Gil Troy and Seth Frantzman who kindly sent me copies of their book proposals, so I could figure out how to write mine.

. . . to my beta readers, Judy Kaplan and Marcia Schoppik, and to the two anonymous peer reviewers my publisher arranged. All of your comments improved this work.

... to the many people who read and provided expert feedback on relevant sections: Jennifer Abadi, Lisa Arking, Rina Barbut, Sarah Benor, Benedetta Guetta, Barbara Kirshenblatt-Gimblett, Andras Koerner, Leon Mizan, Nawal Nasrallah, Aylin Tan, Jeffrey Veidlinger, Susan Weingarten, Anya Zhuravel Segal, Jane Ziegelman, and Yehuda DovBer Zirkind. And to the countless others who quickly responded to a brief question here, an email there, and especially those who kindly gave me even more of their time in a longer interview.

... to my awesome team of recipe testers: Marsha Aaron, Margaret Eugenio, Sylvia Fallas, Penny Joel, Sharon Lebewohl, Judith Levy, Ilana Newman Hernandez, Aliza Rimmon, Bryna Runeman, Jessica Sacks, Shoshana Sturm, Faygle Train, Ethan Wasserman, Jill Wheatley, Daniel Witzling, Debby Yeger, and Hillary Zana. Also, to the many who shared their families' Shabbat stew recipes from around the world.

From Green Bean Books, thanks to my wonderful publisher Michael Leventhal. It's so nice to have a great working relationship and friendship in one. I look forward to many more good times together. Thanks to Donald Sommerville, a true Swiss Army Knife of an editor-plus. We butted heads at times, but I know that your hard and passionate work in both editing and design made this a book I'm extremely proud of. Thanks as well to Orit Magia, who created the whimsical and colorful cover that I dreamed this book would have. I love it! And to everyone on the marketing and sales teams, I am forever in your debt.

Thanks to the National Library of Israel, an incredible resource, and a truly pleasant space to research and write. Thanks as well to Asif, in Tel Aviv, whose free culinary library is small but surprisingly huge, and extremely comprehensive.

Finally, thanks to those who have attended my food talks around the world, listened to my podcast, taken my Jerusalem culinary tours in Machane Yehuda Market, or who are now reading this book. I truly appreciate your support and interest, and would welcome your comments and feedback. Everything I do in this field is for you.

*Todah rabah*, and *b'teavon*! Thanks so much, and bon appétit!

# Foreword

*by Adeena Sussman*

I have known Joel Haber for nearly thirty years, and it has been a pleasure to be witness to his professional journey. Long before he became a thoughtful voice exploring Jewish food history, Joel was helping people understand Israel through its culture, landscapes, and flavors, guiding visitors toward the deeper stories embedded in everyday life. Over the years, I've watched that curiosity sharpen into a scholarly devotion to the ways Jewish history can be told through food. And what a joy that the subject is also one of my own enduring culinary obsessions: *cholent*. Humble, adaptable, deeply comforting, and imbued with memory, *cholent* is never just a stew. It is itself a lesson in Jewish resourcefulness and a long-simmering tale of a people and the way its foodways can mirror its history. In fact, there is perhaps no dish that tells the story of Jewish cooking and continuity more completely than this one.

Which is why Joel's book feels so essential at this moment. Joel's proposition (and one that I share) is that *cholent*, *hamin*, *dafina*, *skhina*, *t'bit*, and countless other overnight Sabbath stews are not separate dishes at all, but rather variations of one evolving Jewish culinary idea carried across continents and cultures. Through these pots, he traces the routes of Jewish migration itself, revealing how communities adapted to exile while preserving a shared spiritual and culinary core.

The deceptively simple premise behind these stews has kept Sabbath cooking rooted in continuity: honor Shabbat with a delicious cauldron of hot food while refraining from cooking at all. But from that *halachic* necessity emerged a sophisticated example of Jewish creativity.

Joel offers a culinary history expressed in an edible map of the Jewish Diaspora, exploring how overnight cooking techniques developed and why ingredients diverged regionally—rice and chicken in the Middle East, wheat and lamb across North Africa, barley and beef in Europe.

From ancient Mesopotamian *harisa* to Yemenite, Kurdish, Persian, and Egyptian descendants, Joel uncovers the original stews of the Jewish world and shows how religious movements, migrations, and local tastes shaped them. In Spain's Golden Age, the stew transformed into *adafina* and *hamin*, becoming more elaborate alongside the flourishing Jewish culture around it. Yet the same dish became dangerous during the Inquisition, when *conversos* risked death by cooking it. It's the Shabbat stew as evidence of identity, sometimes for better and sometimes for worse.

Joel follows the stew northward into medieval France and Germany, dismantling myths about *cholent*'s origins in cassoulet, while tracing linguistic and culinary clues connecting Ashkenazi *schalet* to Sephardi roots. From there the pot travels deeper into Central and Eastern Europe, absorbing paprika, potatoes, *kugel*, *kishke*, and *helzel* along the way.

His discussions of communal ovens, Hasidic reverence for Shabbat foods, and the ingenuity of poor cooks reveal how *cholent* became integral to the emotional and spiritual architecture of Jewish communal life.

Then the book circles back through North Africa and Southern Europe, where regional variations illuminate the complexity of Sephardi identity after expulsion. Venturing outward into Soviet Russia, Anglo-Jewish communities, Latin America, Central Asia, India, and beyond, Joel demonstrates how, even when Jewish traditions were suppressed or fragmented, traces of the stew endured. By the time we arrive in America and Israel, these stews mirrored the evolution of modern Jewish life itself.

And perhaps that is why *cholent* feels especially resonant now.

At moments when Jewish life can feel vulnerable or imperiled, traditions like these take on greater meaning. *Cholent* reminds us that Jewish continuity has always depended on ordinary acts performed faithfully and repeatedly. The stew survives because Jews have survived. It has adapted because Jews adapted. *Cholent* must continue to be tracked closely, since it has proven such an accurate mirror for Jewish life.

Yet this book never reduces *cholent* to symbolism alone. Joel understands that the dish also endures because it is deeply, profoundly delicious. Long cooking transforms inexpensive ingredients into richness and complexity. Fat melts into beans and grains; spices take on more depth as they bloom overnight. Textures soften and deepen, creating new harmonies under the lid. And bonus foods tucked into the pot—eggs, *kugel*, *kishke*, and more modern, creative additions—become treasures discovered at the Shabbat table and folded into this time-honored ritual.

In the end, Joel shows us that the Shabbat stew is Jewish history itself. Our understanding of Jewish food—and the Shabbat table—are better for his efforts.

## Introduction

# The Stew with a Thousand Flavors

Can any one food really be called the *most* Jewish?

As I'm sure you can tell by the title of this book, I obviously think so. But what exactly is *cholent*, and why would I consider it the most Jewish food in the world?

For well over a thousand years, Jews around the globe have eaten some version of stew or casserole as their Shabbat ("Sabbath") lunch.* It contains multiple ingredients, usually including some kind of meat and grain at its core. Only rarely throughout history would you have encountered vegetarian versions of this dish, and it would almost never include dairy ingredients, due to the religious prohibition against consuming milk and meat products together.

However, the key element that distinguishes this dish from other stews is its unique cooking method. It is prepared and partially cooked on Friday afternoon, before Shabbat begins, but then is left to continue stewing *all night* at a low heat. Cooking for fifteen or more hours, its ingredients caramelize and break down, flavors blending and unifying, until the final product is ready to be devoured with gusto in the middle of the day on Saturday.†

This "low-and-slow" cooking method changes the stew in a fundamental way; it does not taste the same on Saturday as it would after just two to three hours of cooking. Trust me, I know. I've sampled many a "midnight *cholent*" on Friday evenings, unable to wait for twelve more hours before digging in! Still tasty, but not remotely the same. To be a true iteration of this dish, it *must* be cooked all night. This unique cooking method, applied to a dish explicitly designed for Sabbath, first qualifies it as a Jewish food.

* The Jewish Sabbath begins on Friday evening at sundown, and lasts 25 hours, until after sundown on Saturday night. As Sabbath and Shabbat are just translations of each other, I use the words interchangeably throughout the book.

† The reason for this peculiar cooking process will be explained in Chapter 1.

That being said, *cholent* actually refers specifically to the Eastern European version of this dish, rather than every different version from around the world. How, then, could it be the most Jewish food possible? There are many Jews who never eat *cholent* at all. When I use that name in the title, I intend it in a broader sense, covering all the versions of the dish of which *cholent* is merely the best known example. Throughout the book, I reserve "*cholent*" for that iteration alone, referring to all versions collectively as "the Shabbat stew." (Admittedly, this term is somewhat inaccurate, as not every example can properly be called a "stew." But as a generic collective term, it will have to do.) Using this name as the book's title, I risk highlighting the already dominant Ashkenazi culture, at the expense of the sizable minority of Jews who are not part of that group.* I simply use that name because it is the most recognized. I do not wish to prop up "Ashkenormativity" within the Jewish world. You'll certainly see that my goal is the opposite: to celebrate the diversity of the Jewish people as seen via the food that best embodies Jewish culture and peoplehood.

## A True Jewish Food

So why do I think the Shabbat stew is more Jewish than any other food? To answer that, I first must address what makes a food Jewish to begin with.

Many have explored this question before me. Answers range from foods eaten specifically for rituals or Sabbath/festival meals, to those which Jews elevate culturally to a different status. Some also point out that, frequently, Jewish versions of foods are different from the versions eaten by their non-Jewish neighbors, meaning the dishes are not actually the same at their core. This, too, makes them Jewish.[1]

While all of these would contribute to making a food Jewish, I think we can point to three things that, even with a very strict definition, must place a dish into the category of "Jewish food."† The broadest category are foods that others associate with our people.‡ Tens of foods around the world are called "Jewish style." *Carciofi alla giudia*—Jewish fried artichokes—are among the famous indigenous dishes of Rome. American

* Terms such as Ashkenazi, Sephardi, Mizrachi, and more will be explained as I first come to them in the course of the book. Ashkenazi Jews are those whose ancestors in the Middle Ages lived in the border territory between France and Germany.

† In my podcast, "18 Jewish Foods," I stuck with foods that explicitly met this narrower definition.

‡ My use of "our" and "we" throughout the book in no way speaks to the audience this book is aimed at. I use that pronoun more for subject than object; I am a lifelong, passionate member of the Jewish people, and use the term to highlight my familiarity with my chosen topic.

supermarkets stock "Jewish Rye Bread" or "Kosher Dill Pickles."* And back in the thirteenth century, an Arabic-language cookbook identified six recipes as explicitly "Jewish." If other people recognize Jewish cultural connections to these foods, why would anyone deny them that status?

Second are those foods that, while not Jewish in origin, were modified by Jews. They feature distinctive ingredients or cooking styles, often due to *kashrut* (the rules of kosher). The Jews of Cochin, India, for example, avoid mixing milk and meat by replacing dairy with coconut milk in meat curries.[2] Italian Jews, make prosciutto out of goose rather than pork.[3] These Jewish foods are distinct from their non-Jewish equivalents, in the same way that American and Mexican burritos are different dishes.

The strictest classification, however, are foods which are unique to Jews. Whether or not a Jew first invented it, if we are the only ones who eat something, it is indubitably Jewish.† And make no mistake, such foods definitely exist. The Shabbat stew, in fact, meets just such a definition. The dish's defining overnight cooking method was a uniquely Jewish innovation. Jews have used this cooking technique since antiquity, and (as I'll explain in the next chapter) for reasons that stem from *halacha* (Jewish religious law). While overnight-cooked dishes exist in other cuisines, most are for the convenience of having a ready-to-eat meal. Furthermore, the Shabbat stew is also consumed almost exclusively by Jews. It must, therefore, be a Jewish food.

But what makes it the *ultimate* Jewish food? Comparing it to matzah—another uniquely Jewish food—explains this. Matzah (the unleavened Passover "bread" cracker) grows straight out of our national heritage and religious texts. The Torah describes Jews eating matzah when they left Egypt, making it perhaps the first food directly identified with our people. Our scriptures further command us to eat matzah every year on Passover to commemorate the Exodus. So in that sense, it is even more religiously significant to us than is the Shabbat stew. Furthermore, it is also rare to find non-Jews eating matzah, because (at least in my opinion) . . . matzah doesn't really taste very good. If a non-Jew eats matzah by choice, and enjoys it, I think that *goy*'s a little bit *meshugge*!‡ So you might think that matzah should win as the "most Jewish" food.

* The word "kosher" here associates it with Judaism. It isn't about permissibility under Jewish dietary laws. Pretty much all pickles are kosher.

† A Jew inventing a food isn't enough to make it "Jewish." If a Jew had invented the ham and cheese sandwich, could we really call it a Jewish food?

‡ Taking this a step further, if matzah is genuinely Jewish, so are all foods made from it: *matzah brei*, *mina*, *chremslach*, and of course matzah balls.

Where the Shabbat stew beats out matzah, however, is in *when* it is eaten. Jews eat matzah primarily for one week a year, but many tuck into the Shabbat stew *every* Saturday. Furthermore, the Shabbat stew gains significant prominence since different Jews eat different versions around the world, but all for the same reasons. Matzah, on the other hand, is more or less the same for all Jews, so it sinks further into the background of our culinary culture.*

However, what most singles the Shabbat stew out for "most Jewish" status is what I will show over the rest of this book. The Jewish people are remarkable. We are the most globalized nation on Earth, having literally spread all over the world. I was curious, so I once did a simple Google search combining the word "Jewish" with each of the world's countries. Well over 90 percent returned results, and those that did not (and which might have if I'd dug deeper), were all tiny Pacific island nations, or countries in Africa where Jews existed in the surrounding area at some point. So, we have truly spread everywhere over our thousands of years of history.

The Shabbat stew, in some form or another, has been eaten by almost every Jewish community, and has truly embodied the complex culture of the Jewish people. As diverse as those worldwide Jewish communities are, so is the Shabbat stew. Matzah may be more Jewish on a religious level, but the Shabbat stew is even more *culturally* connected to the Jewish people (while still relating to our religious values). You can't get much more Jewish than that.

## One Dish, Many Variations

I've spoken of the many different Shabbat stews as variations on a single dish, rather than separate foods. Is this really the case?

In 1949, American literature professor Joseph Campbell published *The Hero with a Thousand Faces*. In it he looked at world mythology and noticed the same "hero's journey" story getting told and retold, with slight variations by place and time. He referred to this story as a "monomyth."

Similarly, I see the many Shabbat stews as a "monodish." Despite the variations in their ingredients and names, they are actually one and the same. They are "The Stew with a Thousand Flavors."

* There are slight variations between different communities, but these pale in comparison to the vastly different Shabbat stew versions.

Historically, as Jews moved from place to place, this modest lunch traveled with us. In each place that we settled, the stew took on new characteristics, changing its ingredients to match what was available or popular locally. I will use the alterations in this stew as a tool, tracing through them the routes of Jewish wanderings around the Diaspora. Certainly, not *every* version we'll encounter descends in this way from the earliest example of the dish. This is particularly true in modern times. Some, for example, apply the overnight cooking method to broadly popular foods. So, while I will discuss those other ones when we encounter them throughout the stew's chronology, the ever-changing nature of this dish guides the book's structure. The vast majority indeed sit on the family tree that I'll sketch here.

By way of illustration, let's look at three Shabbat stew variants. In Eastern Europe, *cholent* is the common name for the dish; the classic Polish recipe includes beef, barley, kidney beans, onions, and potatoes. A popular Moroccan version of the stew, called *dafina*, features lamb, wheat, sweet potatoes, chickpeas, dates, and whole eggs (cooked in their shells). Moving to Iraq, we encounter *t'bit*, which fills a whole chicken with scented rice, then buries it in a pot of more rice, creating two flavors of the grain.

Three dishes, from entirely different parts of the world, with unique ingredients and names. And yet, I'd argue that those distinctions are purely superficial, with more tying these stews together than differentiating them.

First and foremost, they all share the most important element: they are all heated slowly from Friday afternoon, through the entire night until Shabbat day.

Second, though their ingredients differ, they aren't as disparate as they seem. They slide into category "slots." All three feature a grain (barley, wheat, or rice), a type of meat (beef, lamb, or chicken) and usually some vegetables. All are nutritionally balanced one-pot meals.

Even their names—their most distinctive aspect—end up being less disparate than they seem at first glance. While not all the stew names stem from an original one (and are thus not all versions of a single name), they can largely be classified into a few core meanings (though in different languages). I'll highlight those categories as I come to them.

In addition to the major changes in each version of the stew, which help us follow Jewish migrations, some lesser aspects remain significant. For starters, a fourth ingredient "slot" in most stews helps imbue each version with its locale's flavors. Shabbat stews from Mexico might feature tamarind, chili powder and paprika; those from Afghanistan can include quince and cinnamon; and southern Indian versions often utilize spices such as ginger, cardamom and cloves. Without looking at those more minor ingredients, we might not even recognize what makes these stews different.

Another phenomenon I'll explore are foods that are cooked inside the stew but are then pulled out to be eaten separately. Many such "Bonus Foods" (as I title them) exist, and they may be one of the most peculiar elements to the Shabbat stew. I have yet to find any analog foods in other cuisines. Many Bonus Foods have become extremely popular, and are today prepared as stand-alone dishes.

Lastly, the Shabbat stew has had an outsized influence on world cuisine. Despite its simplicity and general lack of recognition by non-Jews, the Shabbat stew has actually impacted dishes in the cultures around it. Throughout the book, when appropriate, I'll discuss some of those items as well.

## A Word on Sources and Terminology

One of the challenges of writing about an ancient dish is the lack of direct evidence about recipes from thousands of years ago. Certainly, as I explored more modern times, there was more concrete information, but with the lack of serious attention paid to food until just the past few decades, even that information remained fragmentary. It is therefore near impossible to declare anything *with certainty* about the ancient Shabbat stew. Thus, much of this study must be seen as speculative. Of course, all my suppositions are based on as much supporting evidence as possible. I've essentially tried to "connect the dots" between numerous pieces of adjacent information.

Those dots that I connect may be found in many areas. I explored surveys of regional cuisines, which helped identify what ingredients were available or popular in a given time and place. Furthermore, non-Jewish recipes exist from ancient and medieval times, which further illuminate the subject. Works of literature and history, and archaeological findings served as valuable secondary sources. Finally, while modern recipes are likely not identical to older versions, modern Jewish Shabbat stews can help us make educated guesses about ancestral ones. Then, after making my conclusions, I consulted with experts on specific regional cuisines to ensure I made no glaring errors, and clarified or corrected any inaccuracies.

Language can also be a challenge in a work of this nature. When I'm covering a few thousand years of history, any specific place's name may have changed tens of times over that period. To make things easy to follow, I use contemporary place names to describe any entity that filled the area the country covers today. Any historic names I use for specific time periods in a region (such as al-Andalus or USSR) are clarified within the text.

Finally, I use a number of non-English words (such as food names). In addition to explaining them as needed, some of them have to be transliterated into the English alphabet. Rather than using the academic notation used by linguists, I have aimed for popular readability. If a specific spelling is recognized, I opt for that. Otherwise, I aimed for a spelling that would be most easily understood.

## A Note on the Recipes

Although this is a book of food writing, a book on Shabbat stews that failed to tell you how they're made would probably disappoint many of you! So throughout the book you'll find recipes for Shabbat stews relevant to each chapter. To develop most of them, I combined recipes found in cookbooks from around the globe with information I garnered from discussions I had with people from different Jewish communities. Some others (which I tested more carefully) were based on guesses about what *likely* might have been eaten in a specific time and place. I mention these in the recipe header notes. Finally, some of the later ones are my own inventions, rather than "traditional" recipes. All recipes have been tested by me, and by a team of volunteer testers. I hope that in addition to diversifying your own Shabbat lunch menus, these recipes will also help you understand the historical changes in the stew, adding an extra layer to this study.

The cooking method for almost all of the recipes in this book is the same; it is just the ingredients that differ. I am therefore including some basic information up front here that should be applied to all. This seemed preferable to stating the same instructions repeatedly.

### *The "Standard Cooking Methods"*

Any good Shabbat stew is cooked for a very long time at a warm, but *not-too-hot* temperature. There are, however, many ways to accomplish this "low-and-slow" cooking technique, with three most prevalent today. One is to use a slow cooker (commonly referred to by the brand name Crock-Pot). Start with the stew on High for an hour or two, then switch to the Low setting for the rest of the night. (Some slow cookers have an "Auto" function that switches from High to Low after two or three hours.) Alternatively, start the initial cooking in a pot on the stovetop and then transfer the food to the slow cooker set to Low.

The second and third methods both use a regular pot, ideally a heavy one (such as a Dutch oven). Then you can either cook your stew overnight in an oven at around 210°F/100°C or leave it on an electric hotplate.* If your recipe is relatively dry to start, and you are using the hotplate method, you might put a heat diffuser beneath the pot to prevent the bottom from burning.

Whichever of the three methods you use, placing foil between the lid and the pot helps keep in the moisture, preventing the stew from drying out. Fold the foil edges up over the top of the lid, so steam does not drip down the sides of the pot, making a mess.

Most recipes may be prepared in any of these three ways. If one is preferable, I say so in the recipe. But in general, trial and error is a great tool. If you use one method and it isn't great, try a different one the next time!

### *Common Elements*

All recipes in this book are designed for **eight servings**. They can easily be scaled up or down in size for more or fewer people, or different appetites.

These recipes were all tested using kosher meat, which is pre-salted. If you are using non-kosher meat, you may need to add more salt. My tastes run generally towards a lower salt content, so if you generally prefer salty food, add more than I list in each recipe. Shabbat stews, however, do not suffer from only having the salt added at the table, so that may also be an option. The salt I use in all recipes is coarse kitchen salt. No specific brand is necessary, as this is relaxed stew cooking, not delicate pastry baking. Whatever you have will work.

I have omitted traditional recipes that include organ meats. I love offal, but I know that many people today do not. In deference to that, I've decided to stick with recipes that more of you will actually want to make.

All eggs used are "large." Many of the recipes contain eggs that are cooked, still in their shells, inside of the stew pot. You obviously can't eat them that way! Before serving the stew, remove them (*carefully* due to their temperature) using a large spoon or tongs. Run them under cold water until they are cool enough to handle. Then peel the eggs, which

* In Israel, this is called a *plata*. It is important, if using one, to make sure it is warm enough that the food will not spoil overnight.

will have turned brown inside (don't worry, this is not only normal, but very good). They can then be served in a separate bowl or replaced in the stew as it is served at table.

When oil is called for (without specifications on type), the quantities are not enough that a specific type of oil changes the flavor. I often use olive oil, simply because it is my standard go-to for all purposes. But you may certainly use others, such as canola, palm, or corn. When olive oil is preferred, I say so.

This may be controversial for some, but in my opinion there is nothing wrong with using canned beans in a Shabbat stew. I recognize that dried are better than canned for a dish in which beans are the focal point. But in Shabbat stews, beans are just a supporting character, and I honestly taste no difference between dried and canned. So I use the latter in all recipes. (Only for legumes that require no pre-soaking, such as lentils, mung beans, or black-eyed peas, do I call for dried ones.) You should drain the liquid from the canned beans before using. Should you choose to use dried beans in place of canned, please soak them overnight, then drain them before starting to cook.

All measurements and temperatures are listed in both US and metric versions. Weights are not always 100 percent identical (better, for instance, to say 225 grams than 227.8 when converting 8 ounces). Similarly, different brands have slightly different quantities in their cans. If yours is slightly more or less than the amount I list, use it anyway! This is not delicate cooking, so there is little need to measure anything precisely. I list exact measurements only to meet convention. I use American food terminology, but since (as Churchill said) the US and UK are "one people separated by a common language," there is a conversion chart on page 235 for foods and cookery terms that are different in these countries (for example, eggplant/aubergine).

Since the Shabbat stew cooks overnight, it is essential to ensure that it does not dry out. I recommend checking the stew in the morning when you wake up, and adding more water if needed. For those who are strictly Sabbath observant, most Orthodox opinions offer specific ways in which to do this permissibly. Ask a knowledgeable source if this matters to you.

### *Can I . . . ?*

People often read recipes and ask things like: "Can I swap this for that?" or ". . . leave that ingredient out?" My answer here is always an emphatic, "Yes!" This is exactly what people have done with this stew from time immemorial! If some family members liked their food a bit spicier, more chilies found their way into the pot. Someone else hated turnips?* They got replaced by carrots and more potatoes.

Shabbat stew cooking is very forgiving. If you're curious how a change would affect the stew, try it and find out! Unless you are changing something fundamental, you will *not* ruin the entire dish. At worst, it won't be the greatest version that you've ever cooked. Make note of why and don't do it again. Be adventurous!

The same holds if you have specific dietary needs—allergies or chosen food restrictions. Some people can't or won't eat gluten, specific vegetables, red meat, or all animal products. While many of the recipes in this book already work for special diets (including vegetarian or gluten-free), *please* feel free to change recipes and try them.

For example, to prepare a gluten-free version of the classic Eastern European *cholent*, one can remove the barley and replace it with naturally gluten-free buckwheat (aka kasha). In fact, this would also be a legitimate *traditional* option. But also, no one should feel beholden to tradition alone.† Who cares if you put rice into a version historically made with wheat or barley? If it works for you, do it! Your great-grandmother will *not* roll over in her grave, I promise. The same holds true if you leave out the meat, onions, or a specific spice from any of these recipes. Just consider replacing what you leave out with something else—plant-based meat, mushrooms, garlic, carrots, whatever.

Alternatively, if you particularly like some aspect of one recipe in this book, consider incorporating it into a different one. Even though the slow-cooked whole eggs originate in Sephardi cuisine, you can put them into an Ashkenazi stew if you so choose.‡ (Many did so traditionally, as well.) The same would hold true of inserting a *kugel*, *jachnun*, or *kubbeh* into a stew of a different community.§

Bottom line, the Shabbat stew has taken on so many forms over our history that you should really feel free to try *whatever* you want. This, too, is part of it being the most Jewish food on Earth. As the humorous cliché goes: two Jews, three opinions! Yours is just as valid as anyone else's.

* Throughout this text 'turnip' always means the white turnip. Some regions of the English-speaking world, in North America and elsewhere, also apply the term to the yellow turnip-like root vegetable otherwise called rutabaga or swede.

† For more on this, see the final two chapters.

‡ Sephardi Jews are those whose ancestors in the Middle Ages lived on the Iberian Peninsula.

§ These foods will all be explained in the course of the book.

## Chapter 1

# The Shabbat Stew: A Prehistory

Are Jews insane?!

Why else would they deliberately leave a pot cooking for *fifteen hours straight*? But that is exactly what Jews worldwide have done with their Shabbat stews for more than 1,700 years. Were early Jews just loafers who wanted a convenient, always-ready meal, even if that turned the food into a big pot of mush? What else could explain the origin of this uniquely Jewish food, most identifiable via its all-night cooking method?

While we can't *completely* discount the "lazy-with-bad-taste" theory, a more logical explanation grows directly out of Judaism itself. Before starting to explore the dish's culinary history, a brief foray into its backstory seems appropriate.

Judaism is a religion that loves its celebrations, so in addition to special-occasion holidays (such as Passover or Rosh Hashanah), we celebrate a weekly "holiday"—Shabbat.* Stretching from Friday evening to Saturday night, the Sabbath is set aside as a day to remember God's creation of the world, as well as His special relationship with the Jewish nation. A verse in the Biblical book of Isaiah promises rewards from God to those who "call the Sabbath 'delight' . . . and honor it" by refraining from day-to-day activities.[1] From this, the rabbis derive the twin imperatives of celebrating the day via *oneg* ("delight") and *kavod* ("honor").[2] Thus, Jews reserve their best possessions, such as their nicest clothes, for Shabbat in order to properly honor the day.

Jews also display *kavod* for the Sabbath by eating better. The rabbis of ancient times mandated eating three meals for Shabbat, rather than the usual two that people ate on weekdays.[3] And at those three meals, Jews serve higher quality foods, often in multiple courses. Meat was always seen as more dignified, so it was preferred for Shabbat dishes.† Poor Jews

* I use the term holiday here in its original definition: "holy day."

† There have been Jewish vegetarians at times, but they've been in the minority. See Chapter 10 for more on vegetarian Shabbat stews.

who could only afford meat once a week saved it for the Sabbath, while the truly destitute might insist on at least cooking with bones, to supply a hint of meaty taste (and to place it technically in the category of a meat-based meal). Finally, warm food was considered more luxurious, and thus appropriate for these meals.*

This last way of satisfying the command to honor the Sabbath, however, presented religiously observant Jews with a problem. Among the many restrictions placed on them by *halacha*, two specifically create challenges for a hot Sabbath lunch. Jews are forbidden on Shabbat from both kindling a fire and cooking.[4] Friday night dinner could still be eaten lukewarm, if it was cooked right up until the Shabbat began. But what about the midday meal on Saturday? How could a Jew eat a hot lunch to honor the Sabbath properly without transgressing the religious strictures of the day?

Faced with these conflicting demands, ancient Jews turned to a time-honored tool: the legal loophole.

## The Mother of Invention

In the book of Exodus, we learn of the Israelite nation being fed with the miraculous food known as manna. Each morning they receive enough to eat that day, but if they leave any overnight, it spoils. But then Moses describes the unique character of the portion they are given on Fridays. They receive twice as much as on the other weekday mornings, to provide enough for Saturday, the Sabbath, as well. When some fear that it too will rot, Moses replies, "This is what God intended: tomorrow is a day of rest, the holy Sabbath . . . Bake what you want to bake, cook what you want to cook, and *set aside whatever is left over to be kept until the morning.*"[5]

While this obviously does not compel Jews to heat their Shabbat lunch through Friday night, I'd like to think that perhaps this phrase provided the recipe from which the cooking method was drawn. Jews already commemorate the manna each week by serving two loaves of bread at the Sabbath table, remembering the double portion. Maybe Moses's description of leaving cooked manna until morning also inspired this second Shabbat food.

* Anthropologist Claude Lévi-Strauss might see this as an extension of the greater degree of culture found in cooked food, particularly that which was boiled in a pot rather than roasted. (See Claude Lévi-Strauss, "The Culinary Triangle," in Counihan, et al., *Food and Culture*, 36 ff.) Many of us agree with this hierarchy, considering hot food fancier than, say, a salad.

To be clear, I'm not suggesting this as anything more than a hint. The Shabbat stew does *not* find its source in the Torah itself. We first encounter it in early rabbinic writings. One legend connects this slow-cooked dish to Shabbat itself, recognizing the dish's unique character. The emperor asked a rabbi what made the Shabbat stew so special, and the rabbi explained that Jews have a unique spice. It is called Shabbat (though in a play on words, it is spelled the same as the Aramaic for "dill," *shevet*). When the emperor asks for some of the spice, so he can enjoy it as well, the rabbi explains that it only works for those who observe the Sabbath![6]

Much as different stew versions share common core elements, the rabbis debated details of the Sabbath laws but agreed on the core parameters. The roots of the *halacha* may be found in the Torah, or Jewish Bible (also known as the Written Law). But that text's many regulations are rarely clear. Thus, the rabbis (in what is traditionally called the Oral Law) expounded the meanings and specific parameters of those commandments.* An earlier group in the Land of Israel, known as *Tanaim* (Aramaic for "reiterators"), debated legal details. Their centuries of discussions were transcribed, then edited and organized by subject (around 200 CE) into a body of work known as the Mishnah.

The Mishnah's sixty-three books (or tractates) supply the basis of later rulings, but the intricacies continued to be explored for centuries. Subsequently, other rabbis known as *Amoraim* ("interpreters"), in both Israel and Mesopotamia, further explained the laws. Their conversations were similarly compiled, and eventually published (alongside the relevant passages of Mishnah) in two separate regional collections. The Hebrew word "Talmud" and the Aramaic "Gemara" are used interchangeably for both. The Israeli work, probably completed by the end of the fourth century, became known as the *Talmud Yerushalmi* or Jerusalem Talmud.† The term *Talmud Bavli*, Babylonian Talmud, refers to the Mesopotamian version which was redacted a few hundred years later.‡ Eventually, the more developed *Talmud Bavli* gained dominance as the authoritative, *halachically*-binding source. If someone refers to the Talmud with no modifier, it is known to mean the Babylonian one.§

* Orthodox Jews consider these rabbinic explanations and extensions just as authoritative and binding as the commandments that are spelled out in the Torah itself.

† Alternatively, it is sometimes referred to in English as the Palestinian Talmud.

‡ Jews kept referring to Mesopotamia as "Bavel" long after the Babylonians faded from history.

§ In my citations, BT denotes the Babylonian Talmud tractate's Gemara passage, while the name without the preliminary BT means the Mishnah from that tractate.

*The first page of the Talmud, in its most standard layout today. The word in the decorative rectangle in the central section is the first word of the Mishnah, which then continues for the next 13 lines. The Gemara that expounds on this Mishnah begins on the next line. The different texts that appear surrounding it on the sides are various later commentaries.*

The evolution of hot Sabbath food developed within this same multi-step, centuries-long process. The core prohibition against creative labor on Shabbat, as well as the passage about honoring the Sabbath are both found in the Torah.* The Mishnah, however, noted the problematic conflict, specifying what types of labor are prohibited, and making explicit the need to honor the Sabbath. The Gemara then dug deeper, exploring various parameters surrounding cooking and lighting a fire, eventually leading them to solve the hot lunch conundrum. They asked, for example, what specific actions are classified as cooking? Similarly, is there a way someone can permissibly use a flame if they didn't actually light it on Shabbat? Ultimately, the rabbis concluded that while active cooking and lighting a new fire were expressly forbidden, leaving cooked food to continue warming on a pre-existing flame was generally acceptable. Jewish cooks stuck their pots straight through this loophole, commonly leaving food warming all of Shabbat and thus creating the first Shabbat stews.

How do we know this? Because we find it mentioned as early as the Mishnah itself. At twilight on Friday, when it is unclear whether or not the Sabbath has officially begun, one of the permitted activities the Mishnah lists is "*tomnin et hahamin*"—"bury [or insulate] the hot [food]."[7] While this phrase is characteristically short on details about what exactly is legal, it clearly indicates the early Jewish desire to find a permissible way to keep the Shabbat food hot. Naturally, any food that is cooked through the night would best be kept at a relatively low temperature, cool enough that the food doesn't burn or completely dry out. Thus, a necessary aspect to using this technique was insulating the pot to maintain as much internal heat as possible. And the passage's matter of fact tone (calling it "*the* hot food," for example) suggests people were already doing this, rather than the Mishnah creating an innovation.

This overnight cooking was a peculiar enough practice that non-Jews noticed it, too. In *Epistle to the Magnesians*, for example, Church father Ignatius (died early-to-mid second century, before the redaction of the Mishnah) differentiates his version of Christianity from that of hybrid Judeo-Christians. He writes, "Let us therefore no longer keep the Sabbath after the Jewish manner . . . *eating things prepared the day before*, nor using *lukewarm* drinks."† Similarly, one of Ignatius' contemporaries,

* Torah here refers to the entire Jewish Bible, including the prophetic books, not just the Five Books of Moses.

† This version of the text is from a late-fourth-century expanded version, sometimes attributed to a "Pseudo-Ignatius." Even if the later dating is preferred, it shows a

the Roman satirist Juvenal, on more than one occasion mentions Jews carrying "a basket and a truss of hay," which modern scholars interpret as a device for insulating their Sabbath food.[8] While neither of these references is entirely explicit (perhaps because they were written by non-Jews, less knowledgeable about Jewish customs), they clearly show the writers taking note of this odd Sabbath practice.

When the Mishnah permitted Jews to leave their Shabbat food warming on a preexisting fire, what were the specific criteria of that ruling? The Talmud stepped into the breach left by the Mishnah, delineating the specifics of this law, while also taking into account the practices that had already developed among various Jews. If, as the early sources suggest, Jews were already looking for ways to keep food warm for Saturday, the Talmud needed to find ways in which they could do so without violating any prohibitions. (Frequently, when Talmudic sages saw that a questionable practice had become widely adopted by Jews, they sought ways to justify it legally, rather than swimming against the tide of established customs.) The Gemara's discussions on the topic highlight various foods that Jews might keep warm for Sabbath lunch, as well as numerous potential methods for heating the pots and insulating them.[9]

Even these discussions, however, failed to cover all relevant details of properly providing a warm Shabbat lunch. So rabbis through the centuries continued exploring those gaps, expanding the laws regarding what was permitted or forbidden. The specifics of these rulings are not entirely relevant to this book, but a brief look at some of the issues they addressed can show us how complex the discussion became:

- When leaving food warming from before Shabbat, what specific precautions must be taken to prevent the cook from adjusting the flame?
- Once the food is cooked before the Shabbat, does it make a difference whether further heating will improve or reduce the quality of the final dish?
- Is there a difference between liquids and solid foods? If so, how do we define various mixtures that fall between these extremes?
- What types of materials can permissibly be used as insulation and what types are prohibited? Is there a difference between covering a pot partially and fully burying it?

---

very early reference to Jews preparing food on Friday to eat on Saturday. (*Epistle to the Magnesians*, Chapter 9 [emphasis added].)

The rabbis were not being pedantic with these discussions. They were addressing fully practical issues. It should be easy to see how new technologies and situations would often raise questions for them to address. What may be overlooked, however, in examining the "whats" or "hows" of warming food for the Sabbath is the "that" of this issue: none of the rabbinic opinions and commentaries forbade the practice outright.

The Shabbat stew therefore finds its origins in both Jewish law and popular practice (and is supported by Jewish legend), placing it in an interesting position within the world of Jewish food. Some of our foods, as we saw with matzah, grow directly out of religious practices. Eating it not only reflects the events of the Exodus story, but is expressly commanded in the Torah. Other popular foods stem purely from folk customs. Examples in this category include Purim pastries that mock the villainous Haman from the Book of Esther, or fried foods eaten on Chanukah. The Shabbat stew falls between these poles, but closer to matzah than to hamantaschen.* People's popular interpretation of the *oneg* and *kavod* concepts played an important role in its creation. And while it is not directly required by religious law, it was still created to meet *halachic* criteria. Clearly, Jews wanted to find ways to balance their avoidance of prohibited labor with their desire to honor the Sabbath with a hot Saturday lunch.

Hence the invention of the Shabbat stew, cooked on Friday, then warmed continually, "low-and-slow," through the entire night.

## Different Strokes for Different Regions' Folks

In outlining the origins of the Shabbat stew, I described why Jews chose to cook their food through the whole night. But an equally fundamental aspect of the dish is the set of core ingredients they selected for that slow cooking. As I noted in the introduction, the two things you find in almost every example are grain and meat. In the next chapter I'll describe the earliest popular version of Shabbat stew, which probably led to this becoming the core of most stews that followed.

However, choosing one grain or meat over another can totally alter the character of a stew. In fact, the most popular choices for these ingredients differ not just from community to community, but broadly by regions of the world.

From the Jews' historical birthplace in the Land of Israel, our point of origin thousands of years ago, we subsequently spread throughout the

* Hamantaschen are triangular, filled Purim cookies.

world, creating what is known as the Diaspora. Israel sits at the meeting point of three continents: Asia, Africa and Europe. Each had its own communities, with Middle Eastern and Central Asian Jews to Israel's east, those of North Africa to the west, and Europe's Jews to the northwest. (These held the bulk of world Jewry throughout history, though some communities existed in other areas, too.) Shabbat stews in Asia most frequently use rice and chicken, those in Africa usually include wheat and lamb, and European versions typically are made with barley and beef. Certainly, this is not universal to *all* stews in any given region, just the predominant choices in each.

The grain selections make the most sense based on history and climate. Though wheat and barley were the ancient grains consumed in the Jewish homeland, rice eventually dominated Asian stews. From its birthplace in southeast Asia, rice had already reached the Middle East by the start of the Common Era.[10] So, when the Shabbat stew was being standardized in late antiquity, rice was a moderately new option, but definitely was known in the area. It grew steadily more popular, rising to dominance by the nineteenth century. Even before then, however, rice was considered more luxurious, and thus better for honoring the Sabbath.*

Why would this not also hold true in Africa? Because rice requires a lot of water to grow, making it unsuitable to most of arid North Africa. We can find some rice in Shabbat stews in Egypt and Morocco (at North Africa's wetter extremities), but they are exceptions. More frequently, wheat serves as the region's primary grain. Many use whole wheat kernels ("wheat berries"), while freekeh (*see* Chapter 2) is popular in Egypt and couscous in the Maghreb (the western part of North Africa).

Of the three main grains, barley was the earliest to be domesticated, so it does appear at times in the Shabbat stews of Asia or Africa as well, not just in Europe. In many places, however, it was considered an inferior grain, fit only for animals and poor people to eat.[11] Despite this attitude, one practical characteristic made barley the grain of choice for European Jews: it grows well in sub-optimal conditions. Barley is fairly drought-resistant and does not require deep plowing before planting.[12] So it could easily be grown even in the colder reaches of Europe. Jews there had few other viable choices, despite its lowly status.

While climate and the global dispersion of ingredients explain the predominant grains, culture seems more responsible for each region's

* In Kurdistan, for example, where wheat was popular, rice was served for festive meals (Brauer, *Jews of Kurdistan*, 99).

chosen meats. In the earliest times, people ate little meat. Domestic animals were typically only slaughtered once they had outlived their usefulness for breeding or physical labor.[13] In time, meat consumption increased, slowly though noticeably. Most of the meat eaten in the Middle East came from sheep and goats. So, how did chickens, instead, come to dominate the region's Shabbat stews?

For much of history, chicken was actually more expensive than other meats. Poultry could only be raised in small flocks since disease could spread very readily through a larger group, which would cause major financial damage. This still held true in early 1900s New York, where chicken cost over twice as much as other meats.[14] Only with mid-twentieth-century vaccines could flocks reach into the thousands, drastically reducing chicken prices.[15] More expensive chickens equaled meat that was more luxurious, and thus more respectable for Sabbath.

A further benefit to choosing chicken is that you can kill one from a flock while the rest remain unaffected. A larger animal couldn't be consumed in a single sitting, but one bird alone could provide a family with its Sabbath meat allotment. Also, the other living hens could keep providing eggs regularly, but slaughtering a ewe meant stopping its milk flow entirely. So, yes, chicken cost more on a per-pound basis, but it remained more practical as a weekly meal option.

These last benefits, of course, held true in Africa and Europe as well, so why didn't Jews there choose chickens for their Shabbat stews? North Africa remained dedicated to lamb, the ancient meat of choice. It is hard to pinpoint with certainty why this was, but it may have been simply a matter of taste or cultural preference. Certainly, lamb was always more popular than chicken as a food in the region.[16] Regardless, the regional distinction between Asia and Africa is merely one of proportions; both meats appear in Shabbat stews of each region, just to differing degrees.*

More peculiar than the North African preference for lamb, is beef's dominance within European stews. Throughout history, cattle were rarely eaten because they were more valuable as draft animals. Particularly notable, however, is that even among the poorest Jews in Eastern Europe, beef became the chosen meat for *cholent*. This apparently stems from a little-known quirk of history. The fourteenth-century Black Death killed between 30 and 60 percent of Europe's population in just a few years, resulting in more open grazing land and fewer people competing for the same food. This created a meat surplus, and a resulting price drop.

* In Chapter 2, I'll discuss another possible explanation for this regional difference.

Eating beef then became much more common, for Jews as well as non-Jews. Alas, the good times only lasted for about 200 years; as Europe's population rebounded, so did meat prices. But the Jews there had already developed a taste for beef, and felt there was no adequate substitute. Poor Jews preferred to include a few scraps of beef, or some bones, rather than more of a cheaper meat.[17]

It's worth noting that this regional meat breakdown has lessened in modern times. With the rise of beef production in the New World in the nineteenth century, and easier international shipping, beef prices dropped worldwide. Compounded by America's cultural dominance, eating habits have changed everywhere. Beef, the favorite meat in the US, has seen its popularity increase all over the world.* Many Jews of North African descent now cook Shabbat stews with beef in place of the traditional lamb, for example.

The fact that grains and meats remain similar throughout each region underscores the food's slow spread within each area. Only as the stew moved farther from its roots did more significant changes take place. But rather than creating a completely new recipe in each place, Jews just swapped a less available grain for a more common one, or chose a meat that better suited the local diet. Only in retrospect, after millennia of compounding evolutions, do the Shabbat stews look so radically different.

So, with that background understood, in the next chapter I'll uncover the original version of the stew, and explore how it grew into the standard upon which most others were based.

* Since much of America's beef has long been exported to Europe, this might have added to beef's dominance there.

# Chapter 2

# Babylon and On: The Original Stew

What exactly did the low-and-slow loophole, discussed in the previous chapter, accomplish? An observant Jew still couldn't cook food from scratch on Shabbat, nor could she adjust the temperature or put something on the fire in the middle of the day. (And back then, it was almost always the women doing the cooking.) It only allowed her to take a fully cooked dish and keep it warm through the length of the Sabbath.

It thus created a framework, the method by which Jews ever after would prepare their hot Shabbat lunch. Still, the loophole itself did not create one stew that could later be modified everywhere it went. Most likely, the technique was originally applied to the wide variety of foods

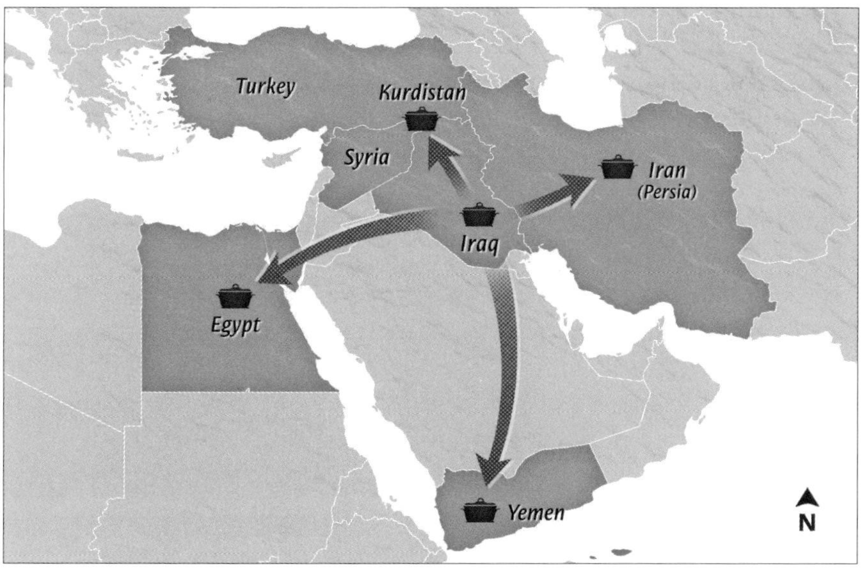


*The map here and those in the following chapters show the regions I discuss, also indicating the Jewish migration path that brought the Shabbat stew to each new location.*

that different women served their families. One might have heated some turnips and carrots in a pot of water, while another mixed mutton chunks with leeks or spiced breadcrumbs.

In time, however, Jewish cooks of the region discovered that some foods held up better than others, and a single specific dish became most popular. Since home cooking was done primarily over a hearth or in a small oven, a one-pot stew best met Jewish Sabbath lunch requirements. It appears that the first example to reach prominence applied the slow-cooking method to an already-popular dish. Primarily combining two simple ingredients, *harisa* was commonly eaten throughout the Middle East, and local Jews realized it would be perfect as a Shabbat stew.

## From a Method to a Meal: Heating and Eating *Harisa*

*Harisa* is an ancient Middle Eastern food in which hulled wheat and meat are cooked together in water, with onions sometimes included.* Once fully cooked, the mixture is mashed into a thick porridge. Typically, *harisa* is served with melted fat drizzled on top, and finished with a sprinkle of cinnamon. It is stodgy, but filling and flavorful, and we find multiple variations of this nutritionally diverse meal in the earliest extant Arab cookbook, from tenth-century Baghdad.

In *Kitab al-Tabikh* (*The Book of Dishes*), Ibn Sayyar al-Warraq compiled over 600 recipes fit for royalty, drawn from the two preceding centuries. Clearly a knowledgeable and well-connected gastronome, al-Warraq provided a comprehensive collection of foods that had become locally popular by the mid-900s. A whole chapter was dedicated to his recipes for different *harisas*. A basic recipe features meat and wheat at its core, but he also offered up other options: a rice-and-wheat blend, various different meats, and a list of ideal fats with which to finish the stew.[1] All of his *harisas* contain milk and are served with *murri*, a salty, fermented barley condiment that was all the culinary rage at the time.

As *Kitab al-Tabikh* shows, *harisa* was beloved in the Middle East, suggesting why Jews might have selected it for Shabbat slow-cooking. It could be eaten as a complete meal, featuring both grain and meat; some *harisas* included simple vegetables, as well.† But is it logical to think that a cookbook containing the dishes of society's upper crust would include

* As is not uncommon in gastronomic terminology, there are now many variations on the name (such as *haris*), or totally different names for the dish (such as *haleem*, as I'll show later). Also, other foods confusingly share the same name; this stew has no connection to *harissa*, North Africa's fiery pepper paste.

† A Christian Lenten *harisa* from the book replaces meat with leeks.

*Manuscript of al-Warraq's* Kitab al-Tabikh.

a commoner's food? Actually, yes, it is. Al-Warraq begins his book with a story that illustrates this point.

Once, the sultan's personal cook was hosted for a night of chess and socializing. The host asks this proto-celebrity chef to honor the group with a dish that he would cook for the sultan himself. So the chef asks the host's servant how *he* cooks. After hearing the response, he tells the lad to make the food . . . exactly as usual! The only difference? The young cook must pay extreme attention to scrubbing the pot and cleaning the ingredients first. Al-Warraq's point is clear: what differentiates high-class food of the time is neither the recipe nor the selected dish, but kitchen hygiene and the care applied to the ingredients used. Furthermore, *harisa*'s constant presence in cookbooks over the next 500 years underscores the admiration it continually enjoyed from people of all classes.

Still, even if it was super-common, how do we know that Jews turned *harisa* into their slow-cooked Sabbath lunch? For this, we turn to another Arab source: the historian al-Baladhuri. In *Ansab al-Ashraf* (*Lineage of the Nobles*), he relates a story about the first caliph of the Ummayad dynasty, Mu'awiya (ruled 661–80).* Mu'awiya was known to

* The word "caliph" is a shortened Anglicized form of the Arabic *Khalifat Rasul Allah*, "Successor of the Prophet of God." His territory became known as a "caliphate."

*Mu'awiya, pictured on an Ummayad coin.*

be a charismatic "people person," flattering when prudent but applying force when needed. Most importantly in the present context, the caliph was also a passionate gourmand.

Al-Baladhuri tells of a party with guests from mixed backgrounds. Mu'awiya asked a Yemenite Jew to recite a poem that the Jew's father had written. The guest obliged, but inadvertently offended some of the Muslim guests. Reflecting his jovial nature, Mu'awiya defused the situation rather than escalating it, deftly changing subjects to another favorite topic (and tactfully dispatching the Yemenite at the same time).

"Does your family," he asked, "still prepare *harisa* as well as it did in pre-Islamic times?"

The Jew replied, "Even better than before!"

"Then go make us some," Mu'awiya answered, sending him off with some money to prepare the Jewish-style *harisa*.[2]

Al-Baladhuri related the story two centuries after Mu'awiya's death, so it may not be historically accurate. But it indicates that at least by the historian's time, in the ninth century, Jewish *harisa* was recognized as distinct from other versions.

## Judaizing *Harisa*

What exactly differentiated a Jewish *harisa* from its non-Jewish lookalike? We can only make educated guesses about that. First, unlike al-Warraq's *harisas*, the Jews certainly did not put milk into their version of the meat porridge, as the mixing of dairy and meat was explicitly forbidden by *halacha*. Still, this minor ingredient change would be unlikely to change the taste enough to make Jewish *harisa* recognizably distinct (and to Mu'awiya, cherished). Furthermore, other Arab recipes include no milk at all, so this change is only a minor one, and likely not unique to Jewish *harisa*.

Beyond that, the Jewish version most likely included onions. Most modern Jewish versions include them, though they are found nowhere in al-Warraq's entire *harisa* chapter. Throughout history, Jews have been famous for their love of onions (as well as other vegetables in the *allium* family, such as garlic). When the Biblical Israelites rejected the miraculous manna that God provided in the Sinai desert, they longed for the foods they ate as Egyptian slaves. Onions and garlic are among the five vegetables they specifically highlighted.[3]

This early passion seems to have been imprinted in our nation's formative DNA, because Jewish foods everywhere embrace these ingredients.* So much so that, historically, garlic (and its related odor) became a well-known antisemitic trope. If our haters attacked us via garlic, we clearly ate it enough for other people to take notice![4] And while the milder onion might not have generated as strong a reaction, it was still associated with Jews and featured prominently in our cuisine.[5] So it seems plausible that, unlike al-Warraq's, Jewish *harisas* probably had onions. If so, it might also explain why onions are so popular in Shabbat stews today, since most descend from Jewish *harisa*.

However, the most likely element that differentiated Jewish *harisa* would be slow-cooking it through the night. Two details support this notion. While the Mu'awiya story does not associate the Jewish version

* Lest you argue that *everyone* likes onion and garlic, many cultures use them less, and some shun them. Korean Buddhist chefs, for example, avoid most *alliums* (*see* Matt Rodbard, "The Korean Temple Food Not Seen on Netflix," *Taste*, Dec. 7, 2021; https://tastecooking.com/the-korean-temple-food-not-seen-on-netflix).

*One of the cuneiform tablets containing the recipes written in ancient Babylonian.*

with the Sabbath, many modern Jews make updated *harisas* for their Shabbat stew. If an antiquated dish like *harisa* is made for Shabbat in the twenty-first century, it seems likely the practice began in antiquity, when the stew was most widely known and consumed.

Furthermore, this theory finds support in later cookbooks in Arabic. A thirteenth-century manual by Muḥammad al-Baghdadi (confusingly for us, also called *Kitab al-Tabikh*), as well as two examples from the same era in Spain, recommend cooking *harisa* through the night.[6] For them, the overnight cooking isn't due to Sabbath restrictions (which Muslims clearly did not face). The overnight cooking was so the dish would be ready to eat for breakfast.* But, wouldn't Arab cooks in the tenth century also have wanted a hot *harisa* breakfast? Why didn't al-Warraq also mention this cooking technique? There were other dishes that he suggested could be cooked overnight, but he doesn't offer that option for *harisa*. Though hard to say with certainty, perhaps this was the influence of the Jewish Shabbat version once it became better known. If so, it may have been the earliest example of something I'll revisit throughout the book: the Jewish Shabbat stew's influence on non-Jewish foods around it.

Some may find it strange that Jews would adapt a food that derives from Arab culture and make it their holy Sabbath meal. But actually, this is neither weird nor uncommon. As the most widely dispersed nation in the world, Jews have come into intimate contact with virtually every other people. Even though we didn't eat at our non-Jewish neighbors' tables, we still discovered their cuisines. Jews have typically eaten the same things as did the Gentiles around them, making minor alterations for *kashrut*, or taste. Specifically Jewish versions of local foods (including many from Muslim cultures) are found in Jewish kitchens worldwide. So a Jewish *harisa* makes perfect sense.

Furthermore, it's inaccurate to describe this as Jews adopting an Arab dish. The two peoples developed side by side, originating in the same Middle Eastern culture and sharing a similar culinary heritage. Digging into that food culture uncovers ancestors of *harisa* that predate the birth of either Jews or Arabs. The oldest recipes ever found were written in cuneiform in the seventeenth century BCE, in southern Iraq.

Among the thirty-five recipes, two slightly resemble *harisa*.† They mix meat (lamb or pigeon, respectively) with a grain ("crumbled cereal-cake"), as well as vegetables from the onion family (as with more modern

* Interestingly, all three also leave out milk, though *harisas* in later Arabic cookbooks, from fourteenth-century Egypt and fifteenth-century Baghdad include options that contain dairy. See Nasrallah, *Treasure Trove*; Perry, "*Kitab al-Tibakhah*," *Petits Propos Culinaires*, 21 (November 1985): 17–22.

† They are more like stew than porridge, and also resemble other later Arab dishes, so these early recipes more accurately represent a class of similar dishes.

*harisas*). The lamb recipe includes added fat, while the pigeon recipe says the vegetables should first be "steeped in milk."[7] Neither recipe calls for pounding into a porridge, but the ingredients are similar to those found 2,700 years later in al-Warraq's cookbook.

Rather than *harisa* being an example of Jews adopting and adapting a popular Arab dish, more likely is that the *harisa* eaten both by Jews and Arabs developed from this preexisting cuisine, hundreds of years before it became a Shabbat stew. Furthermore, Jews had lived in Mesopotamia —where these precursor recipes originate—since the late eighth century BCE, long before the Arab conquest 1,500 years later, and therefore likely ate *harisa* before the Arabs ever encountered it. Either way, the Shabbat version was simply a modification of a regional food that had already been eaten for a long time.

Thus, we have three likely differences between the early Jewish *harisa* and those featured by al-Warraq. Least significantly, it certainly left out the milk. Second, it most probably contained onions, and potentially other similar vegetables. Most importantly, it was almost certainly cooked through the night to be eaten for lunch on Saturday.

One final interesting point about the Sabbath *harisa* relates to its name. As noted in the introduction, Shabbat stews around the world have diverse names, but the names typically fall into a few broad categories. Some simply describe the food as "hot" (the main point of overnight cooking), some highlight a central ingredient, and others describe the cooking process. *Harisa* is an example of this last category, deriving from the Arabic term "to pound" or "to mash," a late step in preparing the dish. Later, we'll also see the cooking process highlighted by names that describe the lengthy cooking time, or the means of keeping the stew warm.

## First Steps of a Moveable Shabbat Feast

I have argued here that *harisa* was not just an early version of the Shabbat stew, but actually the one from which all major examples descend. But I've only explained, so far, how we can identify it as an early example. In order for it to become the granddaddy of most others, it would need to move from being a popular choice to *the* standard one. Otherwise, each Jewish community might have chosen a different dish to cook all night. They wouldn't all share the core combination of a meat and a grain, and they wouldn't be a useful means for tracing the routes of our migrations through the Diaspora. The proof that *harisa* indeed grew into the dominant Shabbat stew is its early spread through the Mizrachi Jewish communities of the Middle East.* This standardized the core formula moving forward.

For much of history, from the seventh-century Arab conquest until modernity in the nineteenth century, the entire region was largely controlled by a single power, be it a caliphate or an empire. Cultural ideas, such as recipes, easily spread throughout the region. This is why we can discuss "Middle Eastern cuisine," in addition to the narrower Iraqi, Persian, or Arabian menus. Jewish foods in the Middle East were no different. Thus, *harisa*-like Shabbat stews still appear in modern Jewish cuisines from around the Middle East—Yemen in the south, Kurdistan to the north, Egypt in the west and Persia (Iran) to the east.† As I explore the neo-*harisas* in these four places, I'll also cover other local variants.

### *Yemen*

While many foods spread outwards from the Middle East's cultural center in Mesopotamia, we also encounter food trends from the fringes reaching the cultural center before radiating out to the wider area. This is how Persian culinary styles later dispersed throughout the Arab world. The same may hold true for the Shabbat *harisa*. As noted, our earliest reference to a Jewish version linked it with Yemenite Jews. They may, in fact, have been the original innovators who turned *harisa* into a Shabbat lunch dish. That version may then have traveled to Iraq, then migrated to the rest of the Middle East.

Even in modern times, many Yemenites eat *harisa* as their Shabbat stew. It is so popular that a common claim states, "Sabbath without *haris[a]* is like salt without a pot."[8] The only major difference in today's Yemenite Jewish *harisa* is that usually it is not mashed after overnight cooking. (This also allows them to include bones, which they couldn't if they wanted a uniformly mushy consistency.[9])

The lack of pounding might reflect modern tastes, or it could illustrate a belief that the action was prohibited on the Sabbath. Some other communities used non-Jewish servants to pound their Shabbat *harisa*, rather than the Jewish homemakers doing it themselves.[10] Whatever the reason, the fact that it has been dropped is significant. The porridgy consistency of *harisa* is truly what differentiates it from other stews, yet

* Mizrachi Jews are those from the Middle East and North Africa who were culturally connected with the ancient Torah centers of Bavel.

† The terms Persia and Iran are often used interchangeably, but many who have fled the Islamic Republic (including many Jews) prefer the term Persia to distance themselves from the current regime.

almost all Shabbat stews today lack that aspect. But if one of the earliest Shabbat stew versions of *harisa* dropped this element, it would explain why the later ones are also more stew-like than the original *harisa* was.

Including bones also moves their *harisa* closer to a common Yemenite weekday dish: a gelatinous stew called *marak regel* (Hebrew for "foot soup"). The collagen in lambs' feet results in the soup's thick and smooth texture. This simple food reflects the lower-income, village culture that existed for much of Yemenite Jewish history. In fact, rather than eating *harisa* for Shabbat lunch, some instead "*harisa*-fy" their *marak regel* by adding bulgur or plain wheat to their foot soup.[11]

Throughout the book, I will return to this class of Shabbat stew, with *marak regel* as the first example. Rather than developing in stages from *harisa*, some take a popular dish—Jewish or non-Jewish—and apply the slow cooking method to it. (If this was done originally with *harisa* itself, why not do it again with another food?) As I mentioned in the introduction, most but not *all* Shabbat stews sit on a continuum of continual modifications from *harisa*. These are the outlier exceptions, and often are secondary or later additions to a community's Sabbath menu. Without modifying the *harisa* formula, they preserve the overnight cooking technique.

Modernity brought some change to the Yemenite Jewish diet, and concurrently introduced a third Shabbat stew. With the 1839 British colonization of the southern port of Aden, many Jewish Yemenis joined the stream of immigrants to the newly independent state. They were attracted by equal rights, modernization, and a better quality of life, including a broader diet. As a seaside city, Aden's cuisine features fresh fish, not generally consumed in the rest of Yemen. So some Adeni Jews created *eadam*, a spicy fish stew that cooks overnight on Friday.[12] Since it uses fish heads, tails, and other parts that might otherwise have gone in the trash, many Westerners might be hard pressed to see this as luxurious food, but the very fact that it was made from fish rather than meat raised its status, while also reflecting the community's still moderate means and frugal "waste nothing" mentality. Contrary to American eating habits, this "Adeni bouillabaisse" is not eaten for lunch, but for a mid-morning breakfast![13] Then, the *harisa* itself can be eaten later in the afternoon.

Between the 1880s and 1950, almost all of Yemen's Jews emigrated, primarily to Israel. Foods commonly eaten by Yemenite Jews have now been incorporated into broader Israeli cuisine. For example, many breakfast pastries (*malawach*, *jachnun*, and *kubaneh*) have become standard fare.

*Harisa*, however, did not penetrate the wider cuisine, and remains primarily a Yemenite dish. *Marak regel* is better-known, but still far less so than *jachnun*, for example. But some Yemenite families still eat it for Shabbat, in *harisa*-fied form.[14] Even *eadam*, less common than it was in Aden (possibly due to greater affluence in Israel), persists for some traditionalists as a savory Shabbat morning breakfast.[15]

### *Kurdistan*

Some 1,800 miles north of Yemen, across the Middle East, we come to Kurdistan. A territory, not a country, it sits north of the Tigris and Euphrates rivers, in a mountainous cross-border region that spans northern Iraq and stretches into northeastern Syria, southeastern Turkey and northwestern Iran. The Kurdish Jews' unique character grows out of the area's topography: they share many traits and practices, but since hills and rivers divide the region, different towns and cities that might seem physically close on a map had little contact with each other and developed their own culinary habits. Like their Yemenite sisters and brothers, many Kurdish Jews lived in remote villages, but the available foods in a lush mountainous region contrast strongly with those found in the Yemeni desert. Plenty of water and fertile grazing land made meat more plentiful in Kurdistan, and infused the diet with various vegetables and fruits.[16]

The standard Kurdish Shabbat stew, known as *mebosa*, logically reflects the wide array of available ingredients, as well as the varying food habits of the different towns.* Rather than a stew with a single recipe, many distinct sub-types of *mebosa* exist today. The most basic variety clearly descends from *harisa*, featuring little more than crushed wheat with beef or lamb.[17] I say "little more" because even this simple version includes a sophisticated, and particularly Kurdish addition: *kubbeh*. An adored local food, *kubbeh* is a dumpling of grain (typically bulgur, rice flour, or semolina) filled with spiced ground meat. *Kubbeh* were so frequently added to Shabbat stews in Kurdistan that non-Jewish Kurds referred to them as "Jewish dumplings" or "Sabbath dumplings."[18] This addition also makes *mebosa* the furthest removed from the original *harisa* among the examples that ring the Middle East.

To be clear, Kurdish Jews eat *kubbeh* all week, not only as part of a Shabbat stew. Indeed, tens of varieties of *kubbeh* exist as everyday snacks

* One source translates *mebosa* as "warm food, sealed oven," though that seems too long for a single word. I assume this translation is metaphoric (Brauer, *Jews of Kurdistan*, 420).

## Mebosa

This Kurdish stew is fairly labor-intensive, with multiple stages of preparation. Since Kurdish Jews make numerous versions, I offer an alternative option in the Notes section. Rice flour was more traditional for *kubbeh* in Kurdistan, but semolina replaced it in Israel, during the austerity period of the 1950s. Semolina, therefore, has now become the standard ingredient.

### *Ingredients*

***For kubbeh filling***

1 teaspoon **oil**
½ pound (225 g) **ground beef** (ideally, ground twice for a softer texture)
1 large **onion**, diced
2 cloves **garlic**, minced
1 teaspoon **salt**
¼ teaspoon ground **black pepper**
1 small bunch fresh **parsley**, chopped

***For kubbeh dough***

2 cups (300 g) **rice flour** or **semolina**
1 teaspoon **salt**
1 cup (240 ml) **water** (or more if needed)

***For mebosa***

2 cups (450 g) **bulgur**
1½ pounds (680 g) **lamb** or **beef**, cut into chunks
1 medium **onion**, chopped
1 pound (450 g) small **okra** (fresh or frozen), left whole
2–3 small **zucchini**, cut into chunks
1 teaspoon **salt**
½ teaspoon ground **black pepper**
½ teaspoon ground **turmeric**

### *Method*

*Prepare the kubbeh filling:* Heat the **oil** in a pan over medium heat. Add the **ground beef**, and as it starts to fry, mix in the **onion**, **garlic**, **salt**, and **black pepper**. Stir regularly, breaking up any clumps, until the meat has browned. Remove from the heat and allow to cool. Put the **beef** and **parsley** into a food processor or blender, and pulse to mix together.

or meals, with variants that are baked or fried, and are hand-held or pie-like and cut up. One popular type nestles chewy dumplings in a piquant broth.

*Make the kubbeh dough*: In a bowl, combine the **rice flour** or **semolina** and the **salt**. Slowly add the **water**, and mix the dough by hand. Start with one cup and add more as necessary. The dough should be pliable, but neither runny nor sticky.

*Assemble the kubbeh*: Prepare a bowl of water to wet your hands as needed. Put parchment paper onto a baking tray. Take pieces of the **dough** slightly larger than the size of a golf ball, and roll them into smooth balls. With your thumb, indent the center of the ball to create a small well. Gently press the sides so they will be as thin as possible without breaking. Fill each with a scant teaspoon of **kubbeh filling**, or more if needed. Close the ball up around the filling, smoothing it with a moistened index finger. You may leave them as round balls, or flatten them into patty shape, as you like. Set each one aside on the baking tray. Continue until you use up all of the dough. (Any leftover filling may be used separately to stuff vegetables, eaten as is for a snack, or dumped into the *mebosa* to add flavor.)

Boil a pot of moderately salted water and add the **kubbeh**. Boil for about 10 minutes. Drain and set aside.

*Make the mebosa*: Using a strainer, rinse the **bulgur** well. Pour it into a large pot, along with the **lamb or beef, onion**, **okra**, and **zucchini**. Sprinkle the **salt**, **black pepper**, and **turmeric** over all the ingredients, and cover with water. Stir and bring to a boil, then reduce the flame to medium-low. Let it simmer for around an hour. Add the **kubbeh** to the pot, and continue cooking for about 15 more minutes.

If most of the water has been absorbed by the **bulgur**, add more water to the pot. Cook overnight using any standard method (*see* pages 7–8).

***Notes***

Since the okra and especially zucchini may become mushy through overnight cooking, smaller, firmer ones are preferable.

Alternatively, replace them with a large turnip and 2 medium carrots, chopped roughly. The flavor will be different, but they hold their form better, and are equally traditional in a Kurdish stew.

This stew should be a bit more liquid when served, so the slow-cooker method may be preferable, though it is not the method that was popular in Kurdistan.

Just as some Yemenites upgraded their weekday *marak regel* into a Shabbat stew, some Kurdish Jews thicken a standard *kubbeh* soup to make a *mebosa* that further honors the Shabbat.[19] Nowadays, *kubbeh* as an everyday food has spread beyond Kurdistan; it is admired from Syria through Israel to Egypt. But only among Kurdish Jews does it find its way into a Shabbat stew.*

The variations between *mebosa* recipes can be vast. Complex versions include such items as okra, beets, pumpkin, quince, tomatoes, or lemon juice.[20] Meat type also varies from one *mebosa* to the next. In Kurdistan, the *shochet* (ritual slaughterer) typically lived in a larger city, and periodically circulated through the countryside. Therefore, rural Jews enjoyed fresh meat less frequently, relying instead on various types of preserved meat. It could be packed in rendered fat, pickled, or salted and air-dried. Each was preferred by some group of Kurdish Jews for their *mebosas*.[21]

Meanwhile, even city-dwellers who had access to fresh meat did not all use the same kind. Beef and lamb were common, but chicken held pride of place.[22] Another frequent addition, even today, is stomach or intestines, stuffed with a rice-and-chopped-meat mixture.[23]

As you can see, the Kurdish Shabbat stew reflects a more developed cuisine and comes in many variants. Two things, however, unite these various *mebosas*. All are built around the same basic meat-and-grain core, with other ingredients elevating the stew above the *harisa*-like base. Also, regardless of variety, they're all called *mebosa*. This name (much like the word *harisa* itself) describes an element of the cooking process, referencing the overnight cooking method.[24]

### *Egypt*

When *harisa* arrived in Egypt, at the western edge of the region, it continued to be made in the traditional manner. But one minor tweak created a unique (and still popular) version, called *ferik*. The stew's plain wheat was swapped out for freekeh—unripe, green wheat that is harvested early, then dry-roasted over an open flame. Freekeh was invented as a sort of agricultural insurance: at least part of the harvest was saved in case of a later crop failure. The production process is ancient, with the food mentioned (by a different name) as far back as the Jewish Bible.† Remarkably, freekeh is still made today in virtually the same way as it was thousands of years ago.[25]

Extremely similar to its *harisa* forebear, the basic *ferik* recipe uses freekeh and meat, maybe an onion, and some basic spices. Non-Jewish

* I have come across one non-Kurdish version with *kubbeh*, from a Syrian family in Panama. But that stew appears to be an outlier. The recipe is in Chapter 8.

† Examples include "*kali*" in Ruth 2:14 and "*aviv kalui*" in Leviticus 2:14.

*Freekeh being made in Israel's northern Galilee region. Wheat before roasting on the right, after on the left.*

Egyptian cookbooks indicate that it is regularly cooked and eaten throughout the week by the general Egyptian populace.[26] Egyptian Jews, however, favor a Shabbat stew version that (of course) cooks through the night. Claudia Roden has written lovingly about the foods of the Egyptian Jewish community in which she grew up. She identifies *ferik* as "one of our Egyptian Saturday dishes." Her version is made with lamb and spiced with salt, pepper, cinnamon, and allspice.[27] Other recipes call for tomato paste and paprika, or turmeric, as flavoring agents.[28] These additions depart only slightly from the medieval *harisa* recipe.

There is, however, one aspect of the *ferik* that noticeably differentiates it from the standard *harisa* formula. Most Jewish *feriks* today contain eggs that cook inside the stew all night. Since Cairo Geniza* documents

* The Cairo Geniza was a trove of hundreds of thousands of documents (or fragments), both sacred and mundane, put in a closed room in a synagogue, rather than being thrown in the trash. They were discovered in the late nineteenth century, and intense study continues to the present day.

## Ferik

This simple but flavorful Shabbat stew is similar both to *harisa* and the slightly more complex *haleem* (*see* pages 38–40). But the freekeh's harder (and lighter) consistency, plus its smoky taste, make it stand apart.

### *Ingredients*

2 medium **onions**, chopped
1 tablespoon **oil**
1½–2 pounds (680–900 g) fatty **beef** or **lamb**, cut into chunks
2 cups (330 g) **freekeh**
1 teaspoon **salt**
1 teaspoon ground **turmeric**
1 teaspoon **sweet paprika**
1 teaspoon **hot paprika**
1 head of **garlic**, whole and unpeeled, but cleaned
8 **eggs**, still in their shells (optional)

### *Method*

In a large pot, fry the **onions** in **oil** over medium heat, until they start to get translucent. Remove from heat before they begin to brown.

Add the **beef** or **lamb**. Pour the **freekeh** around and over the meat. Add the **salt**, **turmeric**, **sweet** and **hot paprika**.

Tuck the head of **garlic** and the **eggs** (if using) gently into the top of the **freekeh**. Add water to cover.

Bring to a boil, then reduce the heat and simmer for about 20 minutes. Make sure there is still a significant amount of water inside. Cook overnight using any standard method (*see* pages 7–8).

*To serve*: Slice the top off the head of **garlic**, and place it on a separate plate, so everyone can get a soft clove. All should also get an **egg**.

### *Notes*

If you cannot find freekeh, use bulgur. The taste will not be identical, but the consistency should be approximately right. A seasoning option is to replace the turmeric and paprika with two teaspoons of cinnamon and one of allspice. Some cooks leave the garlic out entirely.

suggest egg consumption was uncommon among Egypt's Jews during the eleventh–thirteenth centuries, these eggs were probably added to the *ferik* at some later date.[29]

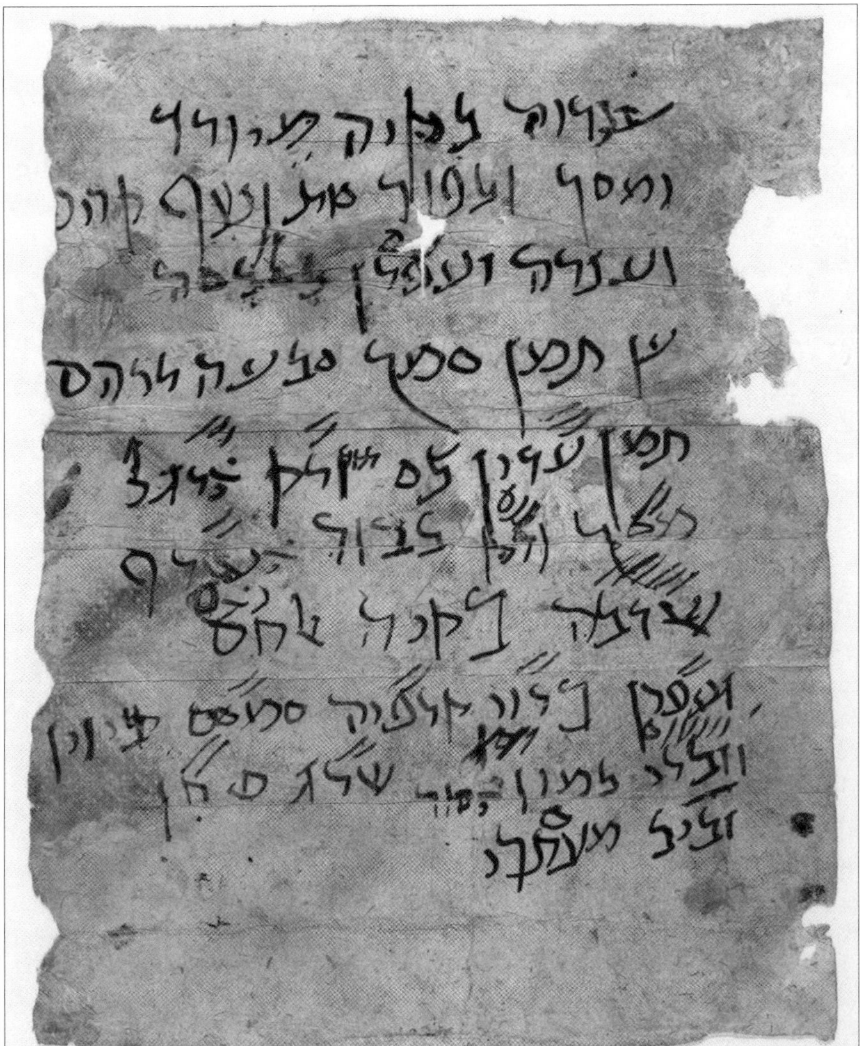

*Documents from the Cairo Geniza include many mundane, non-religious texts. This is a shopping list that includes such items as fish and saffron.*

As I'll describe in the next chapter, cooking whole eggs in the Shabbat stew pot was an innovation of the Jews in Spain, and became a beloved and enduring Sephardi food. So, most likely, after the Sephardi post-Expulsion arrival in Egypt, they influenced the local cuisine, leading to the presence of these eggs in today's Jewish *ferik*.

Those Spanish-Jewish refugees brought more than their beloved slow-cooked eggs. They also introduced an entirely different type of Shabbat stew to Egypt: *sofrito*. In it, meat is slow-cooked in a thick sauce of oil, lemon juice and turmeric. Crispy pre-fried potatoes are added just before serving. To those who know Spanish cookery, the term *sofrito* will be familiar, indicating a dish's base flavors, created by frying a mix of aromatic vegetables in olive oil. Jewish *sofrito* clearly differs, but the shared name and frying medium also help us trace this Shabbat stew back to Spain.[30] It enjoys popularity throughout the Sephardi diaspora today, and is widely eaten in Israel, as well as by Syrian Jews worldwide.

These two distinct Egyptian Shabbat stews, reflect the long history of Jewish presence there. The older community continued to eat a slightly modified version of the medieval *harisa*, and when a wave of Sephardi Jews arrived in the late fifteenth century, they brought a popular addition and a more modern Shabbat stew.

### *Persia*

The fourth corner of the Middle East to look at is Persia. Despite Iran's loss of nearly 90 percent of its Jews after the 1979 Islamic revolution, the approximately 8,000–9,500 who remain make the community the second largest in the Muslim world (after Turkey). Persian Jewry is one of the oldest Diaspora groups, and over their thousands of years in the country, they have spread, moving whenever a new ruler chose a different capital city. Thus, by the twentieth century, the largest Jewish populations were scattered: Tehran in the north, Isfahan in Iran's center with Shiraz to its south, and Mashad in the far northeast.* With the differing climates and histories in each city, different versions of the Shabbat stew dominated in each. But one, from Isfahan, descends directly from medieval *harisa*.

Back in the tenth century, Isfahan was the center of Persian-Jewish life. The area around it had so many Jewish residents that it was referred to as "Yahudistan."[31] The main Shabbat stew of Isfahani Jews is called *haleem*, an alternate name for *harisa* that is used interchangeably in some countries.[32] We can tell that this food does not originate in Persia itself, but rather descends from *harisa* firstly due to its name, which is Arabic for "patient." (Perhaps this relates to the need to wait a long time when the stew is slow-cooked.) But also, Persian *haleem* is made with wheat—particularly notable in a country where rice so heavily

* Smaller but still sizable communities were located in Hamedan to the west and Tabriz in the far northwest near the Caucasus, as well as in other cities, such as Yazd to the southeast of Isfahan.

## Haleem

Like the original *harisa*, this Isfahani stew ends up as a thick and stodgy porridge. It is comforting and filling on a cold winter day. If you prefer a lighter stew, go for the turkey option. If the *haleem* is still too heavy for your taste, see the Notes for a way to loosen it up a bit.

### *Ingredients*

1 pound (450 g) **wheat berries**, or shelled wheat
2 pounds (900 g) **beef**, cut in chunks, or 2 **turkey** legs and 2 **turkey** necks
1 (15-ounce/425 g) can white **beans**
1 large **onion**, chopped
1 tablespoon ground **turmeric**
1 teaspoon **salt**
1 teaspoon ground **black pepper**

*For serving*
Ground **cinnamon** (optional)
**Sugar** (optional)

### *Method*

Soak the **wheat** overnight, or rinse it thoroughly in cold water.

If using **beef**, boil it briefly in water and skim the foam off the top, then drain.

Put the drained **wheat**, **beef** or **turkey**, **beans**, **onion**, **turmeric**, **salt**, and **black pepper** in a pot. Add water to cover, bring to a boil, and simmer for 1–2 hours. Periodically stir the pot, to make sure the bottom doesn't burn. If the stew gets too thick, add some boiling water.

If you are using **turkey**, remove the meat from the pot, let it cool, and pull the meat off of the bones. Discard the bones and return the meat to the pot, with the skin.

Cook by any standard method (*see* pages 7–8).

*Serving option*: sprinkle **cinnamon** and/or **sugar** on top.

### *Notes*

If the *haleem* is too thick, stir some water or olive oil through your bowl.

dominates the diet. Non-Jewish Persians often eat this wheat-and-meat pounded porridge for breakfast, as did thirteenth-century Arabs.[33] Echoing the medieval Jewish *harisa*, Isfahani Jews frequently include onion and/or leek as *haleem* ingredients. Despite all this continuity, modern additions still found their way into the recipe: turkey meat and white beans frequently appear in this stew, both of which did not exist in the region in antiquity.*

Though Shiraz is not that far from Isfahan, a more elaborate stew exists there. Known as *khalebibi*, it features turnip, cabbage, onions, and mixed beans. Adding to the Persian character of this stew, rice is the grain in *khalebibi* and the primary spice is very popular in Persia: turmeric. The cabbage and rice make this stew much lighter than *haleem*. In contrast to the turkey found in an Isfahani *haleem*, no newcomer ingredients appear here. (Some of the beans might be modern arrivals to the region, but older versions of *khalebibi* presumably used only local legumes.) Thus, it is hard to pinpoint when this more complex stew developed, but it likely happened later than the Isfahani *haleem*. The city became a Persian capital later in history, and the Jewish population there enjoyed its greatest freedom in the eighteenth century. While *haleem* is eaten by Jews and non-Jews alike, I have found no parallel to *khalebibi* in non-Jewish Persian cooking. Like another famous Persian Sabbath food, *gondi* (a fluffy and aromatic meatball, typically served in a soup at Friday dinner), *khalebibi* seems to be only eaten by Iran's Jews. Interestingly, the name is unique in that it doesn't comfortably fit into any of the classic Shabbat stew name categories. *Khalebibi* means "aunt-grandmother."† I like to think this reflects the way the recipe was transmitted from generation to generation of home cooks.

A third Persian Shabbat stew, *sirab shirdun*, is like *haleem* in being a slow-cooked version of a widely eaten Iranian food. This festive stew mixes different types of offal with onion, spices and beans. The main-stream Persian version uses only tripe (stomach lining), but a Jewish version may also include feet, stomach, and tongue.[34] This marks a parallel development to the offal dishes encountered in Yemen and Kurdistan. Long before eating "head to tail" became trendy, Jews everywhere avoided wasting any part of the animal, both out of frugality and due to the biblical prohibition known as *bal tashchit* ("do not waste").‡

By finding Shabbat stew descendants of *harisa* in the areas that ring the Middle East, we see the results of its early standardization. Yemenite

* *See* Chapter 3 for a discussion of the "Columbian Exchange."

† Farsi has different words for maternal and paternal uncles and aunts. *Khale* is a maternal aunt. *Bibi* is not the formal name for a grandmother, but an honorific for a respected lady, often applied to a grandmother. It literally means "queen."

‡ The prohibition comes from Deuteronomy 20:19–20, but is extended by the Talmud in many places.

## Khalebibi

From the city of Shiraz, this stew combines many similar but different ingredients into a delicious whole. While you might be able to get away with using fewer types of beans, or only one type of cabbage, I chose to provide this traditional combination. In particular, the mung beans tend to dissolve in this stew, adding a mouth-pleasing thickness. This is based on a recipe I received from Drew Alyeshmerni of Los Angeles.

### *Ingredients*

½ cup (100 g) medium grain **rice**
1 (15-ounce/425 g) can **kidney** or **pinto beans**
⅓ cup (60 g) dried green or brown **lentils**
⅓ cup (60 g) dried **mung beans**
1¼ pounds (560 g) **beef**, cut into chunks
2–3 **marrow bones**
1 large **onion**, diced
1 large **turnip**, peeled and diced
1½ cups (about ⅓ pound/150 g) **red cabbage**, chopped (not shredded)
1½ cups (about ⅓ pound/150 g) **white cabbage**, chopped (not shredded)
1 tablespoon ground **turmeric**
2 teaspoons **salt**
1 teaspoon ground **black pepper**
½ teaspoon **cayenne** pepper (optional)

*For serving*
1 **lemon**, cut into wedges

### *Method*

Put the **rice, kidney** or **pinto beans, lentils,** and **mung beans** into a pot, and stir to mix. Add the **beef** and **marrow bones** on top, then distribute the **onion** and **turnip** around the pot. Pour the **red cabbage** and **white cabbage** over everything, then sprinkle the **turmeric, salt, black pepper,** and **cayenne** (if using) on top.

Add enough water so that the **cabbage** floats on top. Stir to mix.

Cook by any standard method (*see* pages 7–8).

*To serve*: Squeeze **lemon** juice over the top.

*harisa* and *marak regel*, Kurdish *mebosa*, Egyptian *ferik* and Persian *haleem* all provide convincing evidence that *harisa* became the pre-eminent Middle Eastern overnight dish. Over the intervening years, that single stew morphed to varying degrees in each place, but in all cases the modern Mizrachi iterations bear similarities to the medieval one. Later, new stew versions joined the older ones, but like the strong aftertaste left by a hearty meal, the universalized *harisa*'s influence can still be savored today in the region's Shabbat stews.

Oddly, however, the one place where it is *hard* to find a descendant of *harisa* is among Iraqi Jews—the community from which *harisa* disseminated. I now turn to their drastically divergent dish.

## More Than Skin Deep

The main Iraqi Shabbat stew is known as *t'bit*.* To make it, the cook pulls a chicken's meat and bones out of its skin, taking extreme care to not tear the skin itself. Typically, she leaves the wings and drumsticks, and only removes the breast and thigh pieces. The deboned meat and giblets (liver, gizzard, heart, etc.) are chopped and mixed with rice and a spice blend called *baharat*. This blend can include as many as fifteen different spices, with typical recipes favoring cardamom, cumin, coriander, turmeric, ginger and black pepper. The seasoned meat–rice blend is then stuffed back into the empty chicken skin, returning it to the shape of a whole chicken, which is then cooked in a pot, surrounded by more rice. Any Iraqi Jew worth his *baharat* will make sure to get some of each of the *t'bit* rices—the basic one from outside the stuffed chicken and the scented, meat-filled rice from inside the skin.

Ingredients-wise, then, *t'bit* remains close to *harisa*: meat and grain with some seasonings. But the cooking procedure here is completely different, and way more technical. It therefore seems unlikely that *t'bit* descends directly from *harisa*, leaving us with the question of how *t'bit* came to overshadow *harisa* as a Shabbat stew in Iraq.† I can only suggest a plausible explanation.

In time, Iraqi Jewry grew fairly isolated from other Jewish communities of the world. Their land had been conquered multiple times, periodically disconnecting it from the rest of the Middle East.[35] Furthermore, by the end of the Middle Ages, other rabbinical centers overtook that of Bavel in prominence (as I'll describe in the next two chapters). So while new innovations took place in Europe, including culinary ones, few likely made it back to Mesopotamia to influence the locals.

* Other spellings include *t'beet*, *tabyit*, *tabyeet*, and *tabeet*.

† Modern Iraqi Jews also ate *harisa* for Shabbat, at times. Some asked Muslim neighbors to pound it on Saturday mornings (Nawal Nasrallah, email to author, May 13, 2025).

Those who remained in Bavel presumably kept innovating, uninfluenced by (perhaps even unaware of) how universal *harisa* (and its descendants) had become elsewhere. New influences eroded *harisa*'s popularity in Mesopotamia. While Jews around the world altered *harisa*, Iraqi Jews may have simply replaced it with a new Shabbat stew.

That would explain *harisa*'s diminished popularity in Iraq, but what is the origin of *t'bit* itself? It again appears to be a uniquely Jewish iteration of a food drawn from the surrounding culture's cuisine. Thirteenth-century Arabic cookbooks from both Syria and Spain contain recipes for stuffed chicken skin.[36] They fill it with seasoned meat, sometimes supplemented by breadcrumbs or eggs. Only in the Iraqi-Jewish *t'bit* do we encounter rice as the primary stuffing. Perhaps this was a frugal way of using a larger quantity of a less expensive ingredient, much as later Ashkenazi Jews did with *kishke*.* (They all use a mix of meat and grain in the stuffing, but the proportions heavily favor meat in the Arabic recipes, while the Jewish one adds a bit of offal to a lot of grain. I see them, therefore, as distinct dishes at their core.) Iraqi Jews seemingly preserved the technique of emptying and restuffing a chicken skin, conveying it from the medieval to the modern kitchen. According to Iraqi food scholar Nawal Nasrallah, Jews frequently preserved many older Iraqi cooking methods, transmitting them to contemporary times.[37]

Recipes for *t'bit* are found in the first modern cookbooks from Iraq: *Recipes from Baghdad*, published in English in 1946, and an Arabic-language cookbook from the 1960s.[38] While neither states explicitly that *t'bit* is Jewish, Nasrallah indicates that Iraqi Arabs might eat and appreciate it, but definitely associate it with Jews. General Iraqi rice-and-chicken dishes do not stuff the chicken the way Jews do for *t'bit*.[39]

Or perhaps I should say, "the way Jews did for *t'bit*." As Iraqi Jewry modernized, so did their cooking methods. With busier lives and less time for cooking, a simpler version of *t'bit* now prevails. It is nearly impossible today to find an Iraqi-Jewish cook who still removes the chicken from its skin. Typically, the rice-and-giblet stuffing goes directly into the cavity of a whole chicken.[40] Some even prepare an unstuffed version, simply cooking rice and chicken parts together. (I feel this denatures the *t'bit*, moving it closer to non-Jewish Iraqi chicken-and-rice recipes.) Regardless, *t'bit* remains beloved in Iraqi-Jewish kitchens, and was carried elsewhere as Iraqi Jews migrated to other Asian countries in modern times.†

* *See* Chapter 6.

† *See* Chapter 8.

### T'bit

Most *t'bit* recipes are largely the same, with only minor differences in spicing, and the like. One change I've made here is the suggested alternative of using boneless chicken thighs (known as *pargiyot* in Israel), if your chicken does not come with the giblets. Also, this uses the more modern (and easier) method of stuffing the chicken cavity, rather than removing the chicken from its skin, and then restuffing it. *T'bit* works best in a pot in the oven, but can still be made using the other cooking methods.

***Ingredients***

3 cups (600 g) basmati (or other long-grained) **rice**
2 tablespoons **oil**
2 medium **onions**, sliced
3 medium **tomatoes**, diced, or 1 (14.5-ounce/400 g) can diced tomatoes
1 whole large **chicken**
2 tablespoons **tomato paste**
2 teaspoons **salt**
1½ tablespoons **baharat**, or this **spice blend**:
- ½ teaspoon ground black pepper
- 1 teaspoon sweet paprika
- 1 teaspoon ground turmeric
- ½ teaspoon ground cardamom
- ½ teaspoon ground cinnamon
- ¼ teaspoon ground cloves
- ¼ teaspoon ground nutmeg

8 **eggs**, still in their shells (optional)

***For the stuffing***

**Giblets** from the chicken, or 2 small skinless, boneless **chicken thighs** (*pargiyot*), chopped into small pieces
¼ teaspoon sweet **paprika**
¼ teaspoon ground **turmeric**
¼ teaspoon ground **cardamom**
¼ teaspoon **salt**

## From Inclination to Imperative

So far, we've seen how *harisa* came to be the original Shabbat stew, and how its spread through the area surrounding Bavel led to its standardization. But what explains the worldwide popularity of the Shabbat

### *Method*

Rinse the **rice** thoroughly, and cover it in water to soak.

In a large pot, heat the **oil**. Then add the **onions** and **tomatoes**, frying over medium heat for about 5 minutes.

Place the whole **chicken** on top to brown, turning to reach all sides. Add water to barely cover the chicken, along with the **tomato paste**, **salt**, and **baharat** or **spice blend**. Reduce heat to medium and cook for about 1 hour.

Remove the **chicken** from the water and set it aside. Check how much liquid remains in the pot. You want approximately 6 cups/1.5 liters left in the pot. Add more water if needed, or boil it down to reduce if there is too much.

Drain the **rice** that has been soaking, and add it to the stock in the pot. Cover and cook on low for about 10 minutes, or until most of the liquid has been absorbed. Remove the pot from the heat.

*Make the stuffing*: Scoop about 1 cup of cooked **rice** out of the pot, and put it in a mixing bowl. Add the cut-up **giblets** or **chicken thighs**, along with the spices from the stuffing ingredients (**paprika**, **turmeric**, **cardamom**, and **salt**). Mix to combine in the bowl.

*Assemble the t'bit*: Spoon the **stuffing** into the **chicken** cavity. Don't overfill it, but you don't need to leave a ton of space, since the rice is already cooked. Add any leftover stuffing back into the main pot with the bulk of the rice. Tie the legs of the **chicken** together with kitchen twine, and close the cavity with a toothpick or two.

Push the **chicken** down into the center of the **rice** remaining in the pot, making sure that it is surrounded on all sides (except on top). Lay a sheet of baking paper across the top.

If using the **eggs**, place them on top of the paper.

Cook by any standard method (*see* pages 7–8).

*To serve*: Cut the twine, and scoop the stuffing rice out of the chicken cavity and into a separate serving bowl.

Heap the main rice on a serving platter, with the chicken around it in pieces, or place the whole chicken in the middle and let people pull the soft meat from the bones as they like.

stew in general? There must have been some Jews who preferred a nice salad, or a cold chicken-in-flatbread wrap. How did that dish grow into something that lots of Jews feel they *have* to eat, every week?

To answer this, we must delve into one of the more significant—and misunderstood—developments in medieval Jewish history: the rise of

Karaism.* A distinct sect of Judaism, Karaites differ in their practice from most other Jews alive today. Whether Jews are Reform, Orthodox, Conservative or Reconstructionist, virtually all of them fall within the broad stream of "rabbinic Judaism." These denominations are like bagels, naan, focaccia and pita; each is recognizably different, but all are still types of bread. Karaism, in contrast, is like a brownie—another baked good made of wheat flour, but definitely not a bread. It is a different type of Judaism that from its outset was established in direct opposition to Rabbanite Jewry (the term used when contrasting the two groups). *Not* being Rabbanites is practically the *raison d'être* of the Karaite movement.

Karaites overtly reject rabbinic explanations of Judaism, instead appealing directly to the written Torah. (In fact, the word Karaite derives from the phrase *bnai mikra*, "people of the Bible.") Thus, Karaite Jews reject the legal decisions of the Mishnah and Talmud, leading to practical ritual differences between the two groups.† A prominent example relates to separating milk and meat. The Torah commands "Thou shalt not cook a kid in its mother's milk."[41] Famously, the rabbis extended this prohibition to an extreme separation of all milk and meat products, even requiring separate utensils and crockery, and mandating a waiting period between eating meat and dairy. Karaites stick to the explicit but limited Biblical restriction alone, rejecting these many extensions. They might, therefore, have had no issue using al-Warraq's milk-infused *harisas* for their slow-cooked Shabbat lunch.

That is, if they were to eat a slow-cooked Shabbat lunch at all. But medieval Karaites would *never* have allowed any Shabbat stew to be found in their homes. This is because another divergent practice stems from differing interpretations of Exodus 35:3, "You shall burn no fire in your dwellings on the Sabbath day." Early Karaite Jews understood this sentence literally—there should be no fire in your house on the Sabbath. They would even extinguish a fire if it was accidentally left burning on Shabbat.[42] Rabbanites, in contrast, believed the commandment only prohibited actively *lighting* a fire, but allowed for the presence of a pre-lit flame. Thus, while a Rabbanite Jew might have eaten his Friday dinner by candlelight, a Karaite would sit in the dark. More significantly, it meant

* I mainly discuss medieval Karaites here, though there are still Karaites today. Most do not descend from ancient adherents but have adopted Karaite beliefs, just as an Orthodox or Reform Jew may shift to Conservative or Reconstructionist practices.

† Some may question my classification of the Reform movement as rabbinic, since it rejects Talmudic authority. But that rejection came via debate among Reform rabbis.

that no Karaite Jew could possibly have used the rabbinic loophole of keeping food warming through the night for Shabbat lunch!

As should be clear, the practices of these two sects differed significantly. But how widely did this wedge drive them apart? Older theories place the two groups at vicious odds from the very beginning, claiming that Karaism began when a man named Anan was passed over for the position of Exilarch in Bavel, and then spitefully formed his own sect.* Modern scholarship considers this origin story a myth.[43] Furthermore, documents from the Cairo Geniza indicate significant collegial interaction between Karaites and Rabbanites. Members of the two groups married each other (usually Karaite brides to Rabbanite husbands), with Geniza marriage contracts indicating the ways in which leaders helped mixed couples navigate differences in customs.[44]

If Rabbanites and Karaites were like bread and brownies, imagine they'd discovered that the best way for them both to thrive was to establish jointly-operated bakeries.

Still, while their rivalry may not have been as bitter as was once believed, certainly Rabbanite leaders struggled to maintain their dominance, viewing Karaism as a threat.[45] The Karaites were a sizable (though always smaller) population, and enjoyed political power disproportionate to their numbers.[46] By the early tenth century, Israel had become the main seat of Karaite power in the region, while the Rabbanites remained centered in Bavel.[47] Rabbis even tried twice (unsuccessfully) to excommunicate the entire Karaite community, and went so far as to publicly flog some whom they considered rebellious heretics.[48] Despite the civil cooperation, Rabbanites and Karaites clearly remained on bad terms.

Therefore, the rabbis did all they could to shore up their decreasing numbers. Anything that might differentiate a Rabbanite from a Karaite became a litmus test. In an early example of the belief that "you are what you eat," consuming hot food on Shabbat day changed from a permitted act to a required indicator of one's true belief in Rabbanite Judaism.[49] If previously, eating a Shabbat stew was a self-motivated way to show your love for the Sabbath, now it was the main path to proving your bona fides.

This association between hot Sabbath food and faithfulness to "correct" rabbinic Judaism spread across the Jewish world. In twelfth-century Spain, Rabbi Zerachiah ben Isaac HaLevi picked up on this theme in his

* The Exilarch, meaning "Head of the Exile [Community]," was the political head of Babylonian Jewry.

book *Sefer HaMaor* ("The Book of Light"), a commentary on the Talmud. Following a discussion on the detailed laws of warming food on Shabbat, he wrapped up his thoughts with a short, rhymed passage:

> Whoever does not eat **hot food**,
> Must be checked to see if he is a **heretic**,
> Who, if he dies, should be buried by **Gentiles**.
>
> But, one who **prepares** to cook and **insulate** [his food],
> To enjoy the Shabbat and [thus] **gain weight**,
> Is a **true believer** who will merit **eternal life**.[50]
> [Bold phrases rhyme in the original Hebrew.]

If we encounter this harsh (if somewhat whimsical) statement written in Spain, where Karaism was weaker, the stress on eating hot Sabbath food must have been at least as strong back where Karaism was at its strongest. So it makes sense that *harisa*—that had already become the standardized Shabbat stew there—would so universally accompany Jewish migrations around the world.

Interestingly, Karaite practices shifted closer to rabbinic norms in due time. By the fifteenth century, they actually *required* their adherents to light a lamp before Shabbat began.[51] But culinary customs apparently die harder than religious practices, and the Shabbat stew remained a visible divider between the sects. Hundreds of years of *not* eating one meant that even if a Karaite might have some warm food, it would never be the same stew known to rabbinic Jews.[52]

The Rabbanite–Karaite conflict might also explain one other quirk of the stew in the Middle East: the prevalence of chicken as the meat of choice, mentioned in the previous chapter. Early Karaites did not eat chicken, since they were unsure if it was kosher. Unlike for fish and land animals, the Torah gives no signs by which to determine whether a bird is kosher. Instead, it lists about twenty birds that are forbidden and says nothing else on the subject. Karaites, therefore, only ate those types of birds that were sacrificed in the Temple, concluding that they must have been kosher. All other birds (including chickens) were considered, at best, questionable. Rabbanites, in contrast, extrapolated signs of *kashrut* from the list of explicitly forbidden birds in the Torah, as well as relying on tradition; if Jews had eaten a type of bird for ages, it *must* be kosher.[53] With this difference, it is conceivable that, as with consuming hot Shabbat food in general, eating chicken was another way for Rabbanite Jews to prove themselves as true believers, particularly in the region

*Solomon Schechter studying Cairo Geniza fragments at Cambridge University,* c. *1898. Rabbi Schechter was one of the first to recognize the importance of this trove of documents.*

where Karaism was at its strongest. And even better if you could do both with a single dish, such as *t'bit*.

This ingredient no longer sets Karaite Jews apart. As with the change in leaving a fire burning during Sabbath, Karaites eventually accepted the power of tradition in determining the kosher status of chickens.[54] But the effects of that early struggle appear to have pushed chicken into prominence for Middle Eastern Shabbat stews.

* * *

This chapter has uncovered all of the foundational elements of the Shabbat stew. Using the established loophole of slow cooking a Sabbath dish on a pre-existing flame, the Jews of Mesopotamia settled on a one-pot meal called *harisa* as their main option for Saturday lunch. By spreading around the Middle East, it became standardized as a more universal choice for slow cooking. Then, with the threatening rise of Karaism in this region, rabbinic leaders weaponized the Shabbat stew into a near imperative menu item to prove one's fidelity to orthodox observance.

With these stages complete, *harisa* and its culinary descendants took over the Jewish world. From the Middle East the stew would gradually encircle the Mediterranean, and from its many stops along the way would also branch out to reach scattered and smaller Jewish communities. In the next chapter, I'll describe *harisa*'s first port of call, and the earliest developments that began turning it into something new.

Chapter 3

# The Golden Age of Spanish Stewery

From its homeland by the rivers of Babylon, the Shabbat stew headed west, embarking on what would become a grand world tour. Though the rabbis of Bavel had been the leaders of world Jewry for centuries, a new center was rising in Spain—the far reaches of the known world. Jews had lived on the Iberian Peninsula for hundreds of years, but in tiny numbers. We know little about their specific food habits, which presumably were not significantly different from those of the non-Jewish population there, but it is unlikely that any one single dish was eaten universally for their Shabbat lunch. The story of the Shabbat stew's adoption in Spain sets a pattern for the rest of this book; I'll look at how it arrived in each location, and what changes took place there. But before I explore how this ancient Mesopotamian food was welcomed into medieval Iberia, I first must explain how a tiny frontier Jewish group grew into its position of dominance within world Jewry.

Numbers of Jews arrived in Spain at least as early as the third century CE, but may not have been the first. Though we have no direct evidence,

other Jews likely came as slaves following Titus' destruction of the Jerusalem Temple in 70 CE. And some individual Jewish traders may have arrived even earlier, following the Roman conquest in the second century BCE or with pre-Roman Phoenician traders.[1]

Any Jewish slaves in late first-century Spain would likely not have remained as such for long. In the Ancient Roman world, there were multiple ways in which slaves could eventually gain their freedom. Local Jews might have helped monetarily, while other slaves gained release on the death of their owners. These released captives may have established the Jewish communities of Spain. Certainly, by the time the Visigoths swept over the Pyrenees from France in the early fifth century, we know Jews already lived in Iberia.

The anti-Jewish edicts these rulers enacted attests to a Jewish presence.* (They couldn't persecute Jews if none were there, right?) Meanwhile, nearly 3,000 miles away in the Arabian desert, a cauldron called Islam was starting to boil and would soon spill over, with the Arab Conquest altering the course of history and, later, the culture of Iberia. It would also impact the fate of the Shabbat stew—which around that time was becoming standardized in Mesopotamia as *harisa*—and deliver the dish to its new Spanish home. The Islamic faith places Muhammad's first revelation in the year 610. Over the next twenty-two years, the Prophet would gain followers, subdue enemy tribes, and establish the foundation of the religion. He successfully transformed the bulk of the Arabian Peninsula into a single political entity by the time of his death in 632.

Muhammad's successor, Abu Bakr (the first caliph), skillfully maintained control, while adding to Islam's territory. By delegating responsibilities while remaining the political leader, he launched the incredibly rapid and far-reaching spread of Arab culture. Between 634 and 713, he and his successors colonized the Middle East, all of North Africa, and the entire Iberian Peninsula. In a mere eighty years, the Arab armies conquered territory that stretched from the border of China to the Atlantic Ocean and the frontier with France.

As the Arabs made their way to Iberia, Jews apparently accompanied them. With such massive territory taken quickly, there were simply too few ethnic Arabs (or even non-Arab Muslims) to administer it. In many cases, the Arabs used local Jews, Berbers, and others to help in managing

* In an eerie prefiguration of what would transpire 800 years later, King Sisebut decreed Jewish conversion or expulsion in 613. Some fled, while others converted but practiced Judaism in secret (Assis, *Jews of Spain*, 10).

*The evidence of Jewish presence in pre-Arab Spain includes this tombstone. Menorahs flank the bottom, and the word synagogue may be seen at the end of line 2.*

their new lands.[2] Furthermore, by bringing so much area under single rule, the Arab Conquest made it easier for Jewish merchants to traverse the empire. While some Jews came to al-Andalus (the Muslim name for the Iberian Peninsula) from France and Germany, the bulk moved from the vast territory that stretched from Mesopotamia to Morocco.[3]

And with those Jewish immigrants from the East, the Shabbat stew arrived as well.

## From *Harisa* to *Adafina*: The Stew in Al-Andalus

From the time of the eighth-century Arab Conquest, Jewish life in Islamic Spain improved in stages. Jewish history in al-Andalus can be divided into two broad periods. The eighth and ninth centuries were a time of basic integration, while the so-called "Golden Age of Spanish Jewry"—from the tenth to mid-twelfth centuries—brought them significant progress and success in virtually all fields of life. The food of the region in general, and of the Jewish population in particular, also evolved during these 400-plus years. But first, the relationship between Jews and Muslims in al-Andalus.

In contrast to the oppressive Christian rule prior to the Arab conquest, the more tolerant culture of Islam allowed Jews to thrive. Spanish Jewry welcomed the Arab invaders as liberators, even helping in the fight against the Visigothic rulers. Iberia's cultivated land increasingly became Jewish-owned, after the Arabs dispossessed their Christian enemies. Skilled Jewish immigrant farmers brought agricultural knowledge from North Africa, growing produce that would soon become popular in Spain. Jews certainly did not enjoy equality with Muslims in Andalusia. But the local laws did not actively oppress Jews; they merely formalized Jews as second-class citizens.[4]

Over the next 250 years, the Cordoba Caliphate and its successors thrived culturally, with science, art, medicine, education, and commerce all blossoming. Jews fully integrated into the culture and found success in politics as well. The best example of this early prominence is Hasdai ibn Shaprut, who became an advisor and *de facto* foreign minister to Caliph Abd al-Rahman III (ruled 912–29). In addition to interacting politically with Christian Europe, ibn Shaprut parlayed his power into assisting the Jews.

During this period, the Jewish population in al-Andalus increased rapidly, absorbing immigrants from across the Arab world.[5] In response, ibn Shaprut helped shift the center of world Jewry from Bavel to Sepharad (the medieval Jewish name for Iberia). While he still supported Babylonian Talmudic academies, he more significantly appointed Rabbi Moshe ben Hanoch as *rosh yeshiva* (rabbinic academy head) in Cordoba. Legend portrays ben Hanoch as one of four sages of Bavel taken captive at sea and ransomed to various Jewish communities around the Mediterranean region. Too outlandish to be considered a historically accurate tale explaining the Bavel-to-Sepharad shift, the sages-at-sea legend more likely reflects and fictionalizes it. Bavel was already on the decline, and Jewish emigration to the west was already increasing. Compound that with the popularity of the Karaite movement and we see that Bavel's goblet had been nearly drained, even if some sediment remained at the bottom. Moshe ben Hanoch's move to Cordoba helped shift the rabbinic center of gravity to Spain.

During these same few centuries, Iberia became the most cosmopolitan region in the world. The prior Christian and Jewish residents of the area were joined by Muslims of many ethnicities: Arabs, Berbers, and Mesopotamians, perhaps even Persians. Spain became the first place where the Christian and Muslim worlds met and interacted regularly.

Reflecting this worldly and sophisticated atmosphere, the cuisine on the peninsula changed as well, blending aspects of each population's food practices. As a daily human activity, and a typically informal one at that, eating habits are generally among the best expressions of cultural mixing. People prepare the foods they know, but exposure to neighbors from different backgrounds can broaden culinary awareness. If you like the food your neighbor serves you at a shared meal, you might start cooking it yourself. And even if dietary laws (such as *kashrut*) preclude your sampling their food, you'll still smell your neighbor's cooking, or might ask her in the marketplace how she makes her famous goat-and-fava-bean stew.

A modern example of this phenomenon is the popular Irish-American custom of eating corned beef (UK salt beef) and cabbage (with potatoes) on St. Patrick's Day. This dish has become so emblematic that many think it is the core of the Irish diet in general. In reality, the combination was not a popular St. Patrick's Day food in Ireland. Beef was barely eaten there, only consumed by the rich. In America, however, with neighborly relations between Irish and Jewish immigrants (along with low beef prices), Irish people adopted Jewish-style corned beef, fusing it with inexpensive cabbage and their beloved potatoes. Without their exposure to Jewish food in America, that specific combination would have never existed.[6]

Similarly, foods of different cultures mixed in medieval al-Andalus. Produce from the Arab world, such as eggplants, citrus fruits, almonds and spinach met and mingled with local agricultural staples, such as wheat, olive oil and wine. Rice came on the scene, benefitting from newly introduced irrigation techniques. The cosmopolitan culture fostered an atmosphere of culinary experimentation.[7]

This gastronomic cross-pollination also left its mark on the Shabbat stew. *Harisa* arrived in Spain early, while Islamic culture there was still immature, and the adventurous food culture had yet to take root. Mesopotamia was no parochial backwater, but *harisa*'s move to Spain must have brought on the type of culture shock an Indianapolis native might feel on a first visit to New York City. So, while it took some time, the stew gradually embraced the adventurous dietary culture, and began its own metamorphosis, probably during the late tenth and early eleventh centuries.

In Iberia, *harisa*'s ingredients diversified, creating more types to choose from. We see this via a thirteenth-century Andalusian cookbook whose author is unknown.* In describing *harisa*, the cookbook details various versions, with the primary recipe offering multiple meat options: "*Harīsa* may be cooked with fatty veal, meat of yearling sheep, or meat from the breasts or thighs of geese or chicken. Each kind of these meats has its own distinctive flavor and taste."[8] A different *harisa* in the book surprisingly replaces the traditional wheat berries with bread-crumbs.

One recipe in the book, featuring rice (rather than wheat) with chicken or mutton, calls for overnight cooking: "Immerse [the ingredients] in plenty of water and let the pot's lid be tightly sealed. Keep the pot in the *furn* [brick oven] overnight."[9] Interestingly, six recipes in this Arabic cookbook were explicitly identified as Jewish, but this *harisa* was not one of them (perhaps because the all-night cooking was only optional). But the slow-cooked dish seemingly resembles the stew that Caliph Mu'awiya requested of the Yemenite Jew.

As the twelfth-century end to the Golden Age approached, the stew went through even more sophisticated changes. The first developments had been tentative (changing the selected meat or grain), but in time they grew more radical. Like an expat getting a haircut or new pair of shoes to blend into a new culture, the Shabbat stew took on different ingredients and changed its look. Legumes—primarily chickpeas or fava beans—first entered the stew, as did green leafy vegetables, such as chard and spinach. Cilantro and eggplants were among the other popular ingredients of later versions of the stew.†

Chickpeas, chard, cilantro, and eggplants would all grow to be known as Jewish ingredients in Iberia, indicating how widespread their consumption had become within the community.[10] Local Christians simply weren't on familiar terms with these vegetables. Later, they actively avoided them, for example using parsley where Jews used cilantro.[11] Jews were not direct enemies of the Spaniards, as were Muslims, and thus became the preeminent "boundary-crossers," traveling regularly between opposing Muslim and Christian cultures. So while Muslims

* Although composed in the thirteenth century, it includes recipes from a few prior centuries.

† Remembering that "stew" is an inherently inaccurate collective term, it is with these additions that the porridge-like *harisa* began transforming into a genuine stew.

also ate these ingredients, Christians associated the foods with Jews, with whom they interacted more regularly.

The addition of new ingredients into *harisa* reveals an open-mindedness that only picked up pace over time. Gradually, more ingredients found their way into the dish, including garlic and cumin. A minor procedural change may have been pre-frying the onions, sometimes with the meat.[12] Since many of the stew's descendants are served in multiple courses—broth as a starter, followed separately by meat and vegetables—some speculate that this also was done by some in Spain, but I've found no direct evidence of this.*

Most importantly, these small changes meant that the lid had been ripped off the pot of culinary liberalism, freeing the cook to apply the Shabbat stew slow-cook method to any number of distinct, albeit similar, food combinations. This blazed the trail for every other change that would take place moving forward.

Since *harisa* had fairly strict rules about its composition (even the ratio of grain to meat was dictated and, at times, legally enforced),[13] this new dish could no longer be called *harisa*. It received a new name: *adafina*, from the Arabic "to bury." This referenced insulating the hot food overnight.[14] Further changes would alter the Shabbat stew during the next phase of Jewish life in Spain.

## From Crescent to Cross: The Stew in Christian Spain

The development of *harisa* into *adafina* reflects the Muslim influence in al-Andalus. But, as the Middle Ages progressed, Christian Spain's culture would also impact the Shabbat stew. Beginning in the mid-tenth century and continuing for a few hundred years, the *Reconquista* ("reconquest") saw unifying Christians of northern Spain recapturing territory they'd lost to the Arabs centuries earlier. Without even moving, some Jews who had been living under Muslim rule in al-Andalus now found themselves living in such Catholic kingdoms as León, Castile or Aragon.

Then, following the 1002 death of Almanzor (al-Mansur), the most successful Muslim military leader of the time, the local caliphate began to disintegrate. Infighting split al-Andalus into a number of smaller Muslim

* Some claim this was done in Spain, but I couldn't source the claim. See Pilar Bravo Lledó, "Las costumbres judeoconversas en Alcalá de Henares" [The habits of Jewish *conversos* in Alcalá de Henares], Museo Casa Natal de Cervantes, https://museocasanataldecervantes.org/wp-content/uploads/2022/01/LAS-COSTUMBRES-JUDEOCONVERSAS-EN-EL-ALCALA-DE-HENARES-DEL-SIGLO-DE-ORO2014.pdf, 8.

### Adafina

In *A Drizzle of Honey*, husband and wife scholars David M. Gitlitz and Linda Kay Davidson reconstructed medieval Sephardi recipes based on Inquisition trial records. I've based this recipe (with permission) on one of theirs, updating quantities and a few ingredients. Theirs originated with Blanca Ramirez, tried in 1523 Toledo, shockingly based on events from fifty years earlier—before the Inquisition had even begun!

***Ingredients***

2–3 medium **eggplants**, cut into 1½-inch (4-cm) cubes
3–4 teaspoons **salt**, divided
4 tablespoons **olive oil**
3 medium **onions**, sliced
2¼ pounds (1 kg) boneless **beef** or **lamb**, cut into chunks
1 (15-ounce/425 g) can **chickpeas**
1 (15-ounce/425 g) can **fava beans**
1 tablespoon **coriander** seeds
1 tablespoon **cumin** seeds
1 tablespoon **caraway** seeds
1½ teaspoons **peppercorns**
8 **eggs**, still in their shells (optional)
20 medium leaves **chard**

city-states. To escape the unrest, waves of Jews began actively moving northward into re-Christianized territories. This migration increased from the late eleventh century into the twelfth, after the religiously zealous Berber Almoravids and the even more fanatical Almohads in turn took over in al-Andalus, eventually forcibly converting people to Islam. The center of Sephardi Jewry irrevocably shifted to Christian-controlled areas.[15]

Like the Jews who fled al-Andalus, *adafina* and *harisa* also found new homes in Christian Spain. It is unclear how similar or different the stew became in Iberia's north, but we know that it at least gained a new name: *hamin di trigo*. While the name *adafina* came from Arabic, this one combines Hebraic and Romance roots. *Hamin* was the Aramaic-tinged Hebrew for "hot food" and *trigo* was early Castilian Spanish for wheat. In time, this name would be shortened simply to *hamin*.[16]

Thus there is something remarkable in the two main names for the stew in medieval Spain. *Adafina* ("cover") and *hamin* ("hot food")

***Method***

Put the **eggplants** into a strainer and sprinkle with 1½ teaspoons **salt** (or up to 1 teaspoon more, as needed to coat all). Let drain for at least 30 minutes.

In a large pot, heat the **olive oil** over medium heat. Fry the **onions** with ½ tsp of **salt** until they start to soften, about 5 minutes. Remove from heat.

Thoroughly rinse the **salt** off the **eggplant** pieces, and dry them on a tea towel. Add the **beef** or **lamb** and **eggplant** to the pot, then scatter the **chickpeas** and **fava beans** around.

In a spice grinder, good blender, or using a mortar and pestle, grind the **coriander, cumin, caraway,** 1 teaspoon of **salt,** and **peppercorns** together. Sprinkle over everything in the pot. Add water to cover.

If using the **eggs,** nestle them gently on top, at least partly submerged.

Cut the stems off the **chard.** Cut the leaves into smaller pieces, about 2 inches (5 cm) square. (No need to be precise about shape or size. They will cook down.) Pound the **chard** stems to soften. Cover the ingredients in the pot with all of the chard.

Cook by any standard method (*see* pages 7–8).

Serve alongside cooked rice or wheat berries.

directly echo (in separate languages) the phrase *tomnin et hahamin* of the original Mishnah discussed in Chapter 1. Even more notable is that these two terms continued forward in history, getting translated into other languages, but remaining the most popular names for the Shabbat stew.*

In the span of a few centuries, then, we find a number of major steps forward in the Shabbat stew's evolution. Following *harisa*'s initial arrival in Spain, minor ingredient additions made it more sophisticated. Eventually, the changes were drastic enough to require a new name, *adafina*. Finally, with the northward shift of Sephardi Jewry, it also acquired a second popular name, *hamin*.

After tracing these developments—the first major stage of innovation for the Shabbat stew—this is an appropriate point to address a legitimate

* There were many other names used in Spain, indicating that none had yet become standard in a dish that was in the midst of development. These two were the most common.

question. I've spoken of these dishes as versions of the same stew, as I will continue to do for the rest of the book. But was *adafina* actually an evolved *harisa* or was it an entirely new food? This question is central to the study of world cuisine, but is, to a degree, impossible to answer. The history of foods shows them constantly being transported, adopted and modified. Virtually no food in the world was created *ex nihilo*. Everything is based on something prior, with all foods sitting along a single continuum. At what point does one dish cease to be a version of a prior food and turn into something new? There is no single answer to this question. Many factors contribute: ingredients (both central and secondary), preparation method, when or how it is eaten, and even its name. To my view, *adafina* and *hamin*'s continuation of the Jewish *harisa*'s essential "low and slow" cooking method, plus their preservation of the grain-and-meat core, places them close enough to consider them as variations, rather than new dishes.

## The Stew of Life or Death

My mention of Jews finding refuge in Christian Spain might seem strange, in light of the persecution Jews faced there before the Muslim conquest. Compound that with our hindsight knowledge of the Inquisition and Expulsion that would wipe out Spanish Jewry, and the contradiction appears stronger. Interestingly, the early *Reconquista* period was actually favorable for Jewish life in Christian Spain, described by the evocative term *La Convivencia*—coexistence.* Like an avocado's tender flesh, sandwiched between its inedible peel and hard pit, the twelfth and early-thirteenth centuries represent an island of symbiosis amid the generally unpleasant history of Christian–Jewish relations in Iberia.

As they had done for the Arab conquerors in al-Andalus, Jews helped the Christian kings manage and rebuild their reconquered territories. They settled as a counterbalance to the local Muslim population, owning and cultivating land.[17] The Christian kings trusted them as neutral bystanders in the peninsula's ongoing conflict, and as Arabic-speakers who had been integrated into Andalusian society, Jews provided cultural intelligence.[18] For example, Alfonso VI of León and Castile granted Jews nearly full equality after conquering Toledo. In appreciation, many joined his army and fought the Almohads. Later, Jews financed various Christian armies and maintained their fortresses.[19]

* Though scholars debate the extent of genuine coexistence, undoubtedly things were *relatively* better for the Jews among Spanish Christians at the time.

Unfortunately, however, this period of cooperation proved relatively short-lived. *Reconquista* Christian–Jewish amicability could best be described as pragmatic. The Christians had resettled most of Iberia by the mid-thirteenth century, and their kings no longer had use for the Jews.[20] The general populace followed the clergy in vigorously expressing religiously inspired hatred. In the early fourteenth century, the Church won increasing numbers of converts via anti-Jewish edicts.[21] Repetitive mob violence murdered thousands of Jews across Iberia. Finally, in summer 1391, spurred by the incendiary antisemitic priest Ferrand Martinez, a traumatic wave of massacres and forced conversions overtook cities and towns throughout northern and eastern Spain. Tens of thousands of Jews were murdered, while significantly more (over 100,000 by some estimates) were forcibly baptized.[22] Others sensed how deep-seated these attacks were. Spanish–Jewish relations were more like a fruit rotting from within, than an apple with a small bruise on it. Thus, many Jews fled the country early, escaping the coming horrors of Inquisition and Expulsion.[23]

Though it wouldn't officially be established for nearly ninety more years, the Spanish Inquisition grew directly out of the nightmarish events of 1391. And within that century's tense environment, the Shabbat stew would transform from a celebratory dish to, quite literally, a matter of life and death.

The Catholic Church singled out converts, labeling them New Christians, and considered them all—forcibly converted or not—to be fully fledged and irrevocably Christian. Any attempts to revert to Judaism were seen as apostasy, to be prevented at all costs. One such "cost" was complete separation between *conversos* (converted Jews) and their former community.* Any hints of maintaining contact or observing Jewish rituals was called "Judaizing." To prevent this, the Inquisition launched in 1480. The Inquisition couldn't punish unconverted Jews; it only targeted *conversos* suspected of secretly following Jewish practice. Such Crypto-Jews, as they are now commonly known, were called by the derogatory epithet Marranos, from the Spanish word for "swine."†

* The term *converso* refers to all those who converted. By calling them (and their descendants) "New Christians," Spanish Christians ensured that conversion couldn't solve a Jew's problems—he was perpetually held in suspicion.

† We also don't know what percentage of *conversos* became Crypto-Jews. It likely varied by time of conversion, economic status, and so on. Rather than questioning the ratio of secret Jews to faithful Christians, perhaps we should view those as the extremes of a spectrum.

But how could Inquisition courts identify such Judaizers? Most commonly, witnesses testified to seeing New Christians engaged in Jewish practices. While some identified Sabbath or holiday observance, many trial records highlight food practices as telltale signs. What Crypto-Jews ate—or didn't eat—could easily give away their secret.

Gitlitz and Davidson, in their fascinating book *A Drizzle of Honey: The Lives and Recipes of Spain's Secret Jews*, reconstruct Crypto-Jewish foods based on Inquisition trial transcripts. They point out that food choices and timing could both land a *converso* in court. Eating a "Jewish" dish or avoiding non-kosher animals were potential giveaways. Similarly, eating special foods around Jewish holidays or Sabbath, or ignoring food prohibitions on Christian fast days could also create trouble.[24] In short, fasting on Yom Kippur, eating meat during Lent, or entirely avoiding shellfish could betray a Crypto-Jew. But probably the most incriminating individual food was that most Jewish of dishes: the Shabbat stew.[25] Preparing it could lead—if such testimony held up—to execution.* Such "heretics" were horrifically burned alive in public *autos-da-fé*.†

It must be said that just because witnesses accused *conversos* of cooking *adafina*, that doesn't mean Inquisition officers (or regular Spaniards) actually knew what *adafina* was. Awareness of the Jewish food name and a vague related suspicion could be sufficient to implicate. One testimony from a trial in the Canary Islands states that "Ana Goncales . . . saw that her mistress cooked mutton with oil and onions, *which she understands* is the Jewish dish Adafina."[26] Note, first, that meat, onions and oil alone could not be a complete *adafina* recipe. More importantly, it was clearly sufficient that Goncales *believed* this was the forbidden food, whether or not it actually was.

That type of speculation didn't spring up in a vacuum. Inquisition officials distributed the ingredients necessary for regular citizens to cook up their malicious accusations. The Inquisition educated the populace about suspect Jewish food practices, via published "Edicts of Grace." In a list delineating details of kosher observance (such as salting meat and removing the sciatic nerve), they also described "cooking on the said Fridays such food as is required for the Saturdays and on the latter

* Nawal Nasrallah points out that couscous served a similar role in incriminating Muslim converts, "revealing" Crypto-Muslim practices (Nasrallah, *Delectable Foods*, 94–9).

† In just the first few years of the Inquisition, thousands were burned alive. Nearly 20,000 more faced punishments from imprisonment to total despoilment (Sachar, *Farewell*, 65).

eating the meat thus cooked."[27] The dead giveaway, therefore, was what has always set the Shabbat stew apart: its peculiar cooking method. Ingredients were less significant.

To avoid detection, some Crypto-Jews found clever ways of appearing to eat *treif* (non-kosher foods), while still adhering to the kosher laws. For example, though most Iberian sausages are made of pork, *alheira* is a Portuguese sausage that originally used bread and chicken, a somewhat indistinguishable and similarly white (though kosher) meat. Its Crypto-Jewish roots are revealed by its common nickname today: "Marrano sausage."[28]

Meanwhile, other *conversos* who genuinely believed in Christianity could prove their faith by conspicuously consuming pork. It was their way of telling the Inquisitors, "Look! I'm a good Christian. I'm eating pig!"

Many culinary historians believe some New Christians went so far as to purposely insert pork into the *adafina* they still loved. With such a blatantly non-kosher ingredient, what accuser could point to this stew as an example of Judaizing? In combining the ultimate *treif* food with the very Jewish *adafina*, these *conversos* created today's Spanish "national dish"—*cocido*.* Notably, *cocido* features the classic low-and-slow cooking method and is typically served in separate courses. Additionally, chickpeas (which you'll recall were identified with Jews) are an absolutely essential ingredient. At the same time, *cocidos* also prominently feature lots of pork.[29]

Thus, in addition to its position in the family tree of Jewish food, *adafina* also became the culinary uncle of some extremely unkosher, Spanish favorites.

## But Wait, There's More: A Bonus Food

In addition to the non-Jewish *cocido*, another descendant of the Spanish Shabbat stew enjoys popularity today among Sephardim everywhere. In the process of expanding the stew's core ingredients, Spanish Jews also created its first "Bonus Food." By that term I mean an add-in item that is not an integral part of the dish—something cooked in the stew pot but usually removed to be served separately on the side. We will encounter many such Bonus Foods in different regions moving forward, but the earliest entered the Shabbat stew in medieval Iberia.†

* The term *cocido* is a collective term applied to many similar Spanish stews. A few common ones are *cocido madrileño* and *olla podrida*.

† The *kubbeh* found in Kurdish *mebosas* might seem like a Bonus Food, but they're not eaten separately. Plus, they were created later, even if mentioned earlier in this book.

*Huevos Haminados* are eggs, still in their shells, that hard-boil with the stew through the full night. The name is Ladino (Judeo-Spanish) for "*hamin* eggs." When they emerge from the stew on Shabbat day, the egg whites have turned a *café au lait* brown, and the yolks are soft and creamy. The eggs' meaty flavor and appealing color stem from the extended cooking, not just the stew penetrating the egg shell. *Haminados* (as they are known for short) were an inexpensive additional protein, pumping up the stew's nutritional value while also filling hungry bellies. But the Sephardi innovation was not in adding these eggs to their Shabbat lunch menu. Rather, it was in the idea of cooking them *inside* of the stew.

Slow-cooked eggs long predate the Spanish Golden Age. First mentioned in the Talmud, they are actually one of the earliest foods that can be specifically connected with Shabbat day. In a legal discussion about eating food that was cooked through Shabbat, the Gemara mentions eggs that shrunk in size after all-night cooking. One rabbi ate such eggs with Rabbi Yehuda HaNasi, the famous head of the Sanhedrin. Shrunken to the size of crabapples, the eggs were so delectable that the two rabbis couldn't eat enough of them.[30] Clearly, these Talmudic sages learned what generations of later Sephardim knew implicitly: the long cooking process transforms the eggs into a recognizably distinct, and immensely tastier food.

The Talmudic eggs shrank because of the dry-roasting process.* For a long time, this was the predominant cooking method, and it remains so in some places today. Some Iraqi Jews, for example, rest eggs on the lid of their *t'bit* pot to cook through the night, while Yemenite Jews have been known to roast them in the oven, alongside their *jachnun* or *kubaneh*.[31] Similarly, in nineteenth-century Hungary, Jews put eggs covered in hot ashes into a tightly-sealed pot that baked in the oven next to their stew.[32]

The notable alteration in Spain was the eggs' move out of the dry heat and directly into the stew. We can't pinpoint exactly when or why this first took place, but we can make some basic assumptions. With more vegetables, *adafina* would have become more liquid than the porridge-like *harisa*. Since the Shabbat stew and slow-cooked eggs were both typical Shabbat lunch dishes, some Sephardi Jews presumably started cooking them in one pot, out of convenience. Gil Marks speculates this happened after the thirteenth century "when the place for cooking the Sabbath stew moved from the home hearth to the local large commercial oven."[33] Stewing the eggs in the pot's moist atmosphere provided the

* Such eggs are properly called *huevos asados*, roasted eggs, rather than *huevos haminados*, as they don't cook inside of the *hamin*.

## Huevos Haminados

The easiest way to make *huevos haminados* is simply to put eggs directly into your Shabbat stew. But since these have grown popular enough to be eaten on their own, I wanted to give you that option as well.

This is the most basic recipe in this book because, in reality, all you truly need are eggs and water. They'll be just as delicious, and will still turn the proper brown color. I've done it that way myself! However, I'm adding here a few optional extras that many recipes include, and which might have some hidden benefits that I've not discovered. Doing it the way generations of mamas and nonas have may be reason enough.

### *Ingredients*

6–10 dry **onion skins** (optional)
8–12 raw **eggs**, still in their shells
**water**
1 cup (240 ml) **coffee grounds** (optional, see Notes)
3 **tea bags** (optional)
2 tablespoons **olive oil** (optional)
1 tablespoon **vinegar** (optional)
1 teaspoon **salt** (optional)

### *Method*

If using the **onion skins**, place them on the bottom of a pot (or slow cooker) large enough to hold all the **eggs** you want. Gently put the **eggs** on top. Add enough **water** to cover the eggs by at least 2 inches (5 cm).

Add any of the other optional ingredients (**coffee grounds, tea bags, olive oil, vinegar, salt**) that you choose to use.

Cook for 8–12 hours, or more in a 200°F/95°C oven (if using a pot), or on Low setting if using a slow cooker.

*To serve*: Drain, cool in cold water, and peel.

### *Notes*

You can use coffee grounds after you have already brewed coffee from them, as they are more for color than flavor.

If you are using any of the other optional ingredients to add more color, you can remove the eggs from the water after about an hour, cool them, and lightly crack (without removing) the shells. Return them to the water for the rest of the time, and you will get a beautiful web pattern on the eggs. This doesn't work well with plain water.

added benefit of having similar eggs, but without them shriveling via dry heat. Whether this was a fortuitous discovery or the result of planned experimentation, the Spanish Jews quickly discovered the pleasures of this new cooking method and widely adopted it.

Like *adafina*, *haminados* were another incriminating food during the Inquisition. Numerous testimonies mention their cooking method and unique color, at times in direct connection with the stew. For example, one Jew in 1492 Aragon was accused of eating a Jewish "stew and vermilioned hard-boiled eggs" for Shabbat.[34]

The Expulsion from Spain in 1492 dispersed Sephardi Jewry, spreading their *haminados* to many other regions as well. It remains a hallmark of Sephardi cuisine today.* These eggs became so beloved among Sephardim that they wanted to eat them during the week as well. This, however, presented a *halachic* challenge since the eggs were cooked with meat, and could therefore not be eaten with dairy foods. In order to eat *haminados* with milky meals, Sephardim started making the eggs in separate pots of water. To ensure the cherished caramel color, inventive (and frugal) cooks added onion skins to the cooking water.† Later, old coffee grounds or tea leaves also became popular for this purpose.‡

The historical development of this first Bonus Food is admittedly convoluted. It originated outside the stew pot, then it was cooked inside, and finally it was moved into its own pot of water. Most of the other Bonus Foods I'll discuss later started, and still remain, inside of the stew. But in Chapter 5, we will explore one other, particularly well-known example that evolved via a different, yet equally convoluted process: *kugel*.

## The Stew After 1492

The final topic to discuss in relation to the stew's sojourn in Spain is what happened at the end of its time there. Spanish Jewish history came to an abrupt halt in 1492 with the Alhambra Decree that expelled all Jews from the newly constituted kingdom of Spain.§

* Recipes abound in cookbooks from across the Sephardi diaspora.

† Apparently this was already done by some Jews while still living in Spain (Gitlitz, *Drizzle*, 75). The onion skins also cushion the eggs, preventing cracking.

‡ In fact, such additives are unnecessary. The brown color derives from the Maillard reaction browning the sugar in egg whites. Cooking them in plain water has the same effect (*see* Harold McGee, *On Food and Cooking: The Science and Lore of the Kitchen, Completely Revised and Updated*, New York: Scribner, 2004, 89). Still, the additives intensify the brown color.

§ Some kingdoms wouldn't be absorbed until later, but the marriage of Isabella I of Castile to Ferdinand II of Aragon unified the bulk of Iberia.

*The Alhambra Decree, expelling Jews from Spain.*

Estimates vary widely regarding how many refugees fled to other lands, but it was at least in the tens of thousands, and potentially as many as 100,000.[35] Many more chose baptism, including some prominent (and wealthy) Jews of the time. Unlike in the past, such conversions now required little Catholic prodding—would-be proselytes practically lined up outside the church doors.[36]

Among the most prominent of those who chose exile over conversion was Don Isaac Abarbanel. His grandfather, Samuel, had fled Seville after the 1391 riots. Though Samuel accepted a forced baptism at the time, he made clear that he'd return to Judaism ASAP, which he did, promptly, on his arrival in Portugal.[37] Isaac, who would later become famous for his Torah commentaries and works of philosophy, served in a high role in the courts of Alfonso V of Portugal and later of Isabella of Castile. Despite his best lobbying efforts, however, the "Catholic Monarchs" refused to revoke the Edict of Expulsion. The following year, after Abarbanel arrived safely in Italy, he described in painful (if slightly exaggerated) terms the hurts and suffering the refugees endured during their travels from Spain.[38]

The importance of Sepharad on the world Jewish stage made the Expulsion particularly catastrophic. But Spain was not the first European territory to expel the Jews. England had done so two centuries earlier in 1290, and France followed suit in 1394 (following a series of halting expulsions and readmissions). The Jewish refugees from Spain, therefore, had limited options for resettlement. About 65,000 fled west to neighboring Portugal, but that proved an ineffective refuge; Portugal expelled its Jews (under even harsher terms) a mere four years later.[39] Those Jews who fled Iberia in 1492 primarily went in three directions: southeast into the Maghreb (Morocco, Algeria and Tunisia), east towards Italy and the Ottoman Empire and north to Holland or, to a lesser degree, southern France. (Provence, just to the north of Spain, only became part of the Kingdom of France some ninety years later, so it could provide some refuge for Jews and Crypto-Jewish *conversos*.)

As with most migrants throughout history, Sephardi Jews continued as much as possible eating familiar foods in their new homes, setting the Shabbat stew on the move once more. Versions of *adafina/hamin* found their way into the cuisines of Sephardim around the world, continuing to develop and alter in each region.

As with the previous century's *conversos*, some of the New Christians who stayed in Spain in 1492 became Crypto-Jews, secretly holding on to their Jewish faith. Thus, Inquisition trials continued "uncovering" Judaizers around the Spanish-controlled world for hundreds of years. By the mid-1500s, the Jewish practice among Crypto-Jewish descendants consisted of little more than vague, isolated customs.[40] But the zeal of Inquisition officials was such that they continued to scour the Spanish empire in search of heretics. Unsurprisingly, the oh-so-Jewish Shabbat stew would remain a key source of accusations.

There was one more direction Crypto-Jews fled from Iberia. A smaller number found refuge in the New World, which proved a significantly safer home in the long run. Christopher Columbus embarked on his first journey west on August 3, 1492, just days after the July 31st deadline for Jews to leave Spain. His arrival in the Caribbean in October that year started the centuries-long process of Spanish colonization, creating what came to be known as Latin America.

Some of Columbus's major financiers and supporters were ex-Jews, as were a number of his crew members.[41] As the colonial era progressed, more *conversos* settled in the relatively permissive climate of the Western Hemisphere.[42] Even in their new homes, however, they were not completely safe.

Many people are not aware that the Inquisition reached the Americas. But it officially arrived just decades after Columbus did, with the first American *auto-da-fé* in 1526.[43] Although the Inquisition in Latin America never operated as intensively as it did in Iberia, Gitlitz and Davidson turn up numerous cases where New World *conversos* were accused of food-related Judaizing activities.

In sixteenth-century Brazil, Isabel Ramos testified about the Shabbat stew of her employer Clara Fernandes: "With the meat she mixed grains and crushed them," showing procedural continuity with the early *harisa*. Gitlitz and Davidson's reconstruction of this distinctively yellow stew mixes beef and fried onions with mangoes, saffron and chili peppers, garnishing each serving with avocados and cashews.[44] This recipe, if accurate, displays an ingredient mix that exemplifies one of the longest-lasting legacies of 1492.

While Columbus's journeys led indirectly to the Shabbat stew's move west, it was in the easterly direction that his explorations more noticeably impacted the dish. Today's Shabbat stews frequently include ingredients that couldn't have been included before Columbus reached the Americas. Potatoes are nearly ubiquitous today. Other popular ingredients include sweet potatoes, bell and chili peppers, tomatoes, and common (*phaseolus*) beans such as kidney, pinto and lima. None of these vegetables (or the avocados and cashews of the Brazilian recipe) ever saw the Old World before Columbus returned from the West.[45]

In part of what is known as the Columbian Exchange, these were just a few of the American food items that transformed Old World diets from the 1500s forward. Some were accepted fairly quickly; the beans, for example, rapidly joined—and to a degree supplanted—the similar chickpeas and favas.[46] But other ingredients, including tomatoes and especially potatoes, took centuries to gain acceptance.[47]

Jews were among the most avid adopters of these new foods in many places. Jewish and *converso* traders were connected via family networks from Latin America to the Netherlands, Spain, the Ottoman Empire, and across North Africa. These mercantile networks facilitated the transfer and spread of these foods in wider society.[48] The degree to which these ingredients have become part of the Shabbat stew worldwide is therefore truly extraordinary. New World ingredients' entry into Shabbat stew pots worldwide may be, in a very small way, a silver lining to the Spanish Expulsion.

* * *

Before we trace the stew's moves throughout the Sephardi diaspora, we must first explore the other major medieval hub from which the stew spread through the rest of the world. In the next chapter we move to the France/Germany border territory, known to Jewry as Ashkenaz.

## Chapter 4

# Le Cordon Stew

As Sepharad became the most prominent Jewish community of the Middle Ages, another Jewish community to its north was steadily growing, destined to overtake it on the world stage. Some 800 miles away, in territory that today spans the France–Germany border, the population of Ashkenaz was coalescing. Long before that term became synonymous (in most people's minds) with Eastern Europe, it was applied to the Rhineland and Alsace regions.

Sepharad and Ashkenaz, applied to the medieval homes of the two most recognized categories of Jews today, are names that derive from the Jewish Bible. Interestingly, however, they almost certainly did not reference European places. Based on context, the words "Sepharad," "Ashkenaz," and "Tzarfat" (the Hebrew name for France) may refer to places in the Levant, Asia Minor, or possibly Crimea.[1] Still, at some time during the Middle Ages, Jews of Europe reassigned these names to their own region. Why?

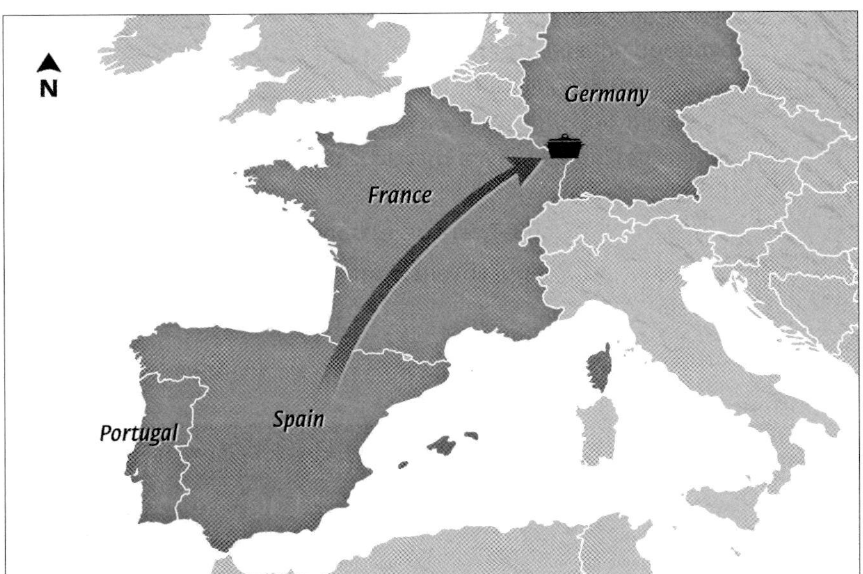

Perhaps appropriating biblical identifiers helped these far-flung Jews feel closer to their homeland. A fourth example suggests they did *not* take the applied terms literally. The famous twelfth-century travelogue of Benjamin of Tudela tells us that Jews near Prague referred to their region as "Canaan."[2] While the other three names derive from obscure biblical references, no Jew could have forgotten that Canaan was the ancient name for the Land of Israel itself. The misappropriated name could not have been an accident.

The Jews of Ashkenaz gradually developed a culture that was distinct from the other medieval Jewish communities. Their liturgy, customs and style of scholarship differed widely from those found among the Jews of Spain, Mesopotamia, North Africa, or Italy (each unique in its own right). And of course, their food was distinct as well. The Shabbat stew they consumed was called *schalet*, a name that would continue to be used (with minor alterations, such as *cholent*) throughout Central and Eastern Europe, until modern times. Just as *schalet* was a new name, it also featured different ingredients than the Sephardi *adafina/hamin* (and its *harisa* forebear). So, while it was still cooked overnight, this medieval French stew differed from its predecessors.

But was the source of *schalet* actually the Sephardi Shabbat stew, or might it have developed from another (Jewish *or* non-Jewish) precursor?

## A Stew by any other Name would Taste just as Savory

Linguistics sometimes help us identify a food's source. Often, when one dish develops into another one, related names illustrate that culinary connection. Unfortunately, however, food terminology also notoriously generates many inaccurate "folk etymologies." With *schalet* and its better-known descendant *cholent*, the most oft-quoted explanations have been proven false.

A common one that appears in many Jewish food books traces it to *shul ende*—Yiddish for "end of synagogue," since that's when it was eaten. As Gil Marks has explained, this couldn't possibly be the source, as the word *schalet* was in use before the Yiddish language developed.*

Another entertaining option suggests it stemmed from the Hebrew *she'lan*, "that rested," which is exactly what the *schalet* pot did all night.[3] While this meaning fits hypothetically, it only works with the later Yiddish variant *cholent*, not the earlier *schalet* (without the "n"), calling this hypothesis into question.

* While *shul*, synagogue, might have come from French or German directly, *ende* could only come from late, German-inflected Yiddish.

Linguists, for their part, have closely examined the derivation of the word *schalet* (and its later Yiddish alterations) to identify its roots. Though they can't pinpoint its immediate precursors, scholarly consensus tells us the word's meaning and its language family.

Researcher Mordecai Kosover says *schalet* certainly has Romance roots, though he offers at least ten possibilities for its direct predecessor. Many of them mean "hot," though at least two others connect it to different words, one that means "concealed" (as in the Mishnaic *tomnin*) and another that comes from a type of onion.[4] German scholars Max Grunwald and Samuel Krauss select two different roots, both of which relate *schalet* to variations on the Spanish word for "hot."[5] And the eminent linguist and Yiddishist Max Weinreich insists the word comes from the Latin root *calentem* ("that is warm") via the Old French *chalt*, meaning "hot" and equivalent of *chaud* in modern French.[6]

These scholars agree the word came to Yiddish from a Latin-derived source, seemingly French or Spanish, and that it most likely meant "hot."* If so, *schalet* would not be a completely new name, but a direct translation of the word *hamin*. In linguistic terms, such a modification is called a "calque"—a literal translation into another language, rather than a "loan word" that mimics, with variation, the sound of its parent—and many Yiddish words are calques of Romance language parallels.[7] If *schalet* simply translates *hamin*, it supports the hypothesis that the Ashkenazi stew was the gastronomic descendant of the Sephardi one.

Further evidence comes from when the word *schalet* first developed. Based on changes in pronunciation and spelling, Weinreich placed the Yiddish word's creation between the ninth and twelfth centuries. Then, in the thirteenth century, about a hundred years after "*hamin*" started being used in Spain, Rabbi Isaac ben Moses used the word *schalet* in his book *Or Zarua* (*Light is Sown*), its first known use in writing. Timing here is important, as Ashkenazi culture was then just starting to emerge as distinct.[8] At the same time, some Sephardim moved north due to increased upheaval in Spain.[9] When people move, they bring culinary culture with them.

Finally, a bit more support comes from the fifteenth-century Rhineland rabbi known as Maharil (R. Yaakov ben Moshe Levi Moelin). Writing about early customs in Ashkenaz, he tells of an episode that

* Another common mistake is the claim that *chulent* comes from the modern French words *chaud* and *lent* ("hot" and "slow"). The *lent* part is incorrect, with the *-lent* suffix deriving from the end of the Old French *chalt*.

## Schalet

This is one of my more speculative recipes, since there are none recorded for a medieval *schalet*. I have chosen ingredients that were available, popular, and would logically have been included at the time (and that taste good together). I use fava beans, but you can use kidney beans if you prefer. They probably replaced favas in the early modern period, anyway. For the mustard, I prefer one prepared using whole seeds. American yellow or English mustard may not be the ideal choices, though feel free to give them a try.

### *Ingredients*

3–3½ pounds (1.35–1.6 kg) **goose** or **duck** (breasts and legs/thighs)
2 large **leeks**, cleaned thoroughly and chopped
3 medium **carrots**, peeled and cut into 3-inch (7-cm) pieces
2 teaspoons **salt**
½ cup (120 ml) prepared **mustard**, plus more for serving
2 cups (400 g) whole **spelt**
1 (15-ounce/425 g) can **fava beans** (or red kidney beans)
10 cloves **garlic**

### *Method*

Start by rendering the schmaltz (poultry fat) from the **goose or duck**. To do this, prick the skin in multiple places with a fork or clean needle. Then place the meat, skin side down, in a large pot over medium heat. The fat beneath the skin will melt and drip into the pot. Move the pieces around if parts are not in contact with the bottom of the pot. Once most has rendered (10–15 minutes), remove the **goose** or **duck** pieces to a plate.

Let the pot cool for a few minutes. Then pour the schmaltz through a strainer into a measuring cup. Discard any bits caught by the strainer. Pour ¼–½ cup of the schmaltz back into the pot (enough to leave a thin layer on the bottom, more than just coating it). There will likely be more schmaltz than you need. You can refrigerate the rest for other uses.

Heat the pot over medium-high heat, cooking and stirring the **leeks** and **carrots**, with the **salt**. Continue until the **leeks** soften, but not until they turn brown. Return the meat to the pot. Add the **mustard** and stir to mix it through the ingredients. Let everything cook for about 5 minutes.

Add the **spelt** and **fava beans**, then scatter the **garlic** cloves around. Add water to cover. Cook by any standard method (*see* pages 7–8).

Serve with extra mustard for people to add to their portions, as desired.

once took place there. Pots of Shabbat stew were in a sealed baker's oven. (Sealing the oven prevented the adjustment of coals inside.) One Friday night, the fire went out, meaning the food would get cold. So the townspeople had a non-Jew relight the fire, then reseal the oven. Maharil permitted the stews that week, to not ruin their Shabbat enjoyment, but prohibited the action for the future. Relevant here is that Maharil refers to the stew as "*hamin*," even though there is no evidence that this was ever used as a name in Ashkenaz.* While he may have simply been using this Mishnaic term as the generic descriptor of hot Shabbat food, rather than referencing a specific dish by name, his application of one of the Spanish stew names may underscore the connection.

So, the name in France means the same thing as a previous one from Spain and appeared at a time in which Sephardi influence in Ashkenaz was increasing. Admittedly, we can't prove with certainty that *schalet* developed out of *adafina/hamin*. The name might have directly translated the Mishnaic term. And just because Sephardi Jews arrived when Ashkenazi culture was emerging doesn't guarantee this theoretical transmission. But the linguistic evidence suggests the claim is at least plausible, and perhaps likely.

## Whose Stew is it Anyway?

Some argue, however, that rather than developing from a Spanish Jewish dish, *schalet* more likely came from a non-Jewish medieval French precursor (of which there are a few possibilities). For example, Jewish food historian John Cooper calls *frumenty* "the probable west European ancestor of *cholent*, although not the only one."[10] *Frumenty*, widely eaten in France and England, was a wheat porridge that was boiled in milk, and sometimes contained eggs or ground almonds as thickeners. Others point to the French *pot-au-feu* as a candidate. It is a stew of meat and vegetables in which the broth is typically served as a first course, followed separately by the core ingredients.

While both of these dishes feature some similarities to *schalet*, neither is close enough to convincingly claim to be its progenitor. For starters, they usually do not cook overnight.† Beyond that, their respective

* *Sefer Maharil* 29a. Interestingly, Maharil also uses the other Mishnaic term, *tomnin*, describing the oven being sealed. As mentioned, this was the source for the other Sephardi stew name, *adafina*.

† Some examples of *pot-au-feu* sit on a fire for extremely long periods, potentially even years. New ingredients regularly refresh the stew. That's clearly a different type of slow cooking.

ingredients show they are unrelated. *Frumenty* is almost purely made of grain, rather than the grain and meat of a Shabbat stew.[11] While a festive *frumenty* might have been "dressed up" with some venison or porpoise flesh, that meat was added when serving, rather than being cooked with it. *Pot-au-feu*, meanwhile, utilizes the opposite ingredients—only meat and vegetables, without any grain.[12] Most likely, these two dishes neither grew out of, nor into, the Shabbat stew.

To many, the southern French dish *cassoulet* appears more promising as a French precursor to *schalet*.* This famous delicacy mixes white beans with various meats, typically including multiple pork products.[13] Though, like *pot-au-feu*, it too lacks grain, the specific meat-and-beans combination reminds many people of particular Shabbat stews. For example, Hungarian *sólet* typically features meat and beans most prominently, with only a minimal amount of barley (though the grain is rarely excluded from the stew entirely).† Cooper also highlights this similarity, suggesting that *schalet* "may have been an adaptation" of *cassoulet*.[14]

On closer examination, however, we see that *cassoulet* could not have grown into *schalet*, for both historical and culinary reasons. *Cassoulet* is most frequently connected with the southern French town of Castelnaudary.‡ Its often-quoted origin story dates its creation to the 1355 English siege of the city.[15] Starving peasants threw any food they had into a large pot. Reinvigorated by this hearty stew, the locals repelled their enemies. They continued to eat the new dish to honor its role in their success (and presumably also because they loved the taste).

This tale clearly smacks of culinary mythology. Many traditional foods are attributed to heroic events in defense of a city, and often are easily disproven by facts.§ That being said, even if it *were* true, this favorite food of Castelnaudary couldn't possibly have developed into the Jewish stew. It would mean that *cassoulet* was "invented" about a hundred years *after* the *Or Zarua*'s reference to the *schalet* that supposedly descended from it!

* Anecdotally, when I lecture on this topic, and I make the *hamin*-to-*schalet* claim, the most frequent audience question is, "But what about *cassoulet*?!"

† *See* Chapter 5.

‡ Though the nearby townsfolk of Carcassonne claim their *cassoulet* is better, most people there don't think they invented it.

§ Another famous example connects the invention of the bagel to the defense of Vienna against the Turks in 1683. Problematically, we have written evidence of bagels in Poland from over seventy years before that battle. (See Maria Balinska, *The Bagel: The Surprising History of a Modest Bread*, New Haven, CT: Yale University, 2008, 20–1.)

But since we've rejected the veracity of *cassoulet*'s origin story, couldn't it be *older* than the legend claims? Then it still might have grown into *schalet*. This, too, seems inaccurate, based on culinary evidence alone. French gastronomy texts and dictionaries from the past 300 years illuminate the development of *cassoulet* itself, and reveal that only recently did it begin to resemble *schalet*.

Described in 1756, *cassoulet* was actually a *frumenty*-like dish, containing only rice or groats, cooked in the oven in a clay pot. Over a century later, a bit of meat began to be added to the grain. Then, in the late 1800s or early 1900s, the grain was entirely replaced with the now-common beans. It was also then that the food actually acquired its current name—the first known appearances of the word *cassoulet* date to the 1800s.* Previously, dictionaries described it using the Occitan words *cassola* or *cassolo*, the distinctive pot in which it is cooked.[16] (Occitan was the regional language then widely spoken around Castelnaudary.) Thus, by the time that *cassoulet* gained its name and most resembled the Shabbat stew, *schalet* had been around for hundreds of years already. *Schalet* could not possibly have descended from *cassoulet*.

With this line of transmission disproved, some go so far as to reverse the proposed direction of influence. Marks claims, "Although the French are loath to admit it, the classic southern French dish *cassoulet* is most certainly a descendant of the Jewish *schalet*."[17] I believe he may have overstated the case. Unlike the direct line of influence we saw from *adafina* to the Spanish *cocido*, the northern French *schalet* seems an improbable source for *cassoulet* in the south, particularly with the two dishes' distinct ingredients. Most plausible is that *schalet* and *cassoulet* independently descended from Spanish foods. (Of course, if the *cassoulet* developed from *cocido*, which in turn came from *adafina*, an indirect lineage from the Shabbat stew remains possible.) Perhaps the best middleground summary comes from cookbook author Joan Nathan: "*Cassoulet* could well be a variation of the overnight Sabbath stews . . . [but it] could also have come from the Arabs [via Spain]."[18]

When *schalet* developed in France from its Spanish precursor, was it just the same food with a new name? This happens in many places; *polenta* and *mamaliga*, for example, are the Italian and Romanian names for the same basic dish. Alternatively, was *schalet* significantly altered from *adafina/hamin*? Since I rejected *frumenty*, *pot-au-feu*, and *cassoulet*

* Anatole France's 1897 description matches what we'd recognize today. The word also appears in a book from southern France in 1867, where it is described as an oven-cooked bean preparation.

as precursors based on their ingredients, can I show the culinary connection between the Sephardi and Ashkenazi stews?

There had to have been at least some changes in Ashkenaz, due to the unavailability of certain ingredients. Marks claims that fava beans are the only *schalet* ingredient that we know with certainty.[19] This wouldn't mark a major change, as they were common in Spanish-Jewish stews as well, though chickpeas were a more prevalent legume. And in fact, American kidney beans overtook both favas and chickpeas shortly after they were introduced in the 1500s. Likely, this was because they were not seen as new foods, but versions of the beans Europeans already recognized.[20]

One of the cooking methods slightly changed in France as well. Spanish Jews fried the onions for their stews in olive oil, but with no olives in northern France, locals fried foods in animal fat. Non-Jews used lard, but Jews opted for schmaltz—rendered poultry fat. Chicken schmaltz is best known today, but in medieval Alsace it always came from geese.* Hence, goose schmaltz replaced olive oil in *schalet*, and more significantly, goose became the common meat for the dish, as well.

Finally, we may presume that Ashkenazim also switched the grain in their stew. The wheat of medieval France was bread wheat, a softer variety than the durum used around the Mediterranean. If Jews had put that into their stew it would have disintegrated into an unappetizing mush.[21] Based on what was available in France at the time, we can guess that they used spelt instead.

Clearly, the ingredients in *schalet* were noticeably different from those in *hamin*. But unlike the differences between *schalet* and *frumenty* or *cassoulet*, here the Ashkenazi dish merely swapped one grain, meat, or fat source for a comparable one. In short, what happened to the Shabbat stew in France is exactly what happened to the stew everywhere else it moved—it was modified based on what was available in that locality. The French *schalet* took the next step in developing the original *harisa*, after the Spanish *adafina/hamin*'s first alterations.

## Well, How Did They Get There?

When *harisa* changed into *adafina*, I portrayed it as the result of the Jewish migration from the Middle East to Iberia. If, as I've just argued, the Sephardi *adafina/hamin* moved to Ashkenaz and became *schalet*,

* The aforementioned Maharil refers to "goose *griben*." These poultry skin cracklings are a cherished by-product of the schmaltz-making process (*Sefer Maharil* 28b).

does that also reflect a Jewish migration route? Answering this is a bit more complicated.

Scholars agree that some Jews had probably moved to Provence during Roman times, around when they settled in Spain.* But those Jews were separate from the ones who would become Ashkenazim, and were culturally influenced by Sepharad.

So, when did Jews reach the northern French and German territory that became Ashkenaz? The first written record of Jews in the region is from the fourth or fifth century.[22] Most moved from Italy via Switzerland and the Rhine River valley in western Germany. Some smaller groups also came from Provence, as traders, settling in Alsace and Champagne, on the French side of today's border.[23] Other Sephardi Jews came in the seventh century, escaping the persecution of the Visigoths. We find evidence of this via some Ashkenazi surnames.[24] In other words, the early Ashkenazi population was primarily of Italian Jewish origin, but was supplemented by minorities of immigrants of Sephardi background.

These early migrations are *not* reflected in the development of the Shabbat stew, since they coincided approximately with *harisa*'s arrival in Spain. But when the stew became popular in France, a few hundred years later, it was during increased interaction between Ashkenaz and Sepharad. Merchants from France and Germany regularly traveled to Spain for business purposes.[25] During the tenth century, a Jewish group known as the Radhanites famously monopolized international trade, and one of their routes passed through Spain on the way between France and North Africa.[26] When traders brought goods back to Ashkenaz, they carried cultural "baggage" as well, including popular morsels and cooking techniques.[27]

Thus, unlike *harisa*'s arrival in Spain, *adafina/hamin*'s move to France did not reflect the primary migration of Jews to the region. When the inaugural Jewish group settled in Ashkenaz, the stew hadn't yet gotten to Europe. The early Jews there probably approached their Shabbat lunch in the same way as others did in early Bavel, each homemaker slow-cooking different foods, without any being universally popular. But once further local migrations took place, accompanying cultural influences may be seen via the introduction of what would become known locally as *schalet*.

Here we see the Shabbat stew reflecting a minor, though important Jewish migratory pattern. The story of the Jewish Diaspora cannot be

* Historically, Jews somewhat inaccurately referred to the entire south of France as Provence.

summed up by the major moves alone. Dramatic events (both positive and negative) are the ones we most remember, but minor changes have shaped Jewish history as well. The kaleidoscopic Shabbat stew embodies the small changes as well as the large.

## Remembrance of Stews Past

Most of what we've seen so far in this chapter surrounded the medieval iteration of the French Shabbat stew—where it came from, what it included, and so forth. Let's now bring it forward, looking at what Jews eat for Shabbat in France today. Alas, contemporary stew versions there show almost no continuity with medieval *schalet*, because today's French Jews, by and large, don't descend from those who were there during the Middle Ages.

As mentioned in the last chapter, France expelled its Jews in 1394, a century after England did and another hundred years before Spain. From that point until emancipation in the early 1800s there were very few French Jews. The intervening four-plus centuries meant that Jewish cultural heritage was not directly passed down. Still, some minor elements of the early Ashkenazi Shabbat stew remain in France today.

You may have noticed I used the phrase "very few," not "no French Jews," above. This was because the expulsion of Jews from France was never as effective, nor as complete, as the English or Spanish decrees. Those countries were essentially Jew-less until readmission in modern times. France instead acted expediently, squeezing as much money as it could out of its Jews. Thus, the country made *multiple* expulsions, periodically letting Jews back in, before the "final" edict of 1394. And even after that edict, enforcement was half-hearted in some regions; Crypto-Jewish Sephardim fleeing Spain and Portugal are known to have settled in such southwestern French cities as Bordeaux and Bayonne, for example.[28]

Beyond that, geography played a significant role in making France's expulsion less effective than England's and Spain's. Britain is an island, and Iberia might as well be one, with water surrounding most of it and the towering Pyrenees blocking its only land border with the rest of Europe. So expelled Jews would have a hard time returning to these two regions. France's borders, however, are long and porous. In an era before surveillance technologies, Jews could easily slip back in quiet times.

Finally, France's boundaries shifted. Provence remained independent for over ninety years after the French expulsion of Jews. In other parts of what is now France, Jews could still live legally. Some remained in the southeastern "Papal States," Comtat Venaissin and Avignon. Similarly,

Alsace remained part of the (culturally German) Holy Roman Empire until the late seventeenth century. So Alsatian Jews were not expelled from France in 1394 because they weren't *in* France then. All of this led historian Esther Benbassa to conclude that despite the fourteenth-century expulsion, as many as 40,000 Jews may have remained in (what is today) France![29]

I asked many Alsatian Jews if they eat a *schalet* on Shabbat, to compare current ingredients with my guesses at the medieval recipe. Unfortunately, this was a dead end. For starters, the word actually now describes a different food. Today's *schalet* is a sort of sweet *kugel* that incorporates fruit.* More than that, the slow-cooked foods for an Alsatian Shabbat lunch in no way resemble the dish that bridged *adafina* and *cholent* on the Shabbat stew continuum. Their shift to eating new foods for Shabbat lunch may reflect the character of the region's Jews.

Alsatian Jews are very proud of their heritage in the original seat of Ashkenaz, resenting how their culture has been overshadowed by that of the more numerous Eastern European Ashkenazi Jews. Perhaps they have consciously rejected any dish that resembles something eaten in Poland or Lithuania. Instead, Alsace's currently popular Shabbat stews reflect the long and continuous Jewish presence in the area, characterized by generally peaceful coexistence with their non-Jewish neighbors. Thus, they slow-cook unique kosher versions of two different dishes which local non-Jews also eat.

*Choucroute* is the French equivalent of the German sauerkraut—shredded cabbage that is fermented (as opposed to just mixed with vinegar). Sauerkraut became popular in Germany in the 1600s.[30] From there, it presumably spread into Alsace relatively quickly.

A common preparation in Alsace is called *choucroute garnie* ("garnished sauerkraut"). Rinsed sauerkraut is cooked with many types of preserved (often pork-based) meats. Typically, it also includes lard, dry white wine, juniper berries, and peppercorns. Luscious and savory, the beloved dish may be rounded out with potatoes or carrots. In Alsace today, a recognized variant is called *choucroute garnie à la juive*—Jewish-style *choucroute garnie*. It uses only kosher meats and goose schmaltz.[31] While it may be eaten throughout the week, many Jews cook it overnight as their Shabbat stew. This places it in line with the Shabbat versions of Yemenite *marak regel* or Persian *sirab shirdun*—weekday foods that were transformed by slow-cooking.

* *See* Chapter 5 for more discussion of *kugels*.

## Choucroute Garnie à la Juive

This is an elaborate show-stopper of a dish. The variety of meats, and beauty of contrasting colors and flavors turns it into a real crowd pleaser. For the proper flavor, make sure to use genuine, salt-fermented Alsatian-style sauerkraut, rather than the industrial vinegar-pickled type.

### *Ingredients*

1½ pounds (680 g) **sauerkraut**
1½ pounds (680 g) **corned beef brisket**, whole
6–8 medium **potatoes**, peeled
2 tablespoons **schmaltz** (chicken, duck or goose), or oil
2 **goose legs**, split into thighs and drumsticks
1 medium **onion** chopped
2 **carrots** chopped
2½ cups (600 ml) dry white **wine** (e.g. Riesling from Alsace)
1½ cups (350 ml) **chicken broth**
1 small beef **sausage** (such as rosette or salami)
½ pound (225 g) **smoked beef** or **pastrami** cut into chunks

*For spice sachet*
6 cloves **garlic**, lightly smashed
20 **juniper berries**, lightly smashed
12 **peppercorns**
4 **bay leaves**

### *Method*

Rinse **sauerkraut** thoroughly in a strainer to remove excess salt. Drain. Rinse again under warm water and drain. Squeeze handfuls of the **sauerkraut** to remove as much water as possible and place in a large mixing bowl. Then, pull the clumps apart into separate strands.

Place the **corned beef** in a large pot of water and bring to a boil. You may continue with other steps while this takes place, and just keep an eye on the

Another of today's Alsatian Shabbat stews, while also a kosher adaptation of a non-Jewish dish, may actually show a different aspect of the Shabbat stew's legacy. *Baeckeoffe* is a stew that traditionally contains three kinds of meat (one of which is pork), along with potatoes, onions, and dry white wine.[32] Typically a basic bread dough is used to seal between the pot and its lid, keeping the moisture inside as the stew is cooked overnight. While few believe the dish itself is of Jewish origin, meat. After boiling for a few minutes, spill out the water and bring to a boil in a fresh pot of water. (This process is to reduce the saltiness of the meat.) Drain again and set the meat aside to cool.

Boil the **potatoes** in well-salted water until they just start to get soft. Drain and allow to cool. This, too, may be done alongside the following steps.

Preheat the oven to 325°F/165°C. This recipe works best in a standard pot, rather than a slow cooker.

Melt the **schmaltz** in a large Dutch oven (or if using oil, just pour it into the pot). Put the **goose legs** in, rendering some of their fat and browning on all sides. Remove legs to a plate.

Put **onion** and **carrots** into the pot, cooking and stirring in the **schmaltz**. Continue until soft, but not brown, approximately 5–8 minutes. Add the **sauerkraut** and mix with the **onions** and **carrots**, continuing to cook for about 3 more minutes.

*Create the spice sachet*: Place the **garlic**, **juniper berries**, **peppercorns**, and **bay leaves** on a small piece of cheesecloth and tie the cloth into a loose sachet. Put the **spice sachet** into the pot with the **sauerkraut**.

Add the **wine** and **chicken stock** to the pot. Let it simmer, covered, for 5 minutes.

Bury the **goose legs**, **sausage** (cut in half if necessary to fit in pot), **smoked beef**, and **corned beef** in the **sauerkraut** mixture. Place **potatoes** around the edges, also partially submerged in the **sauerkraut**. Put in oven for about an hour.

Leave the tightly-covered pot overnight on an electric hotplate, or in a 225°F/110°C oven.

*To serve*: Remove and slice the **corned beef** and the **sausage**. Discard the **spice sachet**. Place the **sauerkraut** with the vegetables and **smoked beef** chunks in the middle of a serving platter. Arrange the **goose legs**, **corned beef** slices, and **sausage** slices around it. Serve accompanied by mustard.

the cooking *technique* appears to be. *Baeckeoffe* literally translates to "baker's oven," and it is believed that Alsatian Christians saw local Jews slow-cooking their Shabbat stews in communal ovens, and used the idea for their own purposes. There is no way of proving this, but we know that the baker's oven was a commonplace cooking spot for Shabbat stews in many areas (including Germany), and the bread seal beneath the lid was also popular. Today, many Jews make their own kosher version of *baeckeoffe*, applying the Jewish technique to a non-Jewish dish that may have been inspired by that very same method!

Most of today's French Jews, however, are even further removed from the original Ashkenazim, so their stews are even less connected. Rather, they reflect the Jews who moved into France following emancipation. France was the epicenter of the nineteenth-century Jewish equality movement, with Napoleon I as one of its early driving forces. With the early twentieth century "Great Migration," hundreds of thousands of Eastern European Jews moved to France seeking a better life. (Some, without even realizing it, may have been returning to their ancestral homeland.) They brought modern Ashkenazi foods that had grown out of medieval Alsatian roots, but had also incorporated other influences.

In France, these new immigrant Jews kept eating the same kind of *cholent* they had eaten in Eastern Europe. Between the world wars, the non-Jewish, Polish-French food writer Édouard de Pomiane published *The Jews of Poland: Recollections and Recipes*, in which he sought out what he saw as the authentic dishes of an ancient people who fascinated him. Despite its name, the book includes passages about, and recipes of, French Jews as well, not just those in Poland.* After eating in Parisian Jewish restaurants, Pomiane overwhelmingly portrays his experiences as virtually identical to those he had in Poland—not surprising, as immigrant eating habits typically mimic those of their former homelands.

Today, approximately a hundred years after Pomiane's book, Eastern Europeans no longer dominate French Jewry. A second sizable group, from the former French colonies in North Africa, has grown more prominent.[33] Most of them came to France after World War II, with a few hundred thousand arriving from Algeria, Tunisia and Morocco. Like the Ashkenazim before them, these Jews continued eating the foods that they remembered from their former homes, including the many different Shabbat stews of that region, that I'll explore in Chapter 7. Thus, like the Alsatian Jews, the stews of both Eastern European and North African Jews in France reflect foods eaten by people other than the medieval Ashkenazim.

But just as the medieval *schalet* highlighted historical Jewish movements, the modern French stews also reflect the routes of Jewish migrations. And while the medieval population shifts were admittedly minor in scope, the modern waves were substantial enough to make French Jewry the third largest in the world.[34]

* I will discuss his impressions of Polish-Jewish cuisine in Chapter 6.

## Chapter 5

# Stuck in the Middle (of Europe) with Stew

The next destination on the Shabbat stew's itinerary was Central Europe. But how exactly did it get there? Did it come straight from Spain, indirectly via Ashkenaz, or from some other source entirely? Also, since the region is fairly large, and made up of numerous countries, how did the dish move around *within* Central Europe? And how similar or different were the versions in each smaller place?

Let's first understand the area itself. For starters, country names here are inherently inaccurate, since the internal borders within the region have been redrawn almost as frequently as knives are sharpened in a Michelin-starred restaurant. The same "country" might have had different names throughout history, and alternatively, the same name might have applied to different areas. Germany and Hungary, the bookends of this chapter, illustrate this well.

In Germany, many small states unified and separated throughout the medieval and modern periods. Numerous countries today include

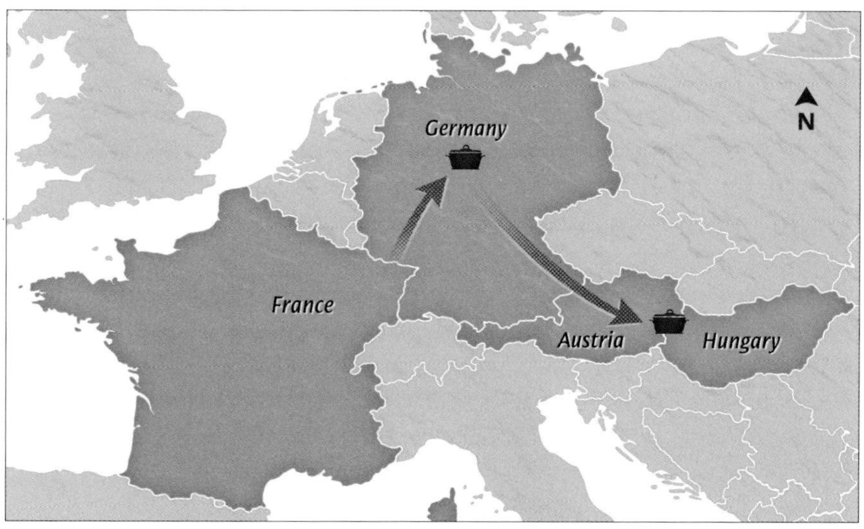

territory that at some point was called "Germany." Furthermore, even when kingdoms united as a single German state, it didn't always bear that name; the Holy Roman Empire, for example, covered most of what in other periods was called Germany.

Hungary at times enjoyed self-rule, while in other periods was controlled from outside. Additionally, parts of what was once considered Hungary may now be found in the Czech Republic, Slovakia, Romania and Serbia. Further complicating matters, though it was never a part of Germany, immigration made German the primary spoken language there for much of the modern era.

Thus, even more than elsewhere in this book, the contemporary place names mentioned in this chapter must be thought of as purely geographic descriptors. Primarily, I will be looking at the Shabbat stew in what is today Germany, Austria, and Hungary, but I also touch on elements in a few other countries as well.*

Noteworthy about the Shabbat stew's Central European history is its name's continuity across the region (and beyond, in Eastern Europe). Popularly, we encounter *schalet*, *shalet*, *scholet*, *sólet*, *cholent*, and more. These names easily answer one of my above questions. Clearly the dish entered Central Europe from Ashkenaz, where it was also called *schalet*, rather than from Sepharad, where it went by the names *adafina* and *hamin*.

This makes perfect sense in light of the known Jewish European migratory pattern. While *some* Jews did move from Spain to Central or Eastern Europe, most Sephardi émigrés did not (either before or during the Expulsion). Rather, most of this region's Jews came from the French–German border territory, periodically moving back and forth between Central and Eastern Europe.[1]

Those mini-migrations, accompanied by dramatic fluctuations in Jewish living conditions, primarily break down into four periods. First, in the tenth–thirteenth centuries, the Jews mainly lived in the western parts of Europe, where they enjoyed fairly positive conditions. Approaching the end of this stretch, anti-Jewish attacks started but were not yet the norm. Next, by the beginning of the fourteenth century, the Jews' economic state had deteriorated, as they were no longer dominant in international trade. Their reduced economic value led to increased attacks by Christians. Through the sixteenth century, numerous local

* While much or all of Poland is *geographically* part of Central Europe, culturally it falls into Eastern Europe, and will be discussed in the next chapter.

population shifts culminated in a more substantial emigration east to Poland. Then the seventeenth and eighteenth centuries saw a reversal of fortunes, with Eastern European Jews' circumstances deteriorating and attitudes towards Jews starting to improve back in central Europe. Parts of Poland's ballooning Jewish population thus returned to Germany, or moved southwest to Habsburg Hungary. Finally, in the nineteenth and twentieth centuries, emancipation brought equal rights to the Jews across Europe, one country at a time, but was soon followed by the horrors of modern antisemitism.

Let's explore how this unstable history affected developments in the Shabbat stew.

## Moving Deeper into Germany

The Shabbat stew's first foray into Central Europe accompanied Ashkenazi Jewry's initial moves there. After the community coalesced into a distinct group in the Rhineland, networks of communication formed between hundreds of Jewish settlements across the region. Students moved between *yeshivot* in various cities, and many people sent *halachic* questions (known as *responsa* literature) to rabbis in faraway places. Traveling Jewish merchants met co-religionists in widespread locations. (This trade also brought luxury items and tax revenue to their Christian rulers, who in turn treated Jews fairly well.) As communications between far-flung Jews increased, so did transmission of culture, including foodways.

Rabbi Isaac ben Moses, often called by the name of his famous work *Or Zarua*, exemplifies this. His life was characterized by mobility. Born in Bohemia (in today's Czech Republic) at the start of the thirteenth century, he began his rabbinic studies in Paris among the prominent group of Talmudic scholars known as the Tosafists (meaning "those who add"). He later returned to Central Europe, and at various times lived, learned or taught in Worms, Speyer, Würzburg, Regensburg, Vienna and in the east German region of Saxony. Thus, his rabbinic travels took him through parts of four modern countries: Czech Republic, Austria, Germany and France.

Rabbi Isaac wrote *Or Zarua* towards the end of his life. While it is primarily a work of *halacha*, many parts shed light on Isaac's biography. As mentioned in the last chapter, one such passage contains the first known use of the word *cholent*. At the time it was written, he was probably living in Vienna, but the passage describes something from forty or fifty years earlier, when he was a young student in Paris. Thus, it's uncertain

*Khal Adath Jeshurun ("Breuer's") is the heart of the German-Jewish community in Washington Heights, NY.*

whether the name he uses was what it was called in his teacher's home or developed later. In fact, his spelling could reflect the early Yiddish of southern Germany or the Old French of early thirteenth-century Paris.* This is not to suggest that Rabbi Isaac himself introduced the Shabbat stew to the deep reaches of Germany. Other travelers between France and Germany likely did. But regardless of when it happened, clearly the Shabbat stew was known in the region by the late 1200s, since he uses the name with no explanation, indicating that his readers would recognize it.

Unfortunately, the *Or Zarua* was only discussing the stew anecdotally, and thus does not supply any information about its ingredients. But with the region's food only just starting to evolve, it most likely remained fairly similar to its French precursor.

Sometime over the succeeding centuries, a new version of the Shabbat stew cropped up in Germany, built around a different grain. While

* Written without vowels, the word may be pronounced in different ways. But he was definitely referring to this dish, spelling it צלנ"ט (*tzadi-lamed-nun-tet*).

spelt was likely the grain in the original Ashkenazi stew, some German Jews began replacing it with unripe spelt, harvested early. Similar to the freekeh used in Egypt, *Grünkern* ("green grain") was a type of insurance against crop losses. Non-Jewish Germans traditionally cooked it into a *Grünkernsuppe*, typically with no meat, or at best a meat broth, and usually including butter and/or cream.* German Jews, however, added beef or poultry (and left out the dairy products, in keeping with *kashrut*), often using it as a Shabbat stew.[2] This meaty version of *Grünkernsuppe* appears to be specifically Jewish. An alternate name is *gesetzte Suppe* ("set soup"), but this generic term could describe any stew left to cook overnight.

Following the Nazi rise to power, many German Jews fled to the United States, largely settling in the Washington Heights neighborhood of Manhattan. For years it held the highest concentration of surviving German Jews in the world, and though many have moved on, a sizable number remain there today. Although *Grünkern* is difficult to find in America, some *yekkes* (as German Jews are nicknamed) still make a Shabbat *Grünkernsuppe*.

## The Winds of Change

As the Middle Ages wore on, Jewish fortunes in Ashkenaz deteriorated, and many emigrated eastwards. This spread the stew throughout Central Europe.

Assaults increased in frequency and grew more catastrophic over time. First in 1096, at the start of the Crusades, the so-called People's Crusade saw mobs of peasants sweep through the Rhineland. They massacred approximately 5,000 Jews, even though the "official" enemies of the Crusades were Muslims.[3] Then, once the Crusaders had finally conquered the Holy Land, the Christian powers replaced Jews as Europe's main international traders. Newly impoverished Jewish merchants lost government protection and were forced into the demeaning and despised profession of money-lending.[4] Public hatred now transformed into physical attacks. Riled up by false accusations such as blood libels, mobs murdered around 20,000 Jews during the 1298 Rindfleisch massacres.[5]

Soon, individual principalities expelled their Jews entirely (often readmitting them later). But since Germany was divided into numerous

* You can see this via numerous online recipes, for example: Fränkische Rezepte, "*Grünkernsuppe*," https://www.fraenkische-rezepte.de/rezepte/gruenkernsuppe-20525.

*The Frankfurt* Judengasse, *as portrayed in 1848 by Jakob Fürchtegott Dielmann.*

loosely confederated kingdoms, Jews often moved locally, permitted entry to one German state when booted from another nearby.

The worst physical attacks came in 1348–9, during the Black Death. The plague killed 30–60 percent of Europe's population, but many survivors blamed the Jews. Coercing "confessions" via horrific torture, some claimed that Jews spread the plague by poisoning wells.[6] While fear or superstition may have played a role here, most historians recognize that the main motivation was to steal Jewish money.[7] Christian mobs attacked Jews in 350 towns, with the entire Jewish population murdered in 210 of them.[8]

While the fruit of Germany's tree might have enticed some, many Jews sensed it was sour and worm-infested. When they fled this time, they didn't just move locally but went further east to Poland. The resulting reduction in Germany's Jewish population further weakened Jewish status there.[9]

Frankfurt am Main, one of the central hubs of the old Rhineland Jewry, exemplifies the declining Jewish fortunes. Established in 1150, the Jewish community there—a wealthy population segment in this market town—gradually grew. By the fourteenth century, they had gone from protection by the Holy Roman Emperor to becoming subjects of the local municipality. This may have brought some initial benefits, but it also subjected them to the whims of narrower interests. In 1462, the Frankfurt leadership buckled under popular pressure and established a closed ghetto for the Jews, probably the first of its kind in Europe.* Called the *Judengasse* (literally "Jewish alley"), it originally housed just sixty people in eleven families, and some basic communal services.

About 250 years later, when much of the *Judengasse* was destroyed by a 1711 fire, the population of this single street had swelled to over 3,000 inhabitants, in the same space!

However, Europe's ghetto walls worked simultaneously as prison and fortress. The ghetto persecuted Jews but also protected Jewish lifestyles; those who lived in Frankfurt's *Judengasse* found ways to thrive culturally. Among the residents were wealthy families, some of whom became internationally known, such as the Rothschilds.† Despite the pressures caused by the overcrowding, such a rapidly growing population also infused Jewish life there with vibrancy. As a testament, many ritual objects, both luxurious and practical, have survived from the *Judengasse*.

One particularly interesting item—and directly relevant to this study—can be found in the Jewish Museum in Manhattan. This brass cooking pot from the late 1500s was made for slow-cooking the Shabbat stew. The hammered Hebrew-language inscription that encircles the pot identifies its owner as Hirtz Popert's wife, who lived at the house marked by a ladder ("*zur Leiter*"). The name is followed by a picture of a ladder,

* The term "ghetto" only dates to the 1500s, but the concept began earlier, as seen here.

† Houses or businesses in the *Judengasse*, as elsewhere in medieval Europe, were marked by logos or colors. Rothschild means "red shield," from the sign in front of the family's house.

*The remains of the Frankfurt* Judengasse *are visible in a small museum, beneath an office building in the city.*

along with a year. But how do we know this two-and-a-half-gallon pot was specifically designed for *schalet*?

The year on the pot is the date on the Hebrew calendar, 5340 (the Gregorian year 1579–80). Jewish years are typically written using Hebrew letters rather than numerals, with each letter assigned a numerical value. Traditionally 5340 would have used just two letters: ש"מ (*shin* + *mem* = 300 + 40 = (5)340).* On this pot, however, the year is written as שאל"ט (*shin* + *aleph* + *lamed* + *tet* = 300 + 1 + 30 + 9 = (5)340). This odd way of writing the year required two extra letters . . . but also conveniently spelled out the word *schalet*!

This rare artifact reflects Jewish vitality in the *Judengasse*. Dedicating a special engraved pot exclusively to one's Shabbat meal suggests the Poperts were affluent. Furthermore, inscribing their family's name on the pot served a practical purpose.

Home ovens were uncommon at that time, so Shabbat stews were cooked in a communal bakery oven. In the *Judengasse*, someone had the specific job of collecting the pots on Friday and arranging them in the oven: the *schaletzetzer* ("*schalet* setter").[10]

* Traditional transcription also often leaves off the millennium.

Later urban legends tell of the mishaps that could occur on Shabbat day at a communal oven. A humorous Jerusalem example speaks of a neighborhood where Ashkenazim and Sephardim lived side-by-side. One Shabbat, an Ashkenazi boy accidentally brought home the wrong pot—one that belonged to a Sephardi family. With no way to locate the correct family on Shabbat, they ate the strongly-seasoned stew, and returned the pot during the week. Next Shabbat, when the father was sending his son to the oven again, he leaned in and whispered, "If you can make the same 'mistake' again, it wouldn't be so bad!"

Presumably, the inscription on the Frankfurt pot ensured that Hirtz Popert would never get stuck eating *schalet* made by another man's wife. (One can only hope that he actually *liked* his own wife's stew.)

*Cooking pot from the Frankfurt ghetto. The word/date* schalet *is at the right side of line 2.*

Cooking the entire neighborhood's Shabbat stews in a communal oven was popular around the world. One man told me he remembered people still doing it during his mid-twentieth-century youth in New York City. A Moroccan Jew related how families would compete to get the alleged best spot in the oven. Wherever they were, gathering the pots after Saturday morning prayers turned into a weekly social hour. As children, teens, or housewives collected their hot Shabbat food they also gossiped, flirted, or made *shidduchim* (marriage matches).

This legacy also left its mark on our own times, even though most Jews now cook their Shabbat stews at home. The slow cooker was actually invented to re-create, on a personal scale, the low-level, enveloping, dry heat of the baker's oven. Irving Naxon (birth name: Nachumsohn), who invented the slow cooker, was inspired by his mother's tales of bringing *cholent* to her communal oven in Lithuania. Naxon received his patent in 1940, and later sold it to Rival Manufacturing (who branded it "Crock-Pot").[11] To this day, many Jews rely on their slow cooker each Sabbath. Few, however, realize how utterly appropriate their choice is. A Crock-Pot *cholent* directly ties them to their ancestors' traditions!

*Communal ovens were found in many places. The low, old building in the foreground here used to be one, pictured in Jerusalem today.*

*Two medieval* kugeltopfs.

## *Kugel*: The Bonus Food that Leapt Out of the Pot

Alongside *cholent*, one of the most beloved of Ashkenazi comfort foods is *kugel*. There are many varieties of *kugel*, but the core recipe combines some kind of starch base with eggs, fat (schmaltz or oil), and some basic spices, baking the mixture as a type of casserole. The term "pudding" was widely used to describe it in most early American Jewish cookbooks, but can confuse Americans today, who only use that word for sweet, milky desserts containing chocolate or vanilla. Here it must be understood in one of its British senses, as a savory concoction, such as Yorkshire pudding.*

One thing that differentiates a *kugel* is that it is made without water. The most commonly used starches today are grated potatoes or egg noodles (*lokshen* in Yiddish), though many other types exist, some of which misapply the word *kugel* beyond its strictest definition. According to Gil Marks, "if the dish lacks any of the basic ingredients [starch base, eggs and fat], it is technically a casserole, quiche, or cake rather than a kugel."[12] Generally, a *kugel* is a simple, filling, and delectable side dish. But its origin was actually *inside* the Shabbat stew, rather than

* In the UK, the term 'pudding' can mean a savory dish of this sort *or* a sweet dessert, and is also often applied broadly to the entire dessert course.

### Mixed Root Vegetable Kugel

Just as *huevos haminados* emerged from the stew pot and became an independent food, *kugel* did as well. But, while I wanted to include at least one *kugel* recipe, there was no need for me to publish another potato or *lokshen kugel* one. A million are easily accessible. In this case, I upgraded a standard potato *kugel* by adding in other root vegetables. Potatoes still dominate, but this adds a variety of flavors, and diversifies the nutrients, too.

***Ingredients***

4 medium **potatoes** (about 1¾ pounds/800 g), peeled
2 medium **onions**, peeled
2 medium **carrots**, peeled
1½ lbs (680 g) mixed **root vegetables** (see Notes)
6 **eggs**
¾ cup (180 ml) plus 2–3 tablespoons vegetable **oil**, divided
⅓ cup (45 g) **potato starch**
½ cup (60 g) **matzah meal**
2 tablespoons **salt**
1 teaspoon ground black **pepper**
1 head of **garlic**, divided into cloves

***Method***

Grate all the **potatoes, onions, carrots,** and **root vegetables** in a food processor or by hand. Work in batches if necessary.

alongside it. In the same way that *huevos haminados* were a Bonus Food to accompany Spanish Shabbat stews, *kugel* was the main example in Central (and Eastern) Europe.

Today's Ashkenazi noshers might not even recognize *kugel*'s precursor. It started as a basic dumpling, to bulk up the Shabbat stew. A simple dough with egg binder was dropped—or . . . "dumped"—into the *schalet*, where it would cook and absorb the stew's flavor. It probably originated in the twelfth or thirteenth century when dumplings generally were entering German cuisine.[13] But while such doughy additions increased the substance and nutrition of a *schalet*, they could also lose their consistency when absorbing liquid through an entire night. So early on, some cooks began putting their dough into a small round pot called a *kugeltopf* ("ball pot" in Middle High German).*

* Not to be confused with a *kugelhopf*, which is a type of cake.

Preheat oven to 400°F/205°C.

Put the grated vegetables into a clean tea towel and squeeze out as much excess liquid as you can. Then dump them into a large mixing bowl. Add the **eggs**, ¾ cup **oil**, **potato starch**, **matzah meal**, **salt**, and **pepper** to the bowl. Mix everything thoroughly by hand. Make sure none of the **potato starch** or **matzah meal** remains dry, and that the **eggs** are evenly mixed through. The overall consistency should be a cohesive goop, but not liquid and wet. If needed, adjust by adding another **egg** (if too dry) or small amounts of **potato starch** or **matzah meal** (if too wet).

Grease an approximately 10 x 13-inch (25 x 33-cm) pan with the remaining 2–3 tablespoons **oil**. Pour the batter into the pan. Insert the whole cloves of **garlic**, evenly spaced throughout the pan, pushing them about halfway into the batter and covering them up. Smooth the top of the batter.

Bake uncovered for approximately an hour. Start checking after 45 minutes. Remove when the top of the *kugel* is uniformly brown and crisp.

***Notes***

In addition to the potatoes, onions, and carrots, a nice mix of other vegetables (rather than just one) is key for flavor. Select based on what is available.

Good options include turnip, sweet potato, Jerusalem artichoke, parsnip, or parsley root. (These should all be peeled before use.) Vegetables that don't work well are celery root, kohlrabi, or fennel.

This earthenware vessel became popular in tenth-century Germany, lending its name to the food and the name stuck even after *kugels* ceased to be ball-shaped.[14] The *kugeltopf* would rest on top of the stew, changing the cooking method from stewing to steaming. Since it no longer absorbed the *schalet*'s flavors, savory ingredients such as onions and pepper had to be added.

The food's consistency changed again with the next stage in its evolution. At some point, the *kugel* emerged from the stew pot to be baked on its own. The advent of home ovens in the mid-nineteenth century popularized the new baked version, though it may have started earlier. With its emergence as a stand-alone item, *kugel* ceased being cooked through the night and was often eaten with Friday night dinner instead of (or in addition to) Shabbat lunch. Some even bake a potato *kugel* in advance, wrap it in foil punctured with holes, and let it sit in their *cholent* pot to absorb more flavor. This mildly recalls the original dumpling version.

However, we encounter an even closer parallel in numerous references from the late nineteenth century. Many people (particularly in Hungary) dropped dough balls into their stews, referring to it as a *ganef* ("thief" in Yiddish), since it "stole" the flavor of the Shabbat stew. The dough varied according to the region, and might have been made of potato flour, matzah meal or even corn meal (the favorite in Romania). It's unclear whether this was a "throwback" version, or a holdover of a long-forgotten original, but the *ganef* clearly recalls the main European Bonus Food's roots.

Finally, not every *kugel* is called a *kugel*. You'll recall that in Germany, Jews eventually started making *Grünkernsuppe* and *gesetzte Suppe*. Those names both describe the dish itself: a soup made of *Grünkern*, or that "sits" through the night. But as these terms grew more common (particularly the latter, as a collective term), the older name *schalet* was free to be transferred. German Jews kept the name *kugel* for savory versions, but applied the name *schalet* to sweet ones. Later, as this sweet *schalet* continued developing into a type of fruity bread pudding, the name lived on, likely the origin of the similarly named "Charlotte" in English baking. All that confusion, just because the German Jews stopped calling their Shabbat stew a *schalet*![15]

## The Qualities of Equality

On the cusp of modernity, the mid-1600s brought major changes for Europe, and consequently for its Jews and their stew. The Thirty Years War (ended 1648) tore Germany apart and left Prussia—its largest state—underpopulated and in dire economic straits. As at so many other times and places in history, the Jews served the dual purpose of repopulating Prussia and increasing commerce to help rebuild its finances. In 1671, Vienna expelled its Jews, and Vienna's loss became Prussia's gain. Prussian Duke Frederick William invited a select group of the expellees to settle in Berlin and the surrounding area. Around the same time, Cossack mobs in Poland killed between 50,000 and 100,000 Jews during the Chmielnicky massacres. Many survivors fled west into the now more-welcoming Prussia or south towards Habsburg Hungary. Despite the upheaval, the population shifts also led to slow but upward Jewish mobility, culminating over the next century in emancipation.

As the European Enlightenment gained steam, Gentiles pushed for Jewish equality almost as much as Jews themselves desired it. Over the course of the 1800s, country after country granted Jews citizenship and equal rights. However, this process was not identical everywhere. Each country's unique situation created a different type of relationship.

Jewish emancipation in Central Europe took off when Napoleon formed the Confederation of the Rhine in 1806, granting full equality to the region's Jews.[16] While the Confederation only lasted seven years, it left its influence regarding the Jews' legal status. Individual German states gradually formalized Jewish equality. However, while French-Jewish equality came as the byproduct of the popular struggle against monarchy, German-Jewish citizenship was granted by self-interested and expedient rulers. Thus, Jewish integration was less successful.[17] Already in 1819, a working class that feared competition attacked Jews in some thirty German cities during the "Hep-Hep Riots."

German Jews responded in multiple ways. There was a growing wave of non-Jewish Germans emigrating, largely to the US, and some Jews simply joined that group.* Assimilation, however, was a more popular solution. To varying degrees, German Jews rapidly secularized during the nineteenth century. The Reform Movement, taking hold in Germany at that time, preached a more liberal approach to religious practice. Shabbat observance was one of the first rituals to be dropped.

As is often the case, since eating is a daily habit, food choices of newly-secular Jews took longer to change. Thus, we hear of many who still ate foods they'd previously consumed as traditional Jews—including *schalet*, but with one significant alteration. Freed from the religious prohibition against cooking on Sabbath, they made their Shabbat stew in one hour, rather than cooking it overnight.[18] Since the Shabbat stew's low-and-slow cooking is at least as important as its ingredients, this undoubtedly altered the dish. But it still allowed these Jews to feel their heritage. This change in the stew directly reflected the unique path to equality that nineteenth-century German Jews experienced.

Some liberal-minded Jews took their assimilationist actions to the extreme, actually converting to Christianity.† One of the best

* From 1820 to 1850, 600,000 Germans emigrated, reaching a total of 5 million by 1910. Approximately 120,000 Jews left Germany by the end of the nineteenth century (Gay, *Jews of Germany*, 143).

† Though some prominent individuals converted, this wasn't the mainstream solution. Only 22,520 German Jews converted in the entire nineteenth century, while 500,000 lived in Germany by the century's end (Gay, *Jews of Germany*, 139).

known—and most illustrative for our purposes—was writer Heinrich Heine. Born in 1797, Heine grew up in a less traditional, but still Jewishly-connected family. When he converted at twenty-eight, he famously referred to it as his "ticket to European culture," turning a formally religious act into a blatantly secular one. Shortly afterward, however, Heine lamented his choice. Rather than helping him reach his goals, he wrote to a friend, it made him despised by Jew and Christian alike. Heine's undying admiration for Jewish culture led him to incorporate the people of his upbringing—and, prominently, Jewish foods—into his work.

Late in life, bedridden and nearing death, he published "*Prinzessin Sabbath*" ("Princess Sabbath"), a long poem that dramatizes the transformative power of Shabbat. In it, the magically personified Sabbath turns a haggard Jewish peddler into a dignified man of leisure.[19] At a turning point in the poem, using his characteristic blend of satire and loving nostalgia, Heine tells how Princess Sabbath denied nothing to her lover . . . except tobacco: "Smoking is forbidden,/Since this is the Sabbath Day." But in place of that deferred pleasure, she offers a superior alternative.

> In return, today at noontime
> At your place a dish will steam,
> That in truth is simply godlike—
> Schalet you shall eat today!

Continuing, Heine then quotes Schiller's "Ode to Joy," replacing the word *Freude* ("Joy") with *Schalet*. In Heine's version, it is the true "spark divine and lovely,/Daughter from Elysium!" The next four stanzas praise this incredible stew as "true God's blessing," "Kosher-style ambrosia," the "bread of paradise," and even "the dish of heaven" which God himself taught Moses in an imagined Sinaitic cooking class.*

To Heinrich Heine, assimilated-Jew-turned-apostate, the visceral memory and evocative symbolism of the Shabbat stew was the very incarnation of the extraordinary Judaism he left behind. And in his undying love for this morsel, Heine also exemplifies a major trend among German Jewry of that period. Despite his assimilation, he remained deeply connected to, and nostalgic for, the Jewish culture of his birth.

* Lest you think Heine edges more towards mocking than admiration, numerous quotes indicate that even after his pragmatic conversion, he never stopped considering himself a Jew.

## Out of Germany's Shadow

While the Jewish secularist movement spread south from Germany, its trail was blazed earlier by the Shabbat stew. Versions from Austria and Hungary (which were at times unified as a single state) display German influences, blended with new local elements. While not identical to each other, the stews from these places have more in common with each other than either do with German *schalet*.

Austria has manifested something of a split personality through its history, in regards to its Germanic culture. It alternately saw itself as a state within greater Germany, a smaller independent entity, or the head of an empire that excluded Germany entirely. This shifting attitude, and the cultural and culinary aspects that accompanied it, stemmed from Austria's location. Austria functioned as the crossroads for a broad swath of European travelers, while Germany mainly bridged two countries: France to its west and Poland to its east. Austria was sandwiched between Germany and Bohemia to its north, with the Balkan Peninsula to the southeast, Italy to the southwest, and France just a short jaunt through Switzerland to the west.

Hungary's political identity similarly fluctuated. From the arrival of the Magyars in the late ninth century, Austria's eastern neighbor was independently ruled. Between then and now, however, it has bounced between the external rule of Ottoman Turks and Austrian Habsburgs, ending with reestablished self-rule. And like Austria, Hungary served as a major crossroads, in this case between Europe and Asia. The Magyars themselves originated in North-Central Asia, and when the Turks occupied the country, it became their deepest penetration into Europe.

These two countries' haphazard histories brought distinctive influences to their cuisines, and specifically changed the Shabbat stew in each place. Reflective of Austria's "German-not-German" mindset, the country's food generally layers Hungarian, Slovak, Czech, and some Balkan and Italian influences onto a Bavarian base. Thus, Austrian *scholet* (as pronounced in the local dialect) added tomato and paprika to the German stew. Barley replaced spelt as the grain of choice in Austria. Common vegetables included turnips, cabbages or leeks. Beans were common (though less than in Hungary), but another regular ingredient in nineteenth-century *scholet* recipes is peas.* An 1856 example comes from Moritz Gottlieb Saphir, another satirist who like his contemporary

* Andras Koerner, scholar of Hungarian-Jewish cuisine, told me these were dried, whole yellow peas.

Heine converted to Lutheranism. Also like Heine, he couldn't escape his deep, enduring love for the Shabbat stew. Writing post-conversion about the Jewish dishes of his youth, he evocatively describes the food as a timeless fusion,

> [W]e take classical barley and romantic peas, combine them the same way as [German romantic poets Ludwig] Tieck and Franz Horn blend Shakespeare and themselves, then add a big piece of smoked beef. People place this dish in the communal Shabbat oven on Friday, naturally after mixing some fat and garlic into it, and they let romanticism and classicism blend there until Saturday noon, to absorb the basic ideas from the smoked beef.[20]

Later in the century, the Viennese Shabbat stew that prevailed was called *ritscher* or *ritschert.* Widely consumed by non-Jews across Austria, southern Germany and Slovenia (where it is known as *ričet*), it combines barley and beans with (in most cases) pork.* But in *fin de siècle* Vienna, *ritschert* typically used beef or goose instead. In an award-winning 2020 study, Susanne Belovari sees Viennese *ritscher* as an example of Jewish–Christian integration in the city, highlighting the resulting Jewish influence on broader Viennese cuisine. She lists it among other newly generic culinary terms that united Jewish and Christian foods into a single cuisine. Other examples include matzah that was called "Easter bread" and the term "lard" being applied not just to rendered pork fat, but also to clarified butter or poultry schmaltz.

While Saphir pointed to the uniquely Jewish reverence for *scholet* in the mid-nineteenth century, it is notable that a popular Viennese cookbook of 1913 featured four *ritscher* recipes, indicating its supremacy over *scholet* at that time.[21]

How did kosher-style *ritscher* become dominant in Vienna? It may not have! Rather, it might be a case of Viennese Jews simply applying the *ritscher* name to their similar dish, *scholet.*† As Belovari also notes, *ritscher* was more frequently identified as a Jewish dish there, even though Christians ate it, too. The Jewish use of the name alone highlights the community's absorption into wider Austrian society.

If the Austrian Shabbat stew reflected positive Jewish–Gentile relations there, the same was even more true of the stew in Hungary.

* Koerner writes that the name was reserved only for stews that contained *both* barley and beans (Koerner, *Taste*, 241).

† Supporting this, the *ritscher* recipe in a Viennese cookbook from the 1950s uses the pork that we would normally expect to find in the dish (Hess, *Viennese*, 160).

Jews there were the most integrated in Europe. Though an ancient Jewish community existed under Roman rule, the modern one dates only to the seventeenth century. Most earlier Jews left (with other Hungarian people) during the 160 years of Ottoman control. The Turks left the country decimated upon their 1686 withdrawal. So, following the Habsburg reconquest, the Austrian rulers invited immigrants to help repopulate Hungary. Jews were an integral ingredient in the tossed salad of the new Hungarian population. Most came from Austria or from the stretch of land to the north that included Bohemia, Moravia and Poland. Later, in 1772, the Habsburgs also took over Galicia, this time bringing Hungary a sizable wave of poor and less worldly Jewish immigrants.[22]

Perhaps reflecting the various origins of nineteenth-century Hungarian Jews, there were also numerous types of Shabbat stew. Rather than mixing all ingredients together, they were divided into numerous, simpler versions: for example, ones that contained beans, rice, or peas.[23] The rice option is interesting, as it may reflect the persistence of Ottoman influence on the local cuisine.[24] Some ate a special wheat version one Shabbat a year, when they read in synagogue about the miraculous manna that Jews ate in Sinai (weekly portion *Beshalach*, Exodus 16).[25]

Hungarian Jewish uniqueness was aided by the 1867 Austro-Hungarian Compromise. Initially creating a "dual monarchy," it opened the door for Hungary's independence. The ensuing decades brought nationalist fervor and a distinct Hungarian identity (a process known as "Magyarization"—becoming more like the native people). The new country's Jews enthusiastically participated in nation-building, more than their co-religionists in other lands did. Emancipated Jews in France or Germany were absorbed into pre-existing societies, but Hungarian Jews participated as equals in their country's identity-forming, passionately adopting Magyar ideals and culture.[26]

We see this in Hungarian Jewry's widespread choice to speak the indigenous language, Magyar. In the thirty years between 1880 and 1910, the share of Hungarian Jews whose first language was Magyar rose from 57 percent to over 75 percent, higher than among any other minority group. The significant Budapest Jewish community prominently abandoned German.[27] This linguistic shift was even promoted by the rabbinic leadership, who offered synagogue sermons in Magyar and brought secular cultural education into many of their religious schools.[28] This expressed the Jews' self-identification as "Magyar in body and spirit, Jewish in religion."[29]

## Sólet

The lack of potatoes and the relatively minimal amount of barley in this stew help maintain its fairly liquid consistency (as is desirable). It should not be thick and dry like some *cholents* are.

Since this dish is often eaten on weekdays in Hungary, the recipe features two cooking options at the end.

I've modified this dish, based largely on a recipe from Joshua Pines of London.

### *Ingredients*

2 medium **onions**, diced
6–8 cloves **garlic**, minced
3–4 tablespoons **schmaltz** or **olive oil**
1 (15-ounce/425 g) can **lima beans**
1 (15-ounce/425 g) can red or white **kidney beans**
1½ cups (325 g) **pearl barley**
1 pound (450 g) smoked **beef** (usually shin), left whole
1 **goose** quarter (leg and thigh), preferably smoked
1 tablespoon sweet **paprika** (or Hungarian paprika paste)
1 tablespoon **salt**
½ teaspoon ground black **pepper**
8 **eggs**, still in their shells

Hungarian *sólet* (pronounced SHOW-let) displays this integration via popular Hungarian ingredients. Barley is common, though not universal. Tomato—chopped or as paste—represents a local ingredient brought by the Turks. Beans feature prominently in *sólet*, which is also typically more liquid than most other Shabbat stews.

Particularly distinctive in the Hungarian stew is the complete avoidance of potatoes; no matter what other variations Hungarian cooks employ, they all agree that if you include potatoes it ceases to be a true *sólet*. This is somewhat surprising, as there are plenty of other beloved potato dishes in Hungary (such as the rich potato-egg casserole, *rakott krumpli*). With no obvious explanation of this potato-in-*sólet*-avoidance, it may simply be a matter of taste specific to this recipe; perhaps potatoes would absorb too much water or weaken the dominant flavors.

And the agents of that flavor are actually *sólet*'s most Hungarian feature of all. Paprika and garlic, two extremely popular spices in the country, dominate the stew. The garlic, in particular, grows more dominant the

***Method***

In a large, heavy pot, over a medium flame, fry the **onions** and **garlic** in the **schmaltz or olive oil.** Once they soften, but before they brown, add the **lima beans, kidney beans**, and **pearl barley.** Place the **beef** and **goose** meat on top, and then add the **paprika, salt**, and **pepper**. Add water to cover by at least an inch (2.5 cm). Gently place the **eggs** around the top of the stew.

Bring to a boil, then reduce heat and simmer for 30 mins.

If making for Shabbat, continue cooking by any standard method (*see* pages 7–8).

If making for weekday use, cook covered on the stovetop over a low flame for two hours, then uncover the pot and put it into an oven set to broil/grill for about five minutes to crisp the top layer.

Before serving, remove, shell, and slice the **eggs** in half. Serve the sliced eggs alongside the stew. Slice the beef also and put some slices on each plate.

***Notes***

The ideal meat blend is beef and smoked goose. Smoked turkey thigh is a decent substitute. Kabanos (dry-smoked sausage) also works.

If no smoked meat is available, add more plain beef plus ½–1 teaspoon of liquid smoke.

You may also pre-cut the beef into chunks and leave it to cook as is. This is less traditional in Hungary, but would be easier.

closer you get to Transylvania, the main garlic-growing region of the territory.* Furthermore, Hungarians of all stripes love the heavy taste of smoked meat, so you will always find some in *sólet*. Traditionally, it was smoked goose leg, but Hungarian emigres today who have trouble finding goose will use any of a variety of replacements: smoked turkey breast, kabanos sausages, or even a hunk of pastrami. Since even more liberal Hungarian Jews typically didn't drop *kashrut* entirely, pork rarely found its way into their *sólet* (though it would not be surprising to discover that some highly assimilated Jews did in fact include it).†

Where you *will* find a pork-filled *sólet*, however, is in the highly popular non-Jewish version of the dish that abounds in Hungary today. In one

* Hungary's main garlic-growing region is Csongrád-Csanád county, in the country's southeast, across the border from Transylvania, Romania.

† Progressive Judaism in Hungary is known as Neolog Jewry, and is more traditional than German Reform Judaism. It falls closer to American Conservative Judaism (*see* Ram, *Jews in Hungary*; Stessel, *Wine and Thorns*, 66).

*Two brands of canned* sólet, *in a Hungarian supermarket today.*

of the most visible examples of Jewish-Hungarian integration, *sólet* is now more commonly encountered in the country's non-Jewish kitchens! Even in the late nineteenth century, it seems that more non-Jews than Jews ate it in Hungary.[30] Restaurants and taverns throughout Budapest serve up decidedly *treif* versions, containing smoked pork as the meat of choice.[31] Many of them drop the low-and-slow cooking method, instead precooking their *sólet* on the stovetop before a short rest in the oven.[32] As far back as 1930, a Hungarian company produced (non-kosher) canned *sólet*, sold in supermarkets.[33] Nowadays, you can find versions from multiple different manufacturers.[34]

This highlights the two-way street of Hungarian gastronomic influence. Even as far back as the late 1920s, we encounter the non-Jewish Hungarian love for *sólet*. "We always reserved some *cholent* for taking it to our Gentile neighbors and acquaintances, since they . . . were always ready to eat some *cholent*."[35] Just as Hungarian Jews incorporated the ingredients and flavors of the country's cuisine into their Shabbat stew, Hungarian Christians incorporated the stew itself into their mainstream menu.

Of all the Ashkenazi variations of the Shabbat stew, *sólet* may be the most distinctive.

# Chapter 6

# A Geshmakte Yiddisher Shabbes Stew

According to Jewish legend, our people settled in Poland because its Hebrew name, *Polin*, sounds like the words for "rest here."[1] Indeed, that phrase accurately typifies the centuries of Jewish life in Poland, and the neighboring Eastern European countries. Poland was a successful resting place for the Jews, offering a period of respite and generally peaceful growth while most of Europe remained inhospitable, or even entirely closed to Jews. Furthermore, general Polish history is intertwined with the story of its Jewry, following similar development patterns. Later, even as Poland began declining overall, its Jews continued their upswing. Finally, in late modernity, those two trends swapped, with Jewish oppression increasing as the Polish nation began to thrive again.

Certainly Polish–Jewish relations were far from perfect over the past 800 years, and they plummeted to their low point during the Nazi era. But claiming Jewish life in Poland was always terrible would be a

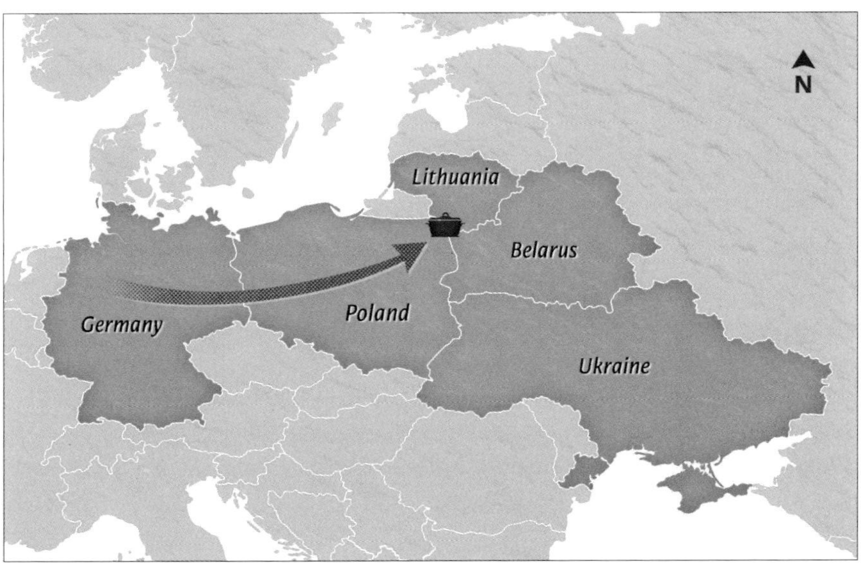

mistake—one that smacks of recency bias. Rather, we can say that Jews and Poles shared a flawed, but symbiotic, coexistence.

## Chronicle of a Country, a People, and a Stew

### *Twelfth–Fourteenth Centuries*

As in Central Europe, the common name for the Eastern European Shabbat stew indicates the origins of the region's Jews.* The name *cholent* (or its variant spellings *chulent*, *chunt*, *tsholnt*, and so on) clearly derives from Ashkenazi precursors, *schalet* and *scholet*. Furthermore, with most early Polish-Jewish settlements located in the west, we can conclude that most immigrated from that direction.

The early growth of Polish-Jewish settlements was largely due to excellent—and/or lucky—timing. Like the *mise en place* prepared by a well-trained chef, the welcome mat in Eastern Europe was rolled out and waiting just as Germany's Jews needed a new home. The 1241 Mongol invasion of Poland highlighted the need for a larger population, a need that was met via immigration from Germany.[2] The Rindfleisch massacres a few decades later, and attacks around the time of the Black Death in the following century, sent many more German Jews fleeing eastward. This "push factor" became paired with a "pull factor" in the 1330s when Casimir III invited Jews to settle in Poland, guaranteeing their rights and privileges.[3] Thus, by the end of the 1300s, the few thousand Jews of Poland (and Lithuania, which was just unifying with Poland) began solidifying into a single community.

The Shabbat stew that Polish Jews ate then was different from today's most recognizable version. As mentioned in the Introduction, it now typically includes beef, barley, kidney beans, potatoes and onions. During this period, however, a number of those ingredients couldn't have appeared in a *cholent*. Barley, for example, only became popular in Poland in the mid-fifteenth century. Back then, Jews most likely used millet. An ancient grain, millet was easily the most popular grain in Poland during the Middle Ages (and even into modern times).[4] Alternatively, a thirteenth- or fourteenth-century *cholent* might have been made with green rye, conceptually similar to German *Grünkern* and the ancient freekeh used in Egyptian Shabbat stews.[5]

* In this chapter, Eastern Europe will primarily mean Poland and Lithuania, two countries that were unified for much of the period I'm examining. The term Poland here is shorthand for areas that may be in either or both countries today. I also touch on parts of Ukraine and Belarus. For Russia, and these latter states during the Soviet era, *see* Chapter 8.

*King Casimir' III's affinity for Jews is reflected in the legend that he had a Jewish mistress, Esterka, portrayed here by Władysław Łuszczkiewicz.*

More significantly, as Columbus had still not reached the Western Hemisphere, neither kidney beans nor potatoes could be found in Poland at all. Turnips likely played the role that potatoes would later on. (Many European potato dishes today were previously made using turnips.[6])

The other major *cholent* ingredients, however, were probably the same then as now. Onions were extremely popular throughout Poland at the time, and meat was eaten frequantly.[7] (How much this applied to Jews as well is difficult to pinpoint, but at least meat was readily available in Poland at the time.) Finally, with offal commonly eaten by impoverished segments of the medieval Polish population, and not uncommon in Shabbat stews worldwide, it seems likely that poor Jews likely chose such "variety meats" for their weekly *cholent*.

### *Fifteenth–Sixteenth Centuries*

The next 200 years brought steady development to Poland, as well as to the Polish-Jewish community. As the feudal system divided Poland into a society of nobles and peasants, the 10,000 Jews who lived there around the beginning of the sixteenth century[8] formed a third group that often mediated between the two. Polish cuisine, in general, improved at the start of this period, with a wider variety of better-quality ingredients. Barley grew in popularity, as did many recently-arrived vegetables.[9]

The year 1569 brought formal confederation between Poland and Lithuania, along with parts of present-day Ukraine and Belarus. Jews moved eastward with the country's geographic and cultural expansion in that direction. With more Jews living in larger communities, *cholent*'s recipe may have started growing more standardized.*

### *Seventeenth–Eighteenth Centuries*

The size of the Jewish population in Poland–Lithuania continued growing rapidly, hitting around 90,000 in 1600 and nearly 170,000 by 1650.[10] New World foods continued to penetrate Eastern European cuisine, starting with beans. Potatoes were only introduced locally during the 1600s and were not yet as popular as they would become in a few centuries. Still, by then, all the pieces of the modern *cholent* were available to be incorporated in time.

Following the ballooning of the Jewish population in the Polish–Lithuanian Commonwealth, the community was about to experience its first major reversal of fortune. The 1648 Chmielnicky uprising decimated Poland in general, but hit Poland's Jews particularly hard. The Ukrainian Cossack who led the revolt saw Jews as representatives of the nobles he was trying to overthrow. Attacks frequently targeted Jews, with Chmielnicky's hooligans murdering thousands (though the total numbers are debated).

* While never identical from kitchen to kitchen, versions made today share a fairly standard recipe, with more in common than what separates them. This period, in which Jewish communities grew more substantial, seems like a logical start time for this standardization, though we can't know with certainty.

*Carrying a pot to the communal oven, in Poland.*

Of the survivors, many fled. Just as Eastern Europe had become a welcoming home specifically when Germany's Jews needed one, the perfectly timed pattern repeated in reverse now. As mentioned in the previous chapter, just when Chmielnicky made life hard for Poland's

## Cholent

This is the recipe that I grew up with. Though my mom didn't like *cholent*, she was kind enough to make it for the rest of the family. So while I have subsequently branched out far from this version, it still tastes like home to me. This is a basic recipe, but over the years I've made numerous substitutions or additions. See the Notes for many additional options.

***Ingredients***

1 cup (215 g) **barley**
1 (15-ounce/425 g) can **beans** (any variety)
2 medium **onions**, peeled and cut into quarters
3–4 medium **potatoes**, cleaned and cut into chunks (peeled or unpeeled as you prefer)
3–4 **marrow bones**
2 pounds (900 g) **beef**, or 3 pounds (1.35 kg) beef flanken (also known as short ribs) on the bones, or a combination, cut into chunks
2 teaspoons **salt**

***Method***

My mother insisted on placing the ingredients into her slow cooker in the following order: **barley, beans, onions, potatoes, marrow bones**, and **beef**.

Jews, Prussia needed to rebuild following the Thirty Years' War, and welcomed them in.* A few decades later, Jews filled another vacuum when the Ottomans withdrew from Hungary. In this way, Ashkenazi culture became the dominant Jewish one across Europe.

Interestingly, despite these emigrations, the Jewish population in Eastern Europe continued to grow. While Poland's overall fortunes took a downturn, birth rates among the Polish-Jewish population remained high, bolstering their segment.[11] Their numbers shot up from about 375,000 in 1720 to 750,000 by 1764, and approximately 1 million by 1800.[12] Polish Jewry had grown into the largest Jewish community on Earth, with some estimates placing them at nearly 75 percent of world Jewry![13] That meant that with their dispersal over the next few centuries, this one specific Jewish cuisine would become particularly recognized and identified as defining "Jewish" food in many countries

* Other Jews moved farther west, joining predominantly Sephardi communities in the rising port cities of Amsterdam, Hamburg and London.

Sprinkle the **salt** on top and add water to cover. She claimed this helped the meat flavor permeate the barley better.

Bottom line, no fancy steps here. Add all of the ingredients to the pot and cook by any standard method (*see* pages 7–8).

***Notes***

Common in America are the use of barbecue sauce or ketchup for flavoring.

Some use beer in place of all or part of the water. I don't taste a noticeable difference, but I sometimes do it anyway, since I do like beer, and it sounds cool.

I've replaced barley with buckwheat (kasha) as the (equally traditional) grain. The result is slightly lighter, a bit sweeter, oddly somewhat smoky, and gluten-free for those who need that.

For a slightly sweeter stew, add 1 peeled turnip and/or 1–2 peeled carrots, cut into chunks. For an earthier flavor, try a handful of mushrooms, or some rehydrated dried mushrooms (each cut up). All-beef frankfurters in addition to, or in place of, part of the meat add a nice smoky taste.

Popular "Bonus Food" additions include (homemade or purchased) *kishke* or a small potato *kugel*. Wrap either in foil and puncture with a fork before resting on top of the stew.

Other possible seasonings: garlic cloves or powder, black pepper, paprika, sugar, honey, cola, or prunes. Add according to taste.

around the world.* It is for this reason that the Eastern European name for the Shabbat stew is now the best known (and why I named this book after *cholent* specifically).

Meanwhile, Poland's neighbors pushed back against the previously thriving country. Between 1772 and 1795, Russia (to Poland's east), Prussia (to its west), and Habsburg Austria (to the southwest) carved off pieces of Polish territory, annexing them to their lands in what were euphemistically known as the "Partitions of Poland." Ashkenazim found themselves living under vastly different circumstances. Those who ended up in Central and Western Europe encountered a gradually liberalizing atmosphere, while those living under Russian rule suffered in the poor conditions of the Pale of Settlement (to be discussed in Chapter 8).

* For example, in Israel today, where only about 45 percent of Jewish residents are Ashkenazim, *ochel yehudi* ("Jewish food") commonly refers to Eastern European foods specifically.

### *Nineteenth–Twentieth Centuries*

It was those Jews who remained in Eastern Europe who became today's popular stereotype of downtrodden "*shtetl* Jewry." Early in the 1800s, however, Jewish life in such Eastern European market towns was far better than what we find portrayed in *Fiddler on the Roof*.[14] Only once Poland emancipated its serfs, in the second half of the century, did economic competition between peasants and Jews develop into popular antisemitism. More and more Jews emigrated from Poland. At first, they followed their predecessors to the western European mainland, but later expanded their destinations to Great Britain, Latin America, South Africa, Palestine, and especially North America.

In both Russian- and Polish-controlled parts of Eastern Europe, many of those who remained behind were the poorest classes, and their food reflected this.* While the *cholent* of the Ashkenazi émigrés was (literally) beefed up in their new homes due to gradually increasing affluence (and cheaper meat), the recipe that remained behind took a step backwards. The inexpensive ingredients (potatoes, barley, and beans) grew in proportion to the more costly beef. They also never saw the addition of upscale spices and flavoring agents that entered the stew in places like the United States. In subtle ways, the Ashkenazi Shabbat stew thought by contemporary Americans to be "classic" and humble might have tasted luxurious to their Eastern European great-grandparents prior to emigration.

Still, as an honored Sabbath food, even the poorest Jews likely made sure their *cholent* wasn't purely poverty fare. Shmil Holland is a Jerusalem-based scholar of Ashkenazi cuisine whose family lived in Galicia, a fairly poor region that spans what today is Poland's southeast and Ukraine's southwest. He mentions a *cholent* from that region made without any beans or barley at all, since they were seen as low-class foods which would be inappropriate for the Sabbath. His modernized recipe is clearly not that of a destitute person; it has a lot of meat, of different kinds.[15] But even the less well-off would likely include a high proportion of potatoes and onions to whatever meat they could afford. They too might have kept the barley and beans to a minimum, or even (as in Holland's example) left out one or the other entirely.

* To be clear, there were also some wealthy Eastern European Jews largely living in urban settings, and their *cholents* might not have matched these descriptions. Not all were impoverished villagers, but many certainly were.

## One Potato, Two Potato . . . Three Million Potatoes

Potatoes play such an outsized role in Eastern European Ashkenazi cuisine, it is difficult to imagine this regional gastronomy without them. But it wasn't until the mid-1800s that they reached such a place of prominence in the region, for Jews and non-Jews alike. Only following the failure of grain crops in Poland in 1839–40 did the government encourage peasants to grow more potatoes, leading to a sharp increase in that vegetable's status in the local diet.* This was due to the many special benefits of potatoes, among other agricultural products. They grow underground, well protected from cold weather. Potatoes are also inexpensive, nutritious, filling, and can be harvested over multiple grow-cycles each year. The resultant boom in available calories and nutrition largely fueled the population growth of Polish Jewry, despite the emigration of many others.[16] For those who remained, this simple tuber became such a dietary staple that many would eat it three meals a day. A popular Yiddish song exemplifies this: "Sunday potatoes. Monday potatoes. Tuesday and Wednesday potatoes. Thursday and Friday potatoes. But *shabbos*, for a change . . . potato *kugel*!"

At a minimum, an Eastern European Jew would eat over 200 pounds of them each winter, with most consuming twice that amount![17] This root vegetable goes by many different names in Yiddish, echoing its name in other European languages. It may, for example, be called *kartofl* (from the early Italian *taratufflo*), *erdepple* ("earth apple," used in many languages, such as the French *pomme de terre*),[18] or *bulbes* (similar to the English "bulb"). In fact, there are nearly twenty different Yiddish words for potatoes, underscoring this single ingredient's centrality to the regional diet.[19] Thus, if a Polish Jew reduced the amount of "low-class" barley in her *cholent*, she likely replaced it with potatoes. Even though they are root vegetables, it appears that many treated potatoes as a grain replacement. This makes particular sense, considering that the increase in Polish potato cultivation followed a local grain shortage.

The "potato-as-grain" attitude is seen in *cholent* recipes that include either potatoes *or* barley/beans, but not both. For example, the first Jewish-American cookbook, Esther Levy's 1871 *Jewish Cookery Book* included a recipe entitled "Coogle."† A combination dish, it featured a basic *kugel*

* The infamous 1840s European potato blight, best known for its impact in Ireland, did not significantly affect crops as far east as Poland.

† Transliterations into English had not yet become standardized, but this clearly means *kugel*.

(made of flour, not potatoes or noodles) cooked inside of a *cholent* pot. The *cholent* itself contained beans and chickpeas, but no potatoes.[20] A few decades later, a synagogue fundraising cookbook from Minnesota had a recipe that called for beans but gave the cook a choice of accompanying them with *either* potatoes or barley.[21] Though both of these examples came from America, they reflect the ideas of recent immigrants, and are based on what was made in Eastern Europe. Another example comes from Europe, but is much more modern. A 1988 Polish-Jewish cookbook features four different *cholent* recipes. One contains potatoes with no beans or barley while the other three all contain beans but no potatoes.[22] Similarly, in an underground cookbook from late Soviet Russia, *cholent* recipes include barley or potatoes, not both.[23]

If these descendants of the earlier Eastern European stew chose between potatoes and beans or barley, the same either/or choice probably existed in Poland, too. And only once potatoes grew in popularity could Jews choose to replace the grain in the Shabbat stew's traditional meat-and-grain pairing in the first place. In their minds, Eastern European Jewish cooks may not have slotted the potato in as a vegetable at all.

## Bonus Foods: Ashkenazi "Sausage"

The potato's prominence in Eastern European cuisine also led to its inclusion in some of the region's Bonus Foods. For example, it was during this time that potato *kugel* grew more popular than the *lokshen* (noodle) variety. Additionally, potatoes were sometimes incorporated into the filling of two other Bonus Foods: *kishke* and *helzel*.

These two classics are rather similar, and might be seen as poor man's sausages. Generally, sausages take a part of an animal that would otherwise be thrown out (most frequently the intestines) and fill it with ground meat. *Kishke* and *helzel*, however, are stuffed with little more than flour (or another starch). They share a common filling; only the casing differs. *Kishke* uses the classic intestine, while *helzel* instead stuffs the neck skin of poultry. In Eastern Europe, goose neck was the most common, though today's (increasingly rare) *helzel*-makers typically use turkey, or even the significantly smaller chicken neck skin.

Sausages are ancient, with recipes known from the collection of the Roman Apicius (compiled in the fourth or fifth century CE). Vague references suggest their potential existence even earlier. This very long history highlights their utility as the quintessential frugal food. In addition to utilizing animal parts that might otherwise be disposed of, they also make less desirable meat cuts more palatable by mincing them and adding seasonings. Most importantly, since not all of the meat of an animal would usually be eaten immediately upon its slaughter, sausages preserved the leftovers via techniques such as smoking, salting, or adding garlic (an anti-bacterial).

Among sausages, however, *kishke* and *helzel* take this thriftiness to the extreme. While they, too, avoid waste with their casings, their filling is ultra-poverty fare—no chopped meat, just flour, cut with schmaltz, and a bit of onion. This grows more noticeable when we contrast *kishke* with its closest non-Jewish relative, the Polish blood sausage called *kaszanka*.* Where *kishke* encases flour and schmaltz in calf intestines, *kaszanka* similarly stuffs pig guts with buckwheat and blood. However, the Polish sausage also contains chopped offal, nowhere to be found in a *kishke*. Clearly, preserving leftovers was not the primary purpose of *kishke* and *helzel*. Rather, they appear to have been created primarily to pump up the calorie content of the Shabbat stew—and in the cheapest possible way. And since these Ashkenazi sausages were cooked inside of the *cholent*, the relatively bland flavor of the stuffing was insignificant, as it would soak up some from the stew itself.

One way we know that *kishke*'s primary role was its filling bulk may be found in a rabbinic discussion on *brachot* ("blessings").† According to *halacha*, when a dish includes ingredients of different categories, the proper blessing is determined by which food is considered essential.‡ For example, if you eat cereal with milk, you recite the *bracha* of *mezonot*—the blessing on grain foods—and not the one for milk. Within the ingredients of a *cholent*, different blessings apply to barley, meat, and vegetables. One might have assumed that the honored meat would be considered the "most significant" part of any *cholent*. But in a book of Hasidic Sabbath customs, various options for the proper blessing appear, based on the specific stew's components. Sometimes the vegetable or meat blessing is prescribed. But, when the stew contains *kishke*, the *bracha* "is unmistakably" *mezonot*.[24] Clearly, at least to the Hasidim of this discussion, the doughy stuffing reigned supreme.§

In Eastern Europe, both *kishke* and *helzel* were common, while the latter seems to have been particularly popular in Hungary. Numerous food accounts of Hungarian Jews mention it as a staple. This was possibly

* Though the two names sound similar, they are unrelated. *Kishke* means "intestine" in Yiddish, while *kaszanka* comes from the word for buckwheat groats, *kasza*.

† The singular of *brachot* is *bracha*.

‡ Different blessings are made, for example, over fruit, vegetables, or bread.

§ I discuss the importance of *cholent* to a Hasidic Shabbat in the next section.

due to higher consumption of goose meat there, meaning more available goose necks. The starch of choice for the filling of both *helzel* and *kishke* varied, and could be regular flour, semolina, breadcrumbs, whole grains (such as barley or buckwheat), grated potato, or some mixture of these. Occasionally, other spices such as garlic, black pepper, or paprika may have accompanied the onion. Despite their frugal nature, these foods were not only eaten by impoverished Jews. Wealthier people ate them too, just in somewhat fancier versions. They might use cow intestines as casings, rather than the smaller calves' guts used by the poor.[25] Edging slightly closer to Polish *kaszanka*, some might also add chicken giblets (hearts, gizzards, and livers), ground meat, or *gribenes*.*

Even greater changes have taken place over the past century or so. First of all, like *kugel*, *kishke* and *helzel* also emerged from the *cholent* pot to be prepared on their own. Today, *helzel* will sometimes be roasted or fried by itself, served with a simple gravy. Similarly, *kishke*—even more recognized and beloved than *helzel*—has become a stand-alone dish, with American delis grilling individual slices.[26] Some cooks even sandwich pieces of *kishke* inside their *kugels*.[27] Beyond that, just as the proportions of the *cholent* ingredients changed with greater affluence in the twentieth century (more on that in Chapter 9), so did the specific ingredients inside of the *kishke* and *helzel*. Chopped meat became more common, and spices broadened to include cinnamon or nutmeg. Some modern cooks even took it to a whole new level, creating elaborate, newfangled fillings.[28]

Nowadays, *helzel* is less popular than *kishke*, but the reason seems obvious. They are essentially the same food, just with a different casing. Nowadays, synthetic cellulose almost always replaces the animal intestines for a *kishke*, and poultry is typically purchased cleaned and without the neck skin. So, if you have neither of the traditional casings readily available, *kishke* is the one that is better known, and also more substantial in size. Still, *kishke* remains a favorite Bonus Food in an Ashkenazi *cholent*, and is also served on its own. Though still beloved, it is unclear whether it would remain the blessing-worthy dominant ingredient of a Hasidic Shabbat stew.

## How to Eat a Divine Cholent

Today, there are hundreds of thousands of Hasidim worldwide, and the movement is well-known and recognizable. But Hasidism as a religious philosophy only began in the eighteenth century. This new brand of

* *Gribenes* are the same as the *griben* mentioned above on p. 78, note.

Judaism exploded on the scene following its founding by the Ba'al Shem Tov (Rabbi Israel ben Eliezer), rapidly picking up thousands of adherents in Poland and southwestern Ukraine. While Hasidim now live all over the world, Eastern Europe remained the movement's heartland until the Holocaust. So this chapter is most appropriate for an exploration of Hasidic attitudes towards the Shabbat stew. Food, in general, holds great symbolic significance to Hasidic Jews. But the traditional foods of Shabbat—and, prominently, *cholent*—are the most revered of all.

Since Hasidism is a religious *philosophy*, we need to unpack some of the movement's beliefs in order to understand why Hasidim view food religiously. It's true that some of their ideas are a bit esoteric, and I won't even claim to fully grasp them all. But hopefully this brief exploration will suffice to explain their veneration of food in general, and of their relationship with *cholent* specifically.

While not all Hasidic sects' beliefs are identical, the basic underpinnings of those philosophies are held in common. At its essence, Hasidism began as a populist movement, drawing on the Jewish mystical beliefs of Kabbalah. The goal was to empower the (at times) ignorant masses. Hasidism preached that any Jew could be as precious to the Lord as the most learned scholar simply by worshipping God with ecstasy. Doing so helped him elevate everyday things and make them holy, a concept known as *avodah b'gashmiyus*—worship via the mundane.*

Philosophically, Hasidism believes that since God created everything known in the universe, "divine sparks" (a sort of holy residue) are contained in all physical things. If we focus on releasing these sparks while we are engaged in daily activities, we can return them to infinite God, imbuing such actions with a transformative holiness. From the outset, Hasidism applied this central concept to eating. The Ba'al Shem Tov's primary student, Rabbi Jacob Joseph of Polonne, wrote the first published Hasidic work, *Toldos Yaakov Yosef.*

In it he describes this foundational Hasidic concept:

> The whole world has nothing big or small that is separated from [God] . . . and therefore a person can create higher unities even with mundane actions, including eating and drinking, sexual relations, business dealings, and all mundane acts between him and his fellow human.[29]

* As this movement developed among Ashkenazim, I am using the Ashkenazi pronunciation, rather than *gashmiyut*. I will use such pronunciation throughout this section.

*One of the earliest copies of* Toldos Yaakov Yosef, *by Jacob Joseph of Polonne, at the National Library of Israel.*

Notably, eating is the first example given in this passage, even ahead of the potentially lewd act of sex. This indicates how central food was within the concept of *avodah b'gashmiyus*. For thousands of years, *halacha* had already explained the holiness of *what* Jews were supposed to eat. Hasidism took things to another level, by sanctifying the physical act of eating itself.[30]

But on a practical level, how does the average Hasid perform this "elevation" while eating? Long before mindfulness became a byword, Hasidism promoted eating with awareness and concentration. Different foods are believed to contain different aspects of Godliness. By looking past the physical pleasure we get from food, focusing instead on each bite's unique essence, we may return the divine sparks to God.[31]

Unfortunately, the reverse also holds true. Unconscious eating runs the risk of degrading the food's Godly elements.[32]

Luckily, at least according to some Hasidic masters, the commandment of *oneg Shabbat* removes this potential danger. Since the Torah actually mandates enjoyment on the Sabbath, the bodily pleasures we get from eating can elevate the divine sparks alone. We do not, in this case, need to have a proper mindset.[33] So, if slurping down some chicken soup or tucking into a gefilte fish could be a religious act in itself, such Shabbat foods naturally became super-important within Hasidic belief.

The sheer volume of Hasidic writings focused on Sabbath foods underscores how significant a part of *avodah b'gashmiyus* they have become.* Such works explore each food's philosophical significance, the proper ways in which to consume them, and even the sequence in which one should eat them. This last aspect grows out of the association of each Sabbath dish with one of the *sefiros*—the divine attributes through which God created the world. Philosophically, the *sefiros* (singular: *sefirah*) were understood as bridging the gap from God's infinite self to a physical and finite universe. I won't even attempt to explain the details of how or why Hasidism associates each food with a different specific *sefirah*. As one scholar of Hasidism told me, it is sometimes better not to ask too many questions, and just to accept the association at face value! But, that being said, Rabbi Shalom of Koidonov, in the early twentieth century, explained that one should eat the Shabbat foods in the sequence of the *sefiros* to which they relate. Fish, for example, represents the first three emanations (all having to do with thought and wisdom), so it is the first food one should eat at the Shabbat meal. Foods such as caramelized onions, chicken legs and *kugel* follow in the sequence of their related Godly attributes. Koidonov places *cholent* as the final food of the meal because it represents the last *sefirah*, known as *Malchus*, Kingship.[34]

Even without fully understanding this esoteric Hasidic belief, I can offer some suppositions about why Hasidism connects *Malchus* with the Shabbat stew. As the final *sefirah*, *Malchus* is considered the most tangible of God's emanations, representing the culmination of everything that preceded it. It was the whole point of creation. *Cholent* embodies this idea, as one of the oldest of all Sabbath foods that has incorporated ingredients and elements from the whole history of Judaism. *Malchus* is also considered a unique *sefirah* in that it didn't directly emanate from

* For a fascinating survey and examination of the Hasidic veneration of one such dish, see Allan Nadler, "Holy Kugel: The Sanctification of Ashkenazic Ethnic Foods in Hasidism," in Greenspoon, *Food and Judaism*, 193–214.

God. Rather, humanity partnered with God to create this one-step-removed attribute. The Shabbat stew reflects this partnership since it was only created to both physically enjoy the Sabbath and religiously cease work on the day. Finally, all of the *sefiros* are seen as representing either masculine or feminine attributes of God. Hasidim believe *Malchus* to be feminine. And since women historically have done most of the cooking, this dish recognizes the valued contributions of women everywhere.*

The Hasidic veneration of *cholent* could not be more appropriate. Via its position at the climax of the weekly Sabbath lunch, *cholent* connects physical pleasures (both filling our bellies *and* pleasing our palates) with the spiritual ideals of our religion.

## Documenting Cholent in an Island (in Time)

As noted earlier, the late 1800s and early 1900s saw a massive exodus of Jews from Eastern Europe, with over 2 million emigrating to the United States alone.[35] Millions more, however, remained behind.† The early twentieth century, and particularly the period between the world wars, was something of an island in time for Eastern European Jewry. The post-World War I rule of Józef Piłsudski brought positive changes for those Jews who had survived the war in Poland.[36] Population shifts continued, but the interwar years were calmer than those that preceded and followed. It was during this period, in 1929, that a unique text was published in Paris—a French-language book, Édouard de Pomiane's *The Jews of Poland*, that examined the culture, and especially the foods, of Eastern European Jewry in a way that was not done before or since.

Pomiane was a French chef and food writer of Polish descent, and though a non-Jew, he was nonetheless captivated by Jewish culture. "It was, therefore, particularly interesting," he writes in the book's prologue, "to familiarize myself with the cuisine of the oldest race in the world still surviving on earth—the Jewish race." He traveled to Poland and studied its Jews and their cuisine, writing down his observations and numerous recipes. He saw this as uncovering "ancient customs and a ritual cuisine."[37]

* Today, many men (myself included) make Shabbat stews. But it was my mother who first taught me how.

† Historian Daniel Pipes, says 3 million Jews lived in Poland between the wars. (Daniel Pipes, "The Impact of World War I and the Russian Revolution on the World of Russian and East European Jewry," *YIVO Institute for Jewish Research*, June 16, 2014. https://youtu.be/ua7whC_ Mafo.) Édouard de Pomiane, in the book discussed here, claims there were 4 million.

What makes this book so engrossing is that it was written by an outsider to the community, one with a special understanding of food and cooking in general, who was attempting to create a portrait of the Jewish people. Of course, Polish Jewry was in no way representative of all Jews or their cuisine, and Pomiane attributed too much significance to one segment to be able to achieve his lofty goal. But that doesn't minimize the book's significance. As Josephine Bacon, the book's translator, writes in her introduction to the recipes, "It takes a non-Jew who is also an expert chef to do for Jewish cuisine what ethnographers seem to prefer to do for exotic Polynesian tribes."[38]

Still, this document is far from flawless. As someone whose study and understanding of Jewish cuisine and culture remained limited, Pomiane made numerous mistakes—for example, about the rules of *kashrut*. Furthermore, though he clearly was not antisemitic, many of his portrayals are tinged by an oblivious condescension that easily offends modern Jewish readers. So, while we might want to hold his observations at arm's length, they still constitute a valuable window onto the food of Polish Jews during the interwar period.

One of Pomiane's primary sources was the family of a Rabbi Chaim Halpern in the southern Polish town of Dobczyce. The two men formed a friendly acquaintance, and the Frenchman joined the Jewish family for many meals, speaking to Halpern and his wife about the foods they ate. Since his first visit came on a Shabbat day, Pomiane learned a lot about *cholent*. As a true Jewish food, and one with a unique and somewhat bizarre slow-cooking technique, the Shabbat stew fascinated him. In more than one place in the book, he gleefully describes re-creating the method at his Paris home (as if his success were shockingly unexpected). He (accurately, I'd say) recognizes that "Certainly, this method of cooking . . . gives the ingredients a special . . . 'gently simmered' flavor. It can consequently be said that cholent cookery is excellent."[39] And who are we to argue about food with such a knowledgeable French gourmand?

Notably, he uses the word *cholent* not only to describe the Shabbat stew specifically, but also the cooking technique. He claims that anything placed in the baker's oven overnight was modified with the word *cholent*. According to Pomiane, Mrs. Halpern said there were over 300 different *cholent* recipes, but seems almost disdainful when reporting that "she had great difficulty in quoting even forty of them to me."[40] (As if that were a small number of such recipes!) In addition to the classic *cholent* stew, Pomiane also lists cholent-beans, cholent-kugel, and "cholent-style" beef tongue and calves' liver. He even describes a "cholent coffee"—mixed coffee and chicory in a water bottle stoppered with paper. "The bottle sits in the baker's oven for 18 hours. All that remains is to decant the liquid and sugar the cups." This breakfast drink is the final recipe in his book, appropriately giving his favored cooking technique the last word.[41]

It's unclear how reliable Pomiane's account here is. Did Polish Jews use the word *cholent* for so many foods? Was it a turn of phrase that the Halperns alone employed? Or was this naming convention a mistake Pomiane made? We can't really say, and that probably is less important than the fact that, by then, they used the communal oven to slow-heat much more than *just* their Shabbat stew. Much as we'll see in the late twentieth century in the US and Israel, what had been standardized through much of history began to break out of its bounds during modernity.

Despite any shortcomings of Pomiane's book, we are lucky it survived to document this snapshot in Jewish culinary history. Because, in just a few short years, the Nazis would deal an almost fatal blow to our knowledge of what this community ate.

## Postscript: What the Nazis Almost Destroyed

As is well known, the Holocaust destroyed massive swaths of Jewish life in Eastern Europe, with Poland and Lithuania the hardest hit countries of all.* The Nazis and their collaborators murdered nearly 90 percent of Poland's Jews.[42] Of course, their heinous acts were not limited to Eastern Europe, but their crimes there overshadowed those elsewhere.

The repercussions of the Holocaust, however, went beyond the 6 million Jewish lives the Nazis stole. They also erased Jewish culture, harming Jewish survivors and their descendants today. Destroying a huge part of a population means interrupting the transmission of communal memory. Jewish gastronomic heritage may have suffered more than other cultural areas, since it was most frequently passed on orally from mother to daughter.

For those who want to explore what pre-Holocaust European Jewish food was like, it is not as simple as visiting the Jewish communities in Europe today. Post-war migrations of European Jews (as well as those that followed the late twentieth-century fall of the Iron Curtain) mean that contemporary populations frequently have nothing to do with the Jews who lived there some eighty-five years ago. Asking a Jew in Berlin

* Poland had by far the largest number of victims. Lithuania had the highest percentage of its Jewish population killed.

today about his Shabbat stew, only teaches us what is eaten there now, not necessarily what Jews there ate before the Nazi era.

As a simple example, a typical *scholet* eaten in Vienna today contains beans, smoked goose, tomato paste, paprika and garlic.[43] You may have noticed that those ingredients typify a Hungarian stew, not the style known in pre-war Austria. Unsurprisingly, this reflects the fact that most Viennese Holocaust survivors moved away after the war, while many others immigrated from Hungary to Vienna after 1945.[44] Does that make this *scholet* "inauthentic" as an example of Austrian cuisine? Of course not! It accurately reflects the most recent chapter in Jewish migrations, but we must also realize that it doesn't really help us learn what Viennese Jews ate before the Nazi atrocities.

Unraveling these threads and uncovering any remaining bits of information is thus of pressing importance to Jewish food history, and to preserving what the Nazis *almost* completely destroyed. With Central and Eastern Europe—the subjects of the previous chapter and this one—the prime territory for the Nazis' crimes, I briefly digress here from a focused discussion of the Shabbat stew to explore some efforts at recovering European Jewry's pre-Holocaust culinary history.

This must begin with the hard work some have undertaken to reconstruct and/or publicize these culinary memories. Well-researched books such as *The German-Jewish Cookbook* by Gabrielle Rossmer Gropman and Sonya Gropman, and András Koerner's *Jewish Cuisine in Hungary* have dug deeply into those countries' historic Jewish foods. But a few other projects relate directly to the cuisine of Holocaust survivors, as well as of the victims who did not make it.

One heartrending but fascinating aspect of the Jewish experience during the Holocaust is the degree to which food sustained Jews' spirits, even while it remained scarce from their stomachs. Many accounts highlight a startling activity that took place in some concentration camps: Jewish inmates who "cooked with their mouths" and minds.[45]

> One of [my Holocaust survivor mother's] favorite stories was about how she and the other ladies would spend their time [in Auschwitz] cooking to survive the daily deprivations, the humiliation, and the hunger.
>
> "Cooking?" I asked her early on. "What about the starvation? What about the hunger?"
>
> She would then explain that "cooking" was when she and the other women would talk recipes and trade cooking secrets. They

> would take turns describing how they had prepared their favorite dishes before the war.[46]

What an incredible affirmation of life! Faced with starvation-level hunger, they did not avoid the thought of food, as might be expected. On the contrary, they indulged in elaborate memories of sumptuous feasts and luxurious dishes, from pirogen and pickles to peach Melba sundaes and even homemade whiskey.[47] Classic Jewish favorites sprang from their memories as well, including the Shabbat stew.

> "Do you make sholet (*cholent*) for Shabbos?" asked one [older lady].
>
> "Of course," replied the other.
>
> "How do you make it?" asked the first one. "With beans and potatoes?"
>
> "Absolutely not!" retorted the second. "No self-respecting Hungarian housewife puts potatoes in her sholet—only beans. If you have it, you can use different types of beans."
>
> . . . The older ladies nodded with approval. But they all had their favorite sholet recipe. Perhaps on another night they each would get the chance to describe their method.
>
> They went to bed hungry but perhaps feeling just a bit more sated from the cooking lesson.[48]

Particularly harrowing is *In Memory's Kitchen: A Legacy from the Women of Terezín*, edited by Cara De Silva. Theresienstadt was a ghetto, that also served as a "model" concentration camp where many Jews from Czechoslovakia were interned.* The Nazis used it to make propaganda to back their claim that they treated their Jewish prisoners well, though behind the facade, conditions were as bad as in any other camp. And the women there also "cooked" from memory. One of them, Mina Pächter, compiled the handwritten recipes into a bound cookbook. It outlived the women who created it (as well as their Nazi murderers) and only made its way to Mina's daughter a quarter-century later. Written entirely from memory, and under circumstances stressful enough occasionally to lead to clear errors (such as omitted ingredients), this translation provides a valuable window onto these women's prior culinary culture and highlights their undying human spirit.

* Terezín is the Czech name; the German name Theresienstadt is somewhat better known today.

While Mina's book, in particular, included no recipe for a Shabbat stew, there are quite a few in the *Holocaust Survivor Cookbook* and its sequel, *Miracles and Meals*, compiled by Joanne Caras. These two cookbooks, that raised funds for a Jerusalem soup kitchen, gathered recipes from survivors who came from all across Europe. Two other recent survivor cookbooks are *Honey Cake and Latkes: Recipes from the Old World by the Auschwitz-Birkenau Survivors* and June Hersh's *Food, Hope & Resilience: Authentic Recipes and Remarkable Stories from Holocaust Survivors.* Like Caras's books, these contain personal stories, bringing the recipes alive on a personal level. Hersh's book, in particular, is well researched, and breaks recipes down in six different regional sections. Admittedly, some of the recipes in these books have been clouded somewhat by post-Holocaust influences, but they still help us explore what might have been cooked in pre-war Jewish kitchens. The breadth of memories they provide complements the focused accounts in the other works.

Clearly, survivors' memories serve as one our best resources for learning about pre-Holocaust Jewish foods. Particularly inspiring is a project that combines this aspect with another handwritten recipe book. During the COVID-19 pandemic period, award-winning chef Alon Shaya found a way to bridge both physical and temporal distance. He saw a family recipe book that had been donated to the United States Holocaust Memorial Museum by survivor Steven Fenves, a museum volunteer. While neighbors looted their home, the Fenves family's cook Maris rescued artifacts she knew they would want. She gave the cookbook to Steven after the war. At Shaya's request, Fenves translated some of the nearly 150 recipes in the book. Most were just ingredient lists with the barest of details, so Shaya spent months discussing them with Fenves, exploring his memories. He cooked and recooked them many times, shipping versions packed in dry ice to Steven to try. Finally, he successfully re-created a few of the survivor's favorite childhood foods, allowing him to taste them again for the first time in seventy-five years! As I write this, the project is ongoing, with the museum trying to raise money to get more of the recipes translated.[49]

Collectively, these projects contribute in one small way to countering the tremendous losses our people experienced during the Holocaust. Hopefully more such projects will further fill the void over the years to come.

## Chapter 7

# The Stew That Circled the Sea

After following the Shabbat stew from medieval Ashkenaz through its travels in Central and Eastern Europe, I must now move back in time to the other hub of medieval European Jewry, Sepharad. During approximately the same period that Jews spread eastward from the French–German border region, Iberia's expelled Jews also sought new places of refuge. Primarily, they traveled along two paths that forked around the Mediterranean Sea.

The northern route took the Jews through today's countries of Italy, Greece and Turkey. Across the sea, other Jews settled throughout what is known as the Maghreb—the modern North African countries of Morocco, Algeria, Tunisia, and Libya.[1] Despite common origins in Spain, the stews in each of these two broad regions differed significantly, reflecting the impact of each local population.

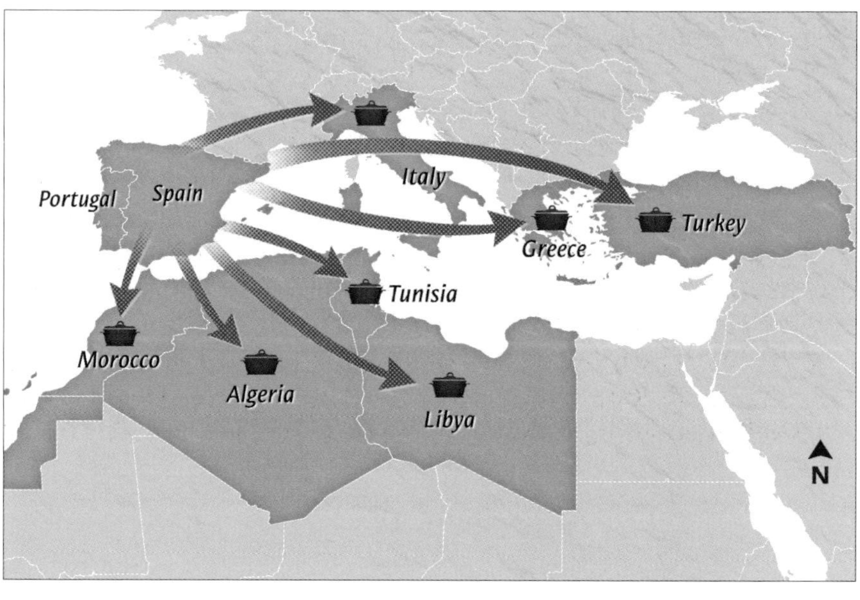

## The Sephardi Stew Splits

The groups of Spanish refugees who moved to North Africa and Southern Europe encountered one common aspect in their new homes: both regions featured deep-seated, preexisting Jewish communities. The Sephardi immigrants, however, were typically better-educated and more worldly than the locals, so their customs and way of life tended to dominate and overwhelm those of the resident Jewry.

Beyond that similarity, however, the two groups had little in common, as seen in their Shabbat stews. Why would two groups coming from the same place consume distinct versions of this dish? Partly, because they were already different before they fled Spain. Those Jews in Northern Spain had lived under Christian rule for significantly longer than those in the south. As most northern and southern exiles moved to Europe or Africa respectively, they brought the separate names, *adafina* and *hamin*, with them. The southern Sephardim used variations of the shortened *dafina* in North Africa, while those from the Christian north largely continued using *hamin* in Europe.

Beyond the stew's names, the Jews in each area also differed fundamentally. Maghrebi Jews were more culturally unified than were their Southern European co-religionists, for geographic and cultural reasons.

North Africa was entirely Muslim-ruled, facilitating trade and intellectual exchange between west and east. The relatively narrow strip of habitable territory between the Mediterranean and the Sahara Desert has few natural north–south boundaries, further unifying the region. Therefore, similar versions of Shabbat stew exist across this vast territory.

In contrast, there was neither cultural nor geographic unity across Southern Europe. Italy was Catholic while Turkey was Muslim, and Greece in between them was controlled by Turkey for centuries but inhabited mostly by Christians. But not the same Christians as in Italy—these were mainly Orthodox, not Catholic. Geographically, a patchwork of peninsulas, bodies of water, and islands disrupted easy travel between east and west. Therefore, unlike in the Maghreb, what southern Europe's Jews ate for Shabbat varied widely between places.

Accepting these broad-strokes distinctions, it's now time to look more closely at the Shabbat stew on both sides of the sea to help gain a better understanding of Jewish life around the Mediterranean over the past 500 years.

## The Jews and Stews of North Africa

While, as I said, the Shabbat stew across North Africa displays a high degree of unity, there are a number of subtle variations due to Jewish diversity there. This similar-but-different aspect is something like what is encountered with Indian curries. People eat curry dishes all over the subcontinent, but tens of individual varieties exist, divided by region and tastes. North African Shabbat stews may not be *quite* as diverse, but still display many variations in otherwise similar dishes.

As described previously, the first known Shabbat stew in North Africa arrived during the seventh-century Arab conquest. But those Jews who it accompanied, coming from Bavel, were not the first of their people to reach the region. Indeed, Jews have lived in North Africa from even before the arrival of the Romans there in 146 BCE, during what is known as the Carthaginian Period (named for the most significant city of the region). Carthage was founded by the Phoenicians (from modern-day Lebanon), who established trading outposts in north Africa that grew into significant population centers; the ethnically similar Jews settled with them.*

Over the following centuries, new transplants came with the Romans (especially after their sack of Jerusalem in 70 CE),[2] and as refugees from seventh-century Visigoth persecution in Spain.† Furthermore, many local Berbers apparently converted to Judaism, or at least culturally assimilated into the community, though scholars debate to what degree.‡

When *harisa* finally reached North Africa, it came with Jews accompanying the seventh-century Arab conquerors. Many of those Jews passed through, continuing on to Iberia, but some settled in North Africa, joining the already mixed local Jews. In time, this diverse multitude took on aspects of Arab culture, while holding on to their own religious practices. They became known as *Musta'arvim*, or Arabized Jews.§

This cultural unification is found in one of the popular North African Shabbat stews. In Libya, a common version is called *orisa* or *arisa*. While

* "Ethnically similar," because Phoenicians and Jews were both Semitic peoples, and originated in neighboring territories in the Levant (*see* Hirschberg, *Jews in North Africa*, 11; Chouraqui, *Between*, xvi).

† *See* Chapter 3.

‡ Some even ascribe Jewish origin to the local tribes, though this remains disputed (Chouraqui, *East and West*, 3–8).

§ Remember that "Arab" is a national culture, not a religion. One may become "Arabized" while maintaining a religious connection to Judaism.

the name clearly derives from *harisa*, it differs more from the original than those already encountered ringing the Middle East. In addition to the familiar wheat, meat, and onions, *orisa* includes more elaborate spicing (paprika, garlic, sugar), and sometimes features the post-Columbian additions of potatoes and/or sweet potatoes.[3]

This stew also appears in other Maghrebi countries, but with the first case of local differentiation, both in name and ingredients. Versions in neighboring Tunisia are fairly similar to Libyan ones, though called by a slightly different name: *arricha*.[4] In Algeria, the dish gets a completely different name: *tafina au blé* ("wheat *tafina*," the latter word to be explained shortly).[5] However, in Morocco, the *orisa* name is preserved, but the recipe changes, incorporating white beans or chickpeas.[6] Thus, with some examples changing the name, and others swapping ingredients while keeping the name, this dish shows the broad unity across the region, with minor differences by place.

As stated, one thing that helped create that broad unity was geography, since no natural borders divide the region from east to west. But within that relatively narrow stretch of land, the southern and northern reaches remained separated by climatic and cultural differences. The area along the Mediterranean coastline was influenced by European and Arab cultures, while the southern band edging on the Sahara maintained an older, Berber-inspired mentality.[7]

Therefore, Jews living in the north and south of the same country often made different types of Shabbat stew from each other. For example, northern Moroccans from Tangier or Fez bore little resemblance to the so-called "Berber Jews" of the Atlas Mountains in the country's south.* As I will soon show, each group's Shabbat stews differed slightly. Similarly, in Tunisia, two large communities existed in Tunis on the northern coast and on the island of Djerba, in the southeast. The ancient Djerba community's food reflected its physical separation. Their unique Shabbat stew uses, in place of meat, the fresh fish that is such a massive part of the island cuisine.[8]

Once the Spanish Jews finally penetrated the region, their influence followed this pattern of general unity with local differentiation. Their impact is best shown by the presence of *haminados* in many of the region's Shabbat stews. Interestingly, they even appear in Libyan *orisa*, mixing influences from the seventh and fifteenth centuries in a single pot.

* "So-called" since their actual origins are disputed by scholars. They may have been Berber converts to Judaism, or just Jews who took on Berber culture.

## Dafina (Skhena)

There is plenty of variation between different Moroccan Shabbat stews. Feel free to leave out one of the two bags here, should you prefer a simpler version. Alternatively, for a more festive option, include a *tamra* (*see* page 150) as a further Bonus Food. Always serve the various stew ingredients separately.

***Ingredients***

*For the wheat bag*
1 cup (200 g) **wheat berries**
1 head of **garlic**, cleaned but kept whole
1 tablespoon **olive oil**
1 teaspoon **cayenne pepper** or hot pepper flakes, or to taste

*For the rice bag*
½ medium **onion**, diced (see below for other half)
1 tablespoon **olive oil**
1 cup (200 g) **rice**
½ teaspoon ground **cumin**
½ teaspoon **salt**

*For the dafina*
½ medium **onion**, sliced
1 tablespoon **olive oil**
1 tablespoon **sugar**
1 (15-ounce/425 g) can **chickpeas**
4 medium **potatoes**, peeled and cut in chunks
2 pounds (900 g) **beef or lamb**, cut into chunks
2 **marrow bones**, or 1 **calf's foot** (cleaned and chopped in half)
2 teaspoons sweet **paprika**
1 teaspoon ground **cumin**
1 teaspoon ground **turmeric**
1 teaspoon **salt**
3 **dates**, pits removed
1 medium **sweet potato**, peeled and cut in chunks
8 **eggs**, still in their shells

Even more indicative of the Sephardi influence, another popular stew across the region descends directly from Spanish *adafina*. Moroccans commonly call their stew *dafina*, while Algerians or Tunisians use the terms *tafina* or *t'fina*. As with *orisa*, the use of this name across the Maghreb shows the region's broad unity. But, even more than with

***Method***

*Assemble the wheat bag*: Place the **wheat berries** in a square of cheesecloth or a fine net soup bag. Put the head of **garlic** in the middle and pour **olive oil** over it. Add the **cayenne** and/or hot pepper flakes. Tie the cloth or close the bag, but make sure to leave space inside for the wheat to expand.

*Assemble the rice bag*: Fry the **onion** in the **olive oil** over medium heat, until it softens but not until it gets brown. Add the **rice**, **cumin**, and **salt** and cook for 1–2 minutes more, stirring periodically. Add 1 cup water, and cook the rice, parboiling it for about 15 mins. (It should not be cooked 100 percent, but to "al dente" with some white still in the middle when you bite into a grain.) Add the **rice** mixture to a second piece of cheesecloth (or soup bag). Tie the cloth or close the bag, leaving enough space for the rice to expand.

*Make the dafina*: In a medium pot, fry the **onion** in the **olive oil** until it softens but not until it gets brown. Add **sugar** and let it caramelize with the onion.

Put the **chickpeas** into a large pot. Arrange on top, in separate sections, the **potatoes**, **beef** or **lamb**, and **marrow bones**. Sprinkle the **paprika**, **cumin**, **turmeric**, and **salt** on top. Add the caramelized **onion** and **sugar** to the large pot. Distribute the **dates** and **sweet potato** around. Add water to cover by at least an inch (2.5 cm).

Put the **wheat bag** and **rice bag** in the main pot. The **wheat** may be submerged, though not packed down into the solid ingredients. The **rice** should sit on top (it can be partially in the water, but it will mostly steam to finish cooking). If using a *tamra*, lay it on top as well. Gently insert the **eggs** around the top of the pot. Add more water if needed to cover the ingredients other than the rice.

Cook overnight using any standard method (*see* pages 7–8).

*To serve*: Each element should be presented in a separate bowl: eggs, meat, wheat (poured out of its bag), rice (poured out of its bag), and everything else.

*orisa*, these similar names are used for stew versions that look and taste rather different. Along with its derivatives, *dafina* has become a generic name for Shabbat stews, as did *cholent* or *hamin* in other parts of the Jewish world. Virtually nothing ties a Moroccan *dafina*, featuring sweet potatoes and chickpeas, to an Algerian *tafina*, that might include

## Orisa

This relatively basic stew can be enhanced with the addition of *kuklas* dumplings (*see* page 148). But even without them, *orisa* is subtly tasty. If you want a stronger flavor, add more paprika and/or sweet potatoes.

***Ingredients***

4 tablespoons vegetable **oil**
2 teaspoons **sweet paprika**
1½ tablespoons **hot paprika** (or less according to taste)
1 tablespoon **sugar**
1½ teaspoons **salt**
2 medium **onions**, sliced
2 medium **sweet potatoes**, peeled and cut into chunks
1¾ pounds (800 g) **beef**, in chunks
2–3 **marrow bones**
2¼ cups (450 g) **wheat berries**
1 whole head of **garlic**, unpeeled but cleaned

***Method***

Heat the **oil** in a large pot, then add the **sweet paprika** and **hot paprika**. Cook, stirring, until it gives off some aroma. Add **sugar, salt**, and about a half-cup of water. Stir and cook for about 2 minutes.

Add the **onions** and cook, stirring periodically, for about 5 minutes. Add the **sweet potatoes, beef** and **marrow bones**, with water to cover. Bring to a boil.

Add the **wheat berries.** Make sure water covers everything. Cook over medium heat until much of the water is absorbed. Mix the **wheat** and **beef** together.

Slice the top off the head of garlic, revealing the tips of the cloves. Insert the **head of garlic** upside down in the wheat. If including *kuklas*, add them now.

Top up the water, and cook overnight using any standard method (*see* pages 7–8).

turnips, or chicken rather than red meat.[9] And neither would ever be confused for a Tunisian *t'fina pkaila*, made with chard and white beans.

Indeed, *t'fina pkaila* alone illustrates the unity-within-diversity of the region's Jews. *Pkaila* is a type of thick sauce that is made by slowly cooking

### Turnip T'fina

Like *orisa*, *t'fina* traditionally has a fairly basic flavor. Should you desire to pump it up a bit (in an unorthodox manner) you could add in another vegetable (such as tomatoes, sweet potato, or green beans) or some extra spicing (hot paprika or cumin can work). With no grain of its own, *kawa* (*see* page 149) often serve that role.

#### *Ingredients*

3 tablespoons vegetable **oil**
1¾ pounds (800 g) boneless **beef** or **lamb** (or a mix), cut in chunks
1 (15-ounce/425 g) can **white beans**
1½ pounds (680 g) **turnips**, peeled and cut into 1½-inch (3.75-cm) chunks
2 medium **onions**, sliced thin
2 teaspoons sweet **paprika**
1½ teaspoons **salt**
½ teaspoon ground black **pepper**
1 bunch **cilantro**, chopped (optional)

#### *Method*

Heat the **oil** in a large pot, then add the **beef** or **lamb**. Brown the chunks on all sides. Next, add the **white beans** to the pot. Continue cooking on medium-low heat until the meat is partially cooked, approximately 10 minutes. If the pot looks dry inside at any point, add a tablespoon or two of water.

Add the **turnips** and **onions** to the pot, followed by the **paprika**, **salt**, and **pepper**. Stir periodically, and brown the **turnips** on all sides. Then add enough water to nearly cover all ingredients.

When everything is cooked, stir the **cilantro** through, if using that option. If using *kawa*, add them now, sprinkled throughout the pot.

If using a slow cooker, transfer everything now. If cooking in the oven or on a hotplate, you can leave it in the cooking pot.

Cook overnight using any standard method (*see* pages 7–8).

down chard or spinach leaves into a dark-colored paste. The stew uses this as its base, and adds in onions, garlic, lamb (or beef), and white beans.[10] We find similar stews in both Algeria and Libya, with minor ingredient differences.[11] Algerians commonly use chickpeas instead of white beans while Libyans utilize a wider array of spices. As with *orisa*, the name of each version varies slightly as well, but the distinctive spinach/chard

## T'fina Pkaila

Ideally, you should prepare some couscous to serve alongside this earthy green stew. Many Tunisian Jews prepare this for the Rosh Hashana holiday, with the *pkaila* serving as one of the holiday's traditional symbolic foods. But it works great as a change-of-pace stew for a regular Shabbat as well.

### *Ingredients*

*For pkaila sauce*

2 pounds (900 g) **chard** or **spinach** leaves (see Notes)
1 bunch fresh **mint** (or 1 teaspoon dry mint, saved for later)
½ cup (120 ml) **olive oil**
1 medium **onion**, diced (optional)

*For t'fina*

2 pounds (900 g) fatty stew **beef**, cut into chunks
2–3 teaspoons **olive oil**
2–4 **marrow bones**
1 (15-ounce/425 g) can **white beans**, or 1 cup (165 g) dried **black-eyed peas**
1 head of **garlic**, peeled and separated into individual cloves
1 teaspoon **salt**
½ teaspoon ground black **pepper**

### *Method*

*Prepare the pkaila*: If using **chard**, remove and discard the hard stems. If using **spinach**, you can leave the stems attached. Chop the leaves into smaller pieces. If using fresh **mint**, pull the leaves off the stems.

Heat the **olive oil** over medium heat in a large pot. If using the **onion**, fry it first in the oil until it softens, approximately 5–7 minutes.

base indicates they are all essentially the same stew. Reinforcing this, none of them includes a grain in the core recipe.*

*T'fina pkaila* also highlights another division. While by and large there is strong unity across the region, as seen by both *orisa* and *dafina*, Morocco has always been more separated from the other countries. It is the physical outlier of the Maghreb, situated at the western edge and extending further south. Also, while the Ottomans ruled the other three

* Typically, *t'fina pkaila* is served over couscous or accompanied by rice, but it is not cooked with the grain inside the pot.

Add the **chard/spinach**, and **mint** (if using fresh leaves). After about 5 minutes, lower the heat to medium-low. Leave everything to cook down, stirring periodically to prevent sticking or burning. As the leaves give off their water, pour or ladle it off into a separate bowl and reserve. The leaves will continue cooking for around 45 minutes to an hour, shrinking in volume drastically, by 80–90 percent. They will also turn very dark, almost black. You will know they are done when you begin to hear some crackling coming from the leaves. As they near this point, be especially careful to avoid burning. If using dried **mint**, stir it in now.

Once the leaves are ready, remove them from the heat. If the pieces are still too large, you may blend them slightly using an immersion blender, though this is not completely necessary.

*Make the t'fina*: About 15 minutes before the pkaila is done, you can start the **beef** in another pot. Brown it in the **olive oil** over medium heat, turning it on all sides.

Add the **marrow bones** and **white beans**. Scatter the **garlic** throughout the pot. Sprinkle the **salt** and **pepper** over everything, and pour in the reserved liquid from the pkaila.

Finally, add the pkaila itself, and stir everything to mix. Add about 2 cups water.

Cook overnight using any standard method (*see* pages 7–8).

Serve with couscous or rice.

***Notes***

Chard is a type of beet leaf. Spinach is in the same family, but since the spinach leaves are smaller and more tender, they may not give off as much liquid. Watch them a bit more carefully. A dash or two of salt may help them soften and reduce.

North African countries from the 1500s, Morocco stayed independent. Thus, it is unsurprising that *t'fina pkaila* cannot be found in Morocco.

As the Sephardi refugees flooded the Maghreb, they clashed to varying degrees with the *Musta'arvi* population. (Imagine that . . . tensions between different groups of Jews!) In Morocco, for example, the locals mockingly called the new arrivals *megorashim* ("exiles"). That group never fully blended with the *toshavim* (established "residents"). While tensions between them lasted a long time, eventually they found paths to peaceful co-existence.[12]

In the primary Moroccan Shabbat stew, we see both its separation from the rest of the Maghreb, and the subtle divisions within the country. You'll recall that *dafina* was a name that tied Morocco to other countries of the region, but that the ingredients were theirs alone. Even more distinctive is the hallmark of any Moroccan Shabbat stew: the various ingredients are eaten separately.[13] Rather than bringing one giant stew to the table, a cook usually serves the grain, meat, vegetables, and *haminados* eggs in separate bowls.

This creates a more elaborate and sophisticated(-looking) Shabbat stew, which perhaps reflects the worldly Sephardi influence. Since Morocco was directly across the sea from Spain, it would logically have been the primary landing place for many refugees.

However, while Moroccans across the country share this "multi-course" serving style, their cooking method varies slightly. Northerners often cook some stew elements (such as the grains) in a porous bag that sits inside the stew. The contents of the bag absorb flavor from the stew but are easily removed to be served independently. In other regions, less formal cooks frequently skip the bag and just put ingredients in different sections of the pot. Another regional difference is that northern Moroccan *dafina* tends to be sweeter, using sugar, caramel, or dates, along with aromatic spices like cinnamon or allspice, while southern stews instead lean towards the savory flavors of turmeric or cumin.*

Even the name of the stew varies by area. The two most popular in Morocco are *dafina* and *skhena*. Interestingly, both names originate in Arabic (or Judeo-Arabic), and go back to the Mishnaic terminology. As mentioned in Chapter 3, *dafina* (or *adafina*) comes from the word for "buried." *Skhena*, meanwhile, derives from an Arabic word for "hot."[14] Nowadays, the names are used interchangeably, and you'd be hard pressed to guess which name someone uses by looking at, or tasting their stew.† Originally, however, the names might also have been regional, with southern recipes skewing more towards the *skhena* name, and *dafina* more popular in the north, since the latter name came from Spain.

The Shabbat stews of the Maghreb therefore reflect the blended aspect of the Jewish community there. This was true of the early immigrants from the Middle East and continued after they were joined by Sephardi refugees. We see this in the stews (by recipe or name), including *orisa*,

* These regional preferences are *not* exclusive, just the dominant choices in each area. But one may easily find a sweet stew in the south, or a bagless one in the north.

† Recipes in many cookbooks include *both* names side by side. For example: Azuelos, *La Table*, 109.

*dafina/tafina*, and *t'fina pkaila*. But differences—distinct stews sharing one name, minor alterations in ingredients and names, and the uniqueness of Moroccan *dafina/skhena* and the Djerba fish stew—show the result of geographical and historical separations.

## Three Countries' Jews, Lots of Shabbat Stews

In contrast to North Africa, where the stews were broadly similar, the opposite is true of Southern Europe. Not only do we encounter different Shabbat stews in different countries across the region, but even within separate parts of the same country.

Take Italy, for example. One of the better-known Italian Shabbat stews is *hamin toscano*, named for Tuscany, where it originates. It combines meatballs and white beans with chard. Some cooks include sausage or chunks of beef alongside the meatballs. Recipes for this famous stew may be found in most Italian-Jewish cookbooks. But I have spoken with many Italian Jews, including the authors of some of those cookbooks, and found something odd. Everyone's heard of *hamin toscano*, and all recognize it as part of Italian-Jewish heritage, but I have yet to encounter an Italian Jew who actually eats it. In fact, all of the cookbook recipes easily trace back to one (sometimes repeated nearly word-for-word), from the first Italian-Jewish cookbook, Ines de Benedetti's 1931 *Poesia nascosta* ("Hidden Poetry"). Presumably, *hamin toscano* was once locally popular, explaining its presence in that book. Since then, that recipe has been continually reprinted as it was the first to be published (and in a beloved and prominent source). A second similar recipe appears in Benedetti's book and has similarly been quoted multiple times. *Hamin di fagioli* ("bean *hamin*") also includes meatballs and white beans, but cooks them in tomato sauce without chard.* The many reprints of Benedetti's recipes suggest a recognition that Shabbat stews are significant in Judaism, and so should be included in a Jewish cookbook. Without other options, the authors referenced the earliest examples known in print.

While these two dishes seem uniquely Italian, other versions in the country make minor modifications to stews from other parts of the world. Some Ashkenazi Jews in northern Italy make a *cholent* that localizes the Eastern European version by replacing the barley with rice. A Sephardi Italian might eat a very similar stew to his Ashkenazi neighbor, changing it only subtly by replacing the beef with lamb.[15] And at least one recipe

* In both cases, Benedetti writes the name as *hamim* not *hamin*, but I've used the more common spelling/pronunciation (Benedetti, *Poesia nascosta*, 100–1).

### Hamin Toscano

This easy-to-make stew is one of my favorites, and not just because I enjoy Italian flavors. Vibrant in color and taste, you'll be amazed that the dish actually cooked overnight.

***Ingredients***

***For meatballs***

1 pound (450 g) **ground meat** (chicken, beef, veal, or a mix)
½ cup (60 g) **breadcrumbs**, or matzah meal
2 **eggs**
½ cup (120 ml) finely chopped fresh **parsley**
½ teaspoon ground black **pepper**

***For hamin***

2 pounds (900 g) **chard**, or **spinach** leaves
2 tablespoons **olive oil**
1½ teaspoons **salt**
3 (15-ounce/425 g) cans **cannellini** or **white beans**, drained
1 medium **onion**, chopped
3 cloves **garlic**, minced
1½ cups (350 ml) **tomato sauce (passata)**
8 **eggs**, still in their shells

I've come across is a true hybrid. The ingredients are largely those of an Ashkenazi *cholent*, but also incorporate Sephardi *huevos haminados*. It is then called by the Italian name *stracotto*. This is particularly interesting since that's the name of a famous Italian roast beef dish, but *not* this dish at all. (However, since *stracotto* literally means "overcooked," it does seem appropriate for a Shabbat stew.)[16]

Clearly, no single Shabbat stew is commonly consumed throughout Italy. The same, in fact, applies across the Ionian Sea in Greece, where cooks also prepare different Shabbat stews.

For example, from Ioannina in the country's northwest comes a *hamin* that combines beef with a local type of bulgur wheat called *pligouri*. It contains no beans, in contrast to the stews of Salonika (Thessaloniki), further north and east. There, beans are actually the primary ingredient, as indicated by two stews' descriptive names.* *Soupa de avikas* means

* The following Greek stew names are in Ladino, the Judeo-Spanish spoken by many Sephardi émigrés.

***Method***

*Make the meatballs*: Combine the **ground meat, breadcrumbs, eggs, parsley,** and **pepper** in a mixing bowl. Gradually work all of the ingredients together, until well-mixed, no more. Roll into balls about 2 inches (5 cm) across. Set aside.

*Make the hamin*: If using **chard** (rather than **spinach**), remove the hard stems from the leaves. Reserve the stems for another use, or discard.

Cut the **chard** or **spinach** into smaller pieces. Heat the **olive oil** in a pot and add the **chard** or **spinach**. Add the **salt**. Stir periodically until the leaves begin to wilt, approximately 3–5 minutes. Then cover, reduce heat to low, and continue cooking for approximately 10 more minutes, stirring periodically to avoid burning.

In a large pot, combine the **beans, chard/spinach, meatballs, onion, garlic,** and **tomato sauce.** Add water to just barely cover. Gently insert **eggs** around the top of the stew. Bring to a boil, then reduce heat.

Cook overnight using any standard method (*see* pages 7–8).

***Notes***

For a meatier stew, add ½ pound of beef chunks or 3–4 Italian sausages (cut into 1½-inch/3.75-cm pieces) with the rest of the ingredients.

"bean soup" and combines white beans, beef, onions, and tomatoes. *Fijones con seboya moraderba con toutano* is a name that translates the main ingredients: beans, sautéed onions, and bone marrow.[17] Again, no single stew dominates within Greek-Jewish cuisine.

What explains the lack of unity in Italian and Greek Shabbat stews? Undoubtedly, many factors have contributed. But perhaps most pertinently, while we generally think of Italy and Greece as countries, they were not singular countries for most of history.

Italy, from the Middle Ages forward, could be divided into three main regions. The south was largely a single kingdom, ruled from Naples. The central Italian Papal States were under Vatican control. The north was the least unified, comprised of a hodgepodge of city-states, led by such great Italian trading cities as Venice, Genoa, and Livorno (traditionally Leghorn in English). The most dominant among the Italian-Jewish communities shifted over time, gradually moving northward, from the Naples area in the days of the Roman Empire to the large but impoverished community of Rome in the center, and eventually the many thriving groups of Jews in Italy's north. Only with Italian unification in the 1800s did the Jews of each region formally blend into one single community.

Greece was similarly divided, with various parts controlled at different times by the Byzantine Empire, Italian city-states, or the Ottoman Turks. As with Italy, Greek unification only began during the 1800s, but it took longer there. The 1820s War of Independence created modern Greece, but today's Greece only developed in stages over the succeeding century, with further strips of the mainland and Greek islands gradually appended, and the final addition (the Dodecanese Islands) only coming after World War II. Historian K. E. Fleming explains there was "no such thing" as Greek Jews until the twentieth century, because there was no Greece as we know it. She points out that "Greek Jewry" ironically only became identified as such after over 90 percent had been killed in the Holocaust, and survivor communities formed in foreign countries.[18]

Just as Jews in Austria and Hungary ate different Shabbat stews, those from different sections of Italy or Greece would understandably do the same. They, too, lived in separate countries! Beyond that, the Italian- and Greek-Jewish communities also blended individuals from different prior homelands. Sizable ancient Jewish communities—known as Romaniote Jews in Greece and Italki Jews in Italy—existed from before the first-century destruction of the Temple in Jerusalem. With the persecutions of Jews in Germany and Poland, Ashkenazim also moved to northern Italy (and, less so, to Greece). But the Sephardim, on their arrival after the 1492 Expulsion, became the dominant group. Different groups of Jews living side by side might understandably choose different foods to slow-cook for their Sabbath lunches. The differences would be reinforced by the previously mentioned geographical divides.

This explains why no single stew dominates in Southern Europe, but there is an even stranger phenomenon that I must explore. Rather than choosing a different Shabbat stew from their neighbors, many Greek and Italian Jews today, along with the bulk of those found in Turkey, have no tradition of a long-simmered stew *at all*. Despite recipes in Italian- and Greek-Jewish cookbooks, many contemporary Jews from these communities say they do not eat a Shabbat stew. And in Turkey, most Jewish cookbooks don't include any Shabbat stew recipes. I have found only one, for a dish called *hamim de kastanya* (more on this later). And it is only questionably a Shabbat stew since, despite the name, the recipe doesn't specify overnight cooking, or say it is meant for Saturday lunch.*

* I've found five Turkish-Jewish cookbooks. Two in English from Edirne and İzmir, one published in Israel in Hebrew, and one more in Turkish, none of which contain

Some people suggest the lack of Shabbat stew in these countries is due to their warm climate, but I don't find that plausible. North Africa is also warm, and the stew itself originated in the Middle East—an area not exactly known for its cold weather. Plus, even in the more temperate, mountainous regions of these three countries, Shabbat stews are no more frequently encountered. I believe the most logical explanation actually connects with the ancient origins of these countries' Jews.

Most of the ancient Jews of Turkey, Greece and Italy came directly from Israel. That original population remained, then grew sizable over hundreds of years before the arrival of Jews from other places. But, as mentioned earlier, the Shabbat stew traveled from Bavel, across North Africa to Spain, and from there onwards through Europe. This meant that Southern Europe's Jews had already been there for over a millennium before they first met the stew that was brought from Iberia. What they ate on Shabbat is unknown, but some probably prepared their personal favorite slow-cooked dish, while others may have become accustomed to eating room temperature foods instead. Since *harisa* never made it to the region, its descendant *hamin* also never became the go-to Sabbath lunch food. In contrast, when Sephardi exiles brought the same tradition to North Africa, the *Musta'arvim* were already familiar with its ancestral predecessor, and likely took to it quickly. Supporting this theory, you'll remember that *orisa* remains popular in North Africa, but isn't found anywhere in Southern Europe.

Reinforcing the idea of a Southern European alternative, there is a popular tradition across the region's Sephardim. They eat an elaborate Shabbat brunch known as *desayuno*.* It typically includes a spread of pastries, such as the "three B's" of Sephardi baking: *bourekas*, *boyos*, and *bulemas*.† *Desayuno* might also include salads, *huevos haminados*, fruit, or cold fish preparations. After consuming such a hearty spread, many might feel no need for a Shabbat stew for lunch. Though a key element that led to creating the Shabbat stew was honoring the Shabbat with hot food, it seems some Jews found a different way to honor the day, via an elaborate (though room-temperature) brunch instead.

---

a Shabbat stew. Only the bilingual (Turkish and English) *Sefarad Yemekleri* (Viki Koronyo and Sima Ovadya, 2012) features the *hamim de kastanya*. The recipe does give the vague instruction "cook over low heat."

* As a popular practice specifically among Sephardim, who would know *hamin*, this shows their culture didn't *completely* overrun the preexisting culture.

† For more on the "three B's" see "The Unknown Jewish History of Bourekas," June 4, 2020, https://www.tasteofjew.com/the-unknown-jewish-history-of-bourekas and

Finally, it is hard to ignore the influence of secularization among these communities. Relatively few Jews in Turkey today remain traditionally observant, and significant percentages of the Jews in Greece and Italy are also secular. So it is conceivable that previously Jews ate slow-cooked stews in those countries, with the practice dying out in modern times. But without written sources, this cannot be confirmed or disproved.*

A few vestigial elements bolster this hypothesis. In Italy each winter, on the Sabbath when the crossing of the Red Sea portion is read from the Torah (Exodus 13:17–15:21), a traditional lunch casserole is *ruota di Faraone*—"Pharaoh's wheel."[19] It combines pasta with sausage, pine nuts, and raisins, and is typically served cold. However, the dish goes by a few other names, one of which is *hamin per Sabato*—"Shabbat *hamin*." This is particularly odd, considering that *hamin* means "hot," which this dish is not.[20] Could it be that the name preserves a memory of Shabbat stews that were indeed served hot after cooking overnight? Similarly, if the Turkish *hamim de kastanya* isn't actually cooked overnight, could it also be an example of something previously made as a Shabbat stew leaving its fingerprints on a food of today? There is no way to know, but those odd names leave open some intriguing and suggestive questions.

As with the Shabbat stew in other regions, its specific characteristics in Southern Europe reflect the unique Jewish communities there. Multiple Shabbat stews eaten across these countries, plus many people not eating a stew at all, typify a region whose Jews are ancient, and stand apart from other communities. While I can't say with certainty why these phenomena developed, some plausible explanations offer a window onto the specific character of these populations.

## The Stew is in the Details

Until now, I've looked at the most prominent characteristics of the Shabbat stew in North Africa and Southern Europe. Sometimes, however, minor details can be at least as instructive. I turn now to a few of those details.

### *Shabbat Stew Roasting on an Open Fire*

The one relevant dish from Turkey was *hamim de kastanya* ("chestnut *hamin*"). As stated earlier, the recipe is unclear about whether this dish should be cooked through the night, and thus whether it is actually a

"Beyond Bourekas: On Boyos and Bulemas," February 3, 2022, https://www.tasteofjew.com/bourekas-boyos-bulemas (Haber, *Taste*).

* Turkish-Jewish food writer Elda Sasun told me she believes secularization is, in fact, the primary explanation for the lack of a popular Turkish Shabbat stew.

Shabbat stew.* That, however, is not its most peculiar aspect, as other people have also shortened Shabbat stew cooking times, for example secularized Jews in Germany. The truly unique element of *hamim de kastanya* is in its name: the chestnuts. It is the only recipe I have come across that includes this ingredient, or even any kind of nut at all.

Chestnuts originated in Western Asia, and were already found in Asia Minor in antiquity. It is from there that they were introduced into Europe.[21] Due to this, they are particularly popular throughout Turkey, eaten as a charcoal-roasted street food, candied, cooked with lamb and rice, or wrapped in cabbage leaves.[22] Turkey is also one of the top exporters of chestnuts in the world.[23] So, to find chestnuts in a Shabbat stew, Turkey is the most logical place to look. After all, Jews regularly add local ingredients to their stew. In some cases (such as this one) these were more distinctive.

Beyond the chestnuts, the recipe for *hamim de kastanya* includes many common Shabbat stew ingredients: beef, potatoes, onions, and tomato sauce. But what is missing is any kind of grain. It is as if the chestnuts take the place of grain, which is in keeping with their history. Due to their high starch content, chestnuts have commonly been used in this way, particularly in ancient times. They were ground into flour to bake into bread by themselves, or as an extension mixed with wheat.[24] The inclusion of chestnuts here, and their old-fashioned use as a stand-in for grain may also (along with the word *hamim*) indicate a vestigial connection to an older Shabbat stew. In addition to illustrating how Jews everywhere adapt recipes to fit local tastes, the chestnuts in a *hamim de kastanya* underscore Turkish-Jewish antiquity.

### *The Stew that Crossed the Sea*

The first stew I looked at from Italy was *hamin toscano*. It was made with chard, white beans, and meatballs. Replace the meatballs with hunks of lamb, and you may notice its similarity to Tunisian *t'fina pkaila*. The meatballs and tomato sauce basically turn it into an Italianized version of that North African stew.

But why is (approximately) the same stew found in Tunisia and Italy? Everything seen until now has indicated stark differences between the Shabbat stews on either side of the Mediterranean. And in this case, the two are even called by each region's distinct modifiers, *hamin* and *t'fina/dafina*. Could their similarities merely be culinary coincidence?

* The Turkish Jews I spoke with said they "doubt" it is commonly cooked overnight, these days.

In light of these two countries' specific geography and history, it actually makes sense to find the same stew in both. First, looking at a map of the Mediterranean, it becomes obvious that there are only two logical crossing points between south and north. While the Straits of Gibraltar between Morocco and Spain mark the easiest option, the fairly narrow Sicilian Strait, between Tunisia and the island of Sicily, clearly ranks second. That's why those were the two points where conquering Arabs crossed into Europe. Tunisia and Italy, therefore, have a historical connection. And while Tuscany is in Italy's north, far from Tunisia, it housed one of the great trading cities, Livorno.

Jews were intimately involved in that city's historic shipping business, living outside a ghetto and enjoying better rights than most Italian Jews. By the 1600s, some of them had moved to Tunisia to create a base for trade with their family members back home.[25] Food ideas regularly traveled with the Jews between these two points. Livorno's Jews introduced couscous to Italy, for example. Thus, encountering a localized version of *t'fina pkaila* in Livorno is no coincidence; it's perfectly logical. More so, in fact, than finding an adapted *hamin toscano* in Tunisia. We may assume the stew emigrated south to north, for a few reasons.

First, we find many more examples of North African foods entering Italy (frequently introduced by Jews) than vice versa. Beyond couscous, other examples include eggplants and artichokes. Second, the Shabbat stew idea was already less popular in Italy than in North Africa. So, a minor local version would be less likely to make an impact across the sea. Third, *pkaila*'s popularity across the Maghreb, beyond just Tunisia, suggests its origins are there.

Finally, however, a deep schism existed between the Livornese and *Musta'arvi* Jews in Tunisia, even more than was mentioned regarding the different groups of Moroccan Jews.[26] After decades of tensions, the two groups formally split in 1710, and only came together again on the cusp of the twentieth century.[27] With such strong opposition to the Italian Jews, it seems unlikely that Tunisian locals would have adopted a Tuscan dish. By contrast, Livornese Jews in Italy had no issue with the far-removed Tunisian Jews, so could easily take *t'fina pkaila* and modify it into a localized delicacy.

Just as the early Ashkenazi stew highlighted the less-significant migration route between Spain and France, the *t'fina pkaila–hamin toscano* connection seems to have grown out of a secondary Jewish relocation.

### *A Bonus Foods Bonanza*

I've already noted that Spain was the birthplace of the Shabbat stew Bonus Food (*huevos haminados*), and have described others in Central and Eastern Europe. But when I look at the stews of North Africa it feels like hitting the jackpot in the Bonus Food Sweepstakes! There is a plethora of options that are widely eaten across the region.

Much like the stews of the Maghreb (and perhaps even more so), these Bonus Foods show the diversity-within-unity of the Jews there. Numerous different names appear in each place for what seem like equally numerous add-ins. But upon further examination, we discover that there are really a few dominant categories, with just slight variation from place to place. And different names *everywhere.*

The most common Bonus Food in North Africa is one I've discussed a few times. As mentioned, *huevos haminados* feature there prominently. This makes sense due to the influence of the Sephardim once they arrived. Beyond those, however, there are three other major categories of Maghrebi Bonus Foods.

One is a sausage, using intestines or sometimes sheep's stomach as casing. But unlike the Eastern European *kishke*, the North African sausage is like most sausages around the world, filled with meat. Typically, it uses some kind of chopped offal, mixed with rice, seasonings, and occasionally further ground meat. Some of the many names this sausage goes by are *osban* or *osbana* in Tunisia and Libya, *m'bhar* in Morocco, and *el enbar, relleno,* or *bobbinet* across the region. These derive from multiple parent languages, further reflecting the cultures that have influenced Jewish cuisine in North Africa.

A second common bonus is a basic dough dumpling, often made using semolina, and most frequently called a *kukla*. It is quite similar to the *ganef* from Hungary, or a dense matzah ball. A similar but different example is found in Morocco and Algeria. Here, the dough is rolled or cut into tiny balls, usually about chickpea size. Some cooks air-dry them overnight, while others pre-fry them. They are then dropped into the stew pot to cook with the other ingredients. These tiny balls get names related to their size and shape: *kawa* or *cafe de masa* recall coffee beans, while others call them *khums*, likely derived from the Hebrew and Arabic for chickpeas: hummus. For some, they *take the place* of chickpeas, and may have originated as a substitute when such legumes were less available.

As if these were not enough variations, a hybrid between these first two Bonus Foods also exists. Some cooks make a type of sausage that

## North African Bonus Foods

Though many of these traditionally work with individual stews (and were suggested in specific stew recipes), I've listed them separately here (opposite and overleaf) so you can mix and match, and add any to whichever stew you choose.

### Kuklas

#### *Ingredients*

2 cups (320 g) **semolina**, plain flour, or a mix of both
2 **eggs**, beaten
2 tablespoons **olive oil**, or 1 ounce (30 g) chicken, lamb, or beef fat
6 cloves of **garlic**, crushed
½ teaspoon ground **turmeric**
½ teaspoon **salt**
1 teaspoon hot **paprika**, or ground black pepper

#### *Method*

In a large bowl, mix the **semolina** with the **eggs**, **olive oil**, **garlic**, **turmeric**, **salt**, and **paprika**. The dough should be soft and pliable. Roll into oval balls about 3 inches (7.5 cm) long and 1½ inches (3.75 cm) wide in the center. (Some like to flatten them into discs.)

Bring a large pot of water to a boil. Cook the *kuklas* in the water for about 5 minutes, until they solidify and gain some color.

Distribute the *kuklas* throughout the stew.

includes no meat, but is filled with a doughy mix of bread crumbs, hard-boiled eggs, animal fat, and spices. This is slightly more elaborate than a *kishke*, but not as luxurious as a North African *osban*, filling some middle ground between them.

The third main Bonus Food in the region is a type of meatloaf. This isn't merely an *osban* without the casing, since the meatloaf uses chopped muscular meat while the sausage is mainly stuffed with offal. We can further divide the meatloaf bonus into two subtypes. The standard has meat, breadcrumbs, eggs, and seasonings. But in Morocco, an enriched version is also popular, adding in raisins, nuts, and spices such as cinnamon. Again, it has many names, including *tamra* and *cara*, but as with *dafina* vs. *skhena*, there appears to be no logic to who calls it by which term.

Still, it seems to have been popular for quite some time. Back in 1851, an American sea captain stranded in Morocco spent time with the Jews there. He wrote about (among other things) their Shabbat food, such as the "*skanah*" they served him, noting that sometimes it came with a "plum pudding."[28] That's a dish of English origin that mixes dried fruits and almonds with suet and spices.[29] Encountering a Moroccan-Jewish *tamra*, he clearly drew a parallel to something more familiar. And mentioning it separately from the (misspelled) *skhena* itself likely indicates that the *tamra* was served separately, in classic Moroccan fashion.

In fact, the Moroccan method of serving the stew in constituent parts seemingly takes the Bonus Food concept and applies it liberally to the entire stew. If it is possible to pull one item out after cooking, why not go through a bit more effort and turn your one stew into a multi-course endeavor, a genuine meal-in-one-pot?

Perhaps that is *why* there are so many different Bonus Foods across North Africa. The *huevos haminados* first seem to have made their way into the Shabbat stew pot for convenience reasons. Rather than bringing

### Kawa

#### *Ingredients*

1½ cups (240 g) **semolina**, plain flour, or a mix of both
1 **egg**
Pinch of **salt**
2 **saffron** threads, soaked in 1 cup (240 ml) warm water

#### *Method*

IMPORTANT: This recipe must be started the night before you make the stew.

Mix the **semolina** with the **egg** and **salt** in a bowl. Add the yellow **saffron** water in small amounts, continually kneading. The dough should be fairly elastic, but not sticky. If you need more than the full cup of water, add a small amount at a time, until you reach the proper consistency.

Then, pull the dough off in small bits, rolling them between your fingers into balls the size of coffee beans. Place them (not touching each other) on a clean tea towel to dry overnight.

The next morning, toast the *kawa* balls briefly in a dry pan over low–medium heat. Then scatter them throughout the stew.

### Tamra

#### *Ingredients*

¾ pound (350 g) ground **beef**
1 cup ground **nuts** (walnuts, almonds, or a mix)
½ cup (60 g) **matzah meal**, or breadcrumbs
2 **eggs**
1 teaspoon ground **cinnamon**
½ teaspoon **salt**
½ teaspoon ground black **pepper**
¼ teaspoon ground **cloves**
¼ teaspoon ground **nutmeg**
1 cup (150 g) black **raisins**
3 **dates**, seeded and chopped (optional)

#### *Method*

Put the **beef, nuts, matzah meal,** and **eggs** in a large bowl and mix by hand. Once all are well-combined, add the **cinnamon, salt, pepper, cloves,** and **nutmeg** and work the spices through the meat. Finally, add the **raisins** and **dates** (if using), and mix them through, until evenly distributed. The mix should be thick and sticky, not loose or liquid. If needed, add more **matzah meal** and/or **raisins** to thicken.

Roll the meat into a thick sausage shape and wrap it in cheesecloth. Tie the cheesecloth at each end. Cook the *tamra* inside the Shabbat stew.

#### *Notes*

Other optional ingredients include 1–2 chopped hard-boiled eggs, or 1 small (peeled and cooked) mashed sweet potato.

two pots to the oven, one could cook two separate courses in the same pot. When this innovation arrived in North Africa, perhaps families who had been cooking *harisa* for hundreds of years saw an opportunity to upscale the sophistication of their Shabbat stews, without a tremendous extra effort.

* * *

With the close of this chapter, I have finished following the Shabbat stew from its ancient Middle Eastern origins, through its two medieval hubs, to the bulk of Europe and North Africa and the cusp of the contemporary age. Before I dive into the story of what happened to the stew during the unparalleled surge of American and Israeli Jewries, I'll take a detour to follow some changes and migrations that brought the Shabbat stew to Jews in more remote places, or which helped create Jewish communities where none had existed before.

## Chapter 8

# The Stew that Grew With the World of the Jew

The Jewish world today is much broader and more diverse than it was just 500 years ago. (While "just 500 years" might sound strange, you can totally say it when you have thousands of years of history behind you.) Jews live in more places than ever before, and in a wider array of political and social circumstances. This has changed not only the face of world Jewry, but also the foods we eat.

As I've outlined in previous chapters, large waves of immigration during the late medieval and early modern periods pushed Jews eastward into Central and Eastern Europe, and from Iberia around the perimeter of the Mediterranean. In time, however, Jewish migrations grew bigger and more frequent. Such moves followed the broader patterns in society. Scholars refer to the period between 1850 and World War I as the "age of mass migration," so the streams of Jews moving from place to place then were teaspoons within the gallons of human population shift. While the influx of Jews to the United States typifies this, other Jewish migrations stood on their own. For example, the Jewish immigration to Israel before and after 1948. I will address these two cases in the next chapter.

Before them, however, this chapter explores communities that changed drastically over the past few centuries, altering the map of world Jewry in their own way. Some created societies where Jews had never lived before, others reinvigorated smaller Jewish populations, and still others connected isolated Jewish groups with the bulk of world Jewry.

Finally, not all moves are physical. Just as a migration from one place to another can create upheaval and lead to changes in foodways, a drastic change in living conditions might also affect what is eaten by people who did not move. In this chapter, I'll explore one community who stayed put, but whose circumstances changed so drastically that it was almost as if they'd migrated. I'm referring here to the Jews of the Soviet Union, and since their story begins in a place already discussed (Eastern Europe, in Chapter 6), I turn to them first, before addressing other groups.

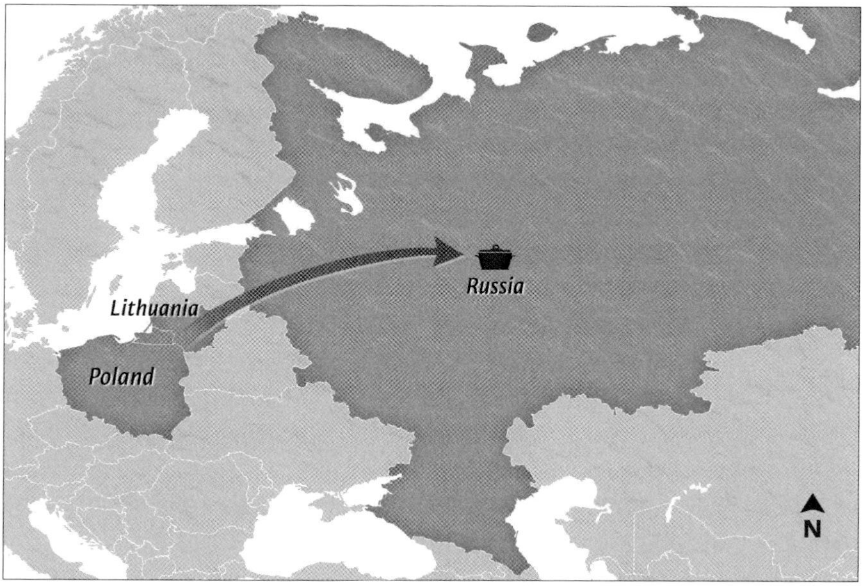


## The Stew That Rescued a Culture

The bulk of Russia's Jews came from the Eastern Europe of Poland and Lithuania. Before the Partitions of Poland in the late 1700s, there were relatively few Jews living under Russian rule. Most European Jews then lived either in Polish lands or the Ottoman Empire.[1] Russia's main goal in annexing large chunks of Poland was purely territorial, but in the process it also "unintentionally acquired some half a million Jewish subjects."[2] At first, Catherine the Great (ruled 1762–96) tried to incorporate the Jews into Russian society.[3] This was easier following the First Partition, when only 27,000 Jews came under her control.[4] But following a flood of many more, Catherine countered anti-Jewish sentiment by confining them to the Pale of Settlement region of the west of Russia, in 1791. This kept Jews out of the Russian heartland and most Russian cities,* while strengthening Russian control over their new territory.[5] In time, Jews gained access to cities within the Pale, such as Kyiv, and eventually they could even move to Moscow and other cities in Russia proper.[6]

While there are few records of specific Shabbat stew versions from Russia during those years, the dish was likely similar to the *cholent* of Poland–Lithuania, since the Jews had only recently left there, and available ingredients were similar. One Jewish cookbook was published in Kyiv in 1889, but it does not contain any Shabbat stew recipes. However,

* Odessa, Ukraine, was a notable exception.

among its tiny section of four "Original Jewish Dishes," a recipe for a "Saturday *Kugel*" gives instructions to leave it in the oven all of Friday night.[7] It was made from soaked bread, schmaltz, and sweet ingredients such as raisins and syrup, but a second recipe for a "Polish *Kugel*" (of the four recipes, three are for *kugels*!) replaces the sweet ingredients with salt, pepper, and onions.* Finding these recipes in a late-nineteenth-century Russian cookbook indicates the similarity between the Jewish cuisine there and its Polish predecessor.

With the founding of the Soviet Union in 1922, government controls dramatically altered Jewish life in the country. Soviet policy attempted to create a unified nation by eliminating, as much as possible, competing loyalties—to nationality, locality, or religion. This obviously affected Jews, targeting them both as a religion and a nation, but these efforts were different from what we had experienced through the previous millennium-plus of life in Europe. While some Soviet leaders were certainly anti-Jewish, antisemitism doesn't fully explain these policies. At times, the Soviets even made weak attempts to combat antisemitism among the populace.[8] A fair assessment is that the Soviets were anti-religious more than explicitly antisemitic.

Because of their attempts at destroying religious sentiment, the Soviets were actually more successful than the Nazis, in at least one significant way. The Germans of World War II murdered 6 million Jews, an unprecedented and utterly incomprehensible act of barbarism. But those who survived kept their prewar memories, and some (incredibly) had even stronger Jewish identities. That's why, as described in Chapter 6, recent efforts have successfully recovered pre-Holocaust food memories for future generations.

In contrast, the Russian-Jewish population that physically survived the Soviet era were a shell of what had preceded the Bolshevik revolution. In a single generation, the Soviets wiped out nearly all Jewish culture; the Jewish body survived, but its soul was destroyed.[9] This understandably damaged Jewish foodways in the Soviet Union.

I say that Jewish culture there was "nearly" all destroyed, because tiny remnants persisted, but without meaningful context. Professor Zvi Gitelman defines this as the loss of "thick" culture—language, customs, dress, and food—leaving the Jews with only the "thin" culture of shared identification.[10] The degree to which this occurred varied by region

* This regional sweet–savory divide is well-documented, applying to gefilte fish as well as *kugels*.

across the massive USSR. Jewish knowledge survived more strongly in smaller towns than in cities, with Jews of the former Pale of Settlement remembering and cooking their grandparents' traditional dishes more than those who moved to Moscow or Leningrad (today's St. Petersburg).[11]

Still, Jewish food memories were degraded. Former Soviet Jews discussing their parents' and grandparents' food is like eating a dish cooked from a 200-year-old recipe. Ingredients, measurements, or cooking times may be missing or imprecise, so the food will be a vague guess at what was intended. These people's food recollections are full of similar gaps. For example, one described *cholent* as being "potatoes, more potatoes and stewing meat with lots of schmaltz."[12] Could this possibly have been the complete ingredient list? Unlikely. Others recall little more than a peculiar aspect of the food—that *cholent* was a Shabbat food, or that it was cooked in the baker's oven overnight.[13]

Further complicating things, through much of the Soviet era there was no popular Russian Shabbat stew at all. Most Soviet Jews did not remain observant and no longer kept the Sabbath. Even when I've spoken with Soviet Jews who did remain moderately religious, nearly all say they never ate a Shabbat stew of *any* kind in Russia. Such was the degree of secularization that the Soviets forced on their populace.

So how, then, did even fragmentary memories survive? Interestingly, that too may be attributed to the Soviets. Government policy separated religion from culture, forbidding the former while embracing the latter. The government believed a singular Soviet nation could blend numerous ethnicities and individual cultures into one great whole. As historian Jeffrey Veidlinger says, "[M]inorities were encouraged to retain visible markers of ethnic difference, such as dress and food, *provided that they were emptied of any national sentiment.*"[14]

The Soviets even published Jewish cookbooks, including one during Stalin's Great Terror in the 1930s. It contained nothing religious, but how surprising that it was even published at all. Throughout the Soviet Era, Jewish foods were "Sovietized" and cleansed of religious content by "coding" their names. Challah, the Jewish Sabbath bread, was available but sold as *pletenka* ("braid" in Russian). A 1973 Soviet cookbook included Jewish-style stuffed cabbage,* but identifies it euphemistically as "Oriental Style."[15] Jewish dishes persisted under the Soviets in debased form.

* It avoided the non-kosher mixture of meat and sour cream, and contained the recognizably Jewish sweet-and-sour sauce.

What value were half-memories and disguised dishes? Gitelman includes food within thick culture, but could these shreds of heritage constitute a slight thickness, or were they neutered to the point of becoming empty symbols in a thin culture? While the USSR existed, they were little more than blurry markers, but in the post-Soviet era they became a tool that facilitated the return to substantial culture. Those memories went beyond a recognition of Jewish origins. Many bizarre practices were vestiges of forgotten but important Jewish food traditions.

Jewish Studies scholar Anna Shternshis relates that former Soviet Jews frequently speak of eating kosher pork in Russia. You read that right: kosher pork! When questioned about this impossible practice, they explain that they bought it from a Jewish butcher who somehow knew how to make pork kosher.[16] (To be clear, there is no way within traditional Jewish laws to make pig meat kosher.) Beyond buying their "kosher pork" from special butchers, some mention cooking it in separate pots, or eating it by a windowsill rather than at the table. Clearly, they knew something was "off" about Jews eating pork, but not enough to prevent them from doing it. Perhaps most surprising are those who only ate meat from the front half of the pig.[17] Ashkenazi Jews customarily do not consume the hindquarters of an animal to avoid the forbidden sciatic nerve. But there is no difference between the front or rear half of a pig—they're both *treif*! Doing this preserved a long-forgotten Jewish food practice . . . whether it made logical sense or not.

Other residual but camouflaged Jewish food practices included ways to avoid the forbidden milk-and-meat combination, or cooking non-traditional (kosher) recipes for common Russian foods.[18] Most relevant to this book's topic, one woman told Shternshis of her *cholent*, that included fish, onions, carrots, and beets. While she only cooked it for five–six hours, she said that "Old Jewish women used to leave it overnight in the oven." Not only is this a recipe I have never seen elsewhere, but she would make this fish *cholent* any day of the week. So this woman knew that *cholent* was a Jewish food, meant to be cooked overnight, but had no idea that it was intended for Shabbat.[19]

These lingering Jewish food practices acquired real value once the Iron Curtain fell. Any Jew who then chose to reconnect to their religion could use these odd customs as their entry point. They knew these practices were uniquely Jewish, and now they could explore *why* Jews did these peculiar things. What was the significance of keeping separate meat and dairy pots? Why did they eat pork differently than other meats? And why would anyone leave that fish *cholent* cooking for the entire night?

Following the dissolution of the Soviet Union, Russia saw a mini-explosion of Jewish cookbook publishing. In one, the introduction strikes a somber tone, but discusses this very activity of mining the old memories:

> Every new generation desires to rummage in the treasure chest that holds the culinary inheritance of its distant ancestors. And every generation finds there interesting recipes that . . . have fallen out of use or changed in fundamental ways . . . Nonetheless, we try to catch these recipes that have slipped through time.[20]

Could they succeed? Even the pre-Soviet Jewish cookbook barely featured traditional recipes. Still, in case after case, former Soviet Jews have used food to slowly reconnect to their Jewishness.

Project Kesher focuses on strengthening Jewish identity among women from the former Soviet Union. In their 2008 cookbook, many of the testimonials highlight this exact pathway. A Ukrainian woman, who learned of her Jewish heritage only after marriage, describes how chicken-and-carrot *tzimmes* connected her to her family's past generations. Another woman bridged past and future by cooking old family recipes with her young son.[21]

But the best example of food helping Jews reconnect to Judaism began *before* the end of the Soviet era. Tamara Krasilnikova compiled an underground cookbook in pre-Glasnost Soviet Leningrad. Produced surreptitiously, thousands of copies circulated among the *refusenik* population.[22] The effort they made to disseminate the book indicates how significant Jewish food can be to Jewish identity. After Krasilnikova emigrated to the US, an Israeli organization printed her book and sent copies to Jews still stuck in the Soviet Union. When fundraising for the project, the organization wrote, "Imagine . . . you are a Jew with virtually no Jewish education or background . . . who has just received this book . . . Suddenly, you are exposed to a world of Jewish cooking and Jewish ideas of which you never dreamed!"[23]

The book contains five slightly different *cholent* recipes. Two, however, feature an odd addition, laying the other ingredients on an egg-enriched flatbread dough filling the bottom of the pot.[24] It is called *lepeshka* in the recipe, which is a type of Central Asian flatbread, but the version here isn't a standard *lepeshka*. The original is made with milk and no eggs, baked on the walls of an open-faced oven.

The "bread" in these recipes is placed unbaked in the pot, then covered with the rest of the watery stew. Presumably, the name merely recalls the

*Uzbeki-style flatbread, traditionally baked on the walls of an oven.*

round, flat shape of *lepeshka*. This slightly odd practice seems inspired by the idea of a basic *kugel* dumpling cooked in the stew.

Yes, the Soviets were extremely effective in their efforts to destroy Jewish knowledge. But they allowed Jewish cooking practices to persist, even if only in a heavily corrupted form. However, once the Soviet Union fell, those who wanted to dig into their heritage had the chance to do so. Cook the foods their ancestors made, and learn the meaning behind their "strange" practices. *Cholent*, along with other traditional foods, provided a powerful vehicle for reanimating Jewish culture in the former Soviet Union.

## How Do You Say Cholent in English?

Americans dominate world Jewish culture today.* It is, therefore, easy to forget that English-speaking Jews are relatively new in our history.† Pockets of Anglophone Jews existed previously, but only in the mid-1800s did English-speaking Jewry reach its tipping point. So, while I defer US Jewry to next chapter, I'd like to turn now to the smaller, though still significant, Anglo-Jewish communities.‡ As relative newcomers to their countries, many eat foods that resemble their families' pre-immigration roots. But often, interesting innovations express each community's uniqueness.

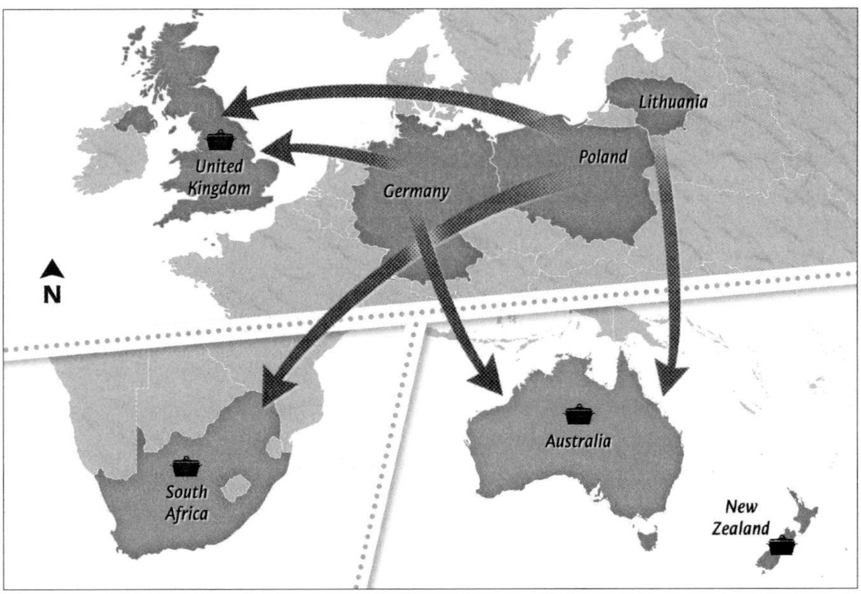


* About 40 percent of world Jewry currently lives in the USA.

† A sizable community of Jews lived in medieval England, but I refer here to Jews who speak Modern English.

‡ I'm focusing only on those countries where I identified notable or unique aspects to the Shabbat stew. Alas, no Canada, for example.

*Lady Judith Montefiore.*

The first English-language Jewish cookbook was published in London in 1846. *The Jewish Manual* was published anonymously by "A Lady," though the scholarly consensus accepts that its author was Lady Judith Montefiore, a philanthropic British Jew. Her Shabbat stew recipe bears a peculiar (and telling) name: "Kugel and Commean."

A fairly straightforward combination of beef and chickpeas, it also includes a simple (though sweetened) *kugel*, cooked in a small container within the stew pot.[25] While the *kugel* is Ashkenazi, she identifies the stew using a Sephardi name—"Commean" is clearly her spelling of *hamin*, before that English spelling had become standard. Using chickpeas as the legume underscores the Sephardi style of her stew.*

This "Ashkephardi" combination may seem surprising at first glance. But it makes sense in light of English-Jewish society at the time. Modern English Jewry bears no connection to the population that lived there in the Middle Ages since, in 1290, England became the first country to expel its Jews. Only after 1655, when Oliver Cromwell began turning a blind eye, did Jews start moving back to Britain.† The first were Dutch Sephardim, who remained dominant among English Jewry for some time. However, as the nineteenth century wore on, Ashkenazi Jews overtook Sephardim as more prominent in English society. Lady Judith's personal biography reflects this. She was Ashkenazi, while her husband Sir Moses Montefiore was of Italian Sephardi origin. When they married, the Sephardi community (centered around London's Bevis Marks Synagogue) did not allow unions between their members and Ashkenazim. But the marriage of these two prominent individuals, personally opposed to separation between Jews, helped eliminate that policy.

* Chickpeas also appear in Ashkenazi stews, but are more common in Sephardi and Mizrachi versions.

† The policy only became official about a hundred years later. There may also have been a few Crypto-Jews living in England prior to Cromwell's changes.

Reflecting the Montefiore family's blended heritage, *The Jewish Manual* includes recipes from both Jewish groups, and some that blend them (as with "Kugel and Commean"). Further disguising the foods' Ashkenazi or Sephardi origins, Lady Judith upscaled them all. (The recipe at right, for example, suggests upgrading the *kugel* with "a sweet sauce flavored with lemon and brandy.") They thus blend into a homogeneous whole, like the English Jewry the Montefiores envisioned.

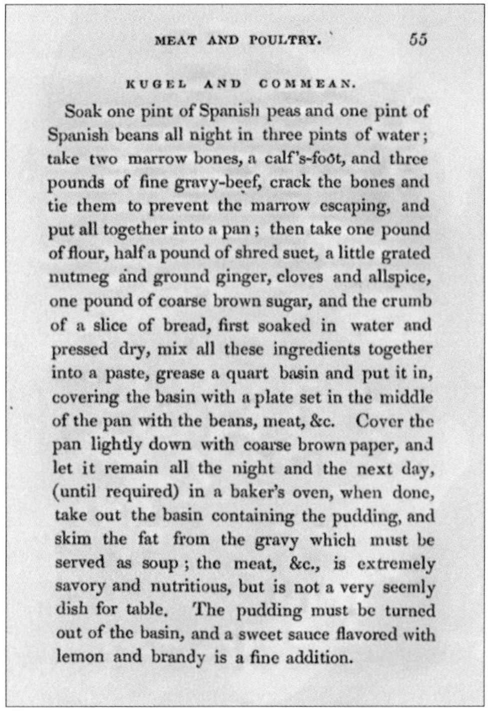

MEAT AND POULTRY. 55

KUGEL AND COMMEAN.

Soak one pint of Spanish peas and one pint of Spanish beans all night in three pints of water; take two marrow bones, a calf's-foot, and three pounds of fine gravy-beef, crack the bones and tie them to prevent the marrow escaping, and put all together into a pan; then take one pound of flour, half a pound of shred suet, a little grated nutmeg and ground ginger, cloves and allspice, one pound of coarse brown sugar, and the crumb of a slice of bread, first soaked in water and pressed dry, mix all these ingredients together into a paste, grease a quart basin and put it in, covering the basin with a plate set in the middle of the pan with the beans, meat, &c. Cover the pan lightly down with coarse brown paper, and let it remain all the night and the next day, (until required) in a baker's oven, when done, take out the basin containing the pudding, and skim the fat from the gravy which must be served as soup; the meat, &c., is extremely savory and nutritious, but is not a very seemly dish for table. The pudding must be turned out of the basin, and a sweet sauce flavored with lemon and brandy is a fine addition.

*Shabbat stew recipe from* The Jewish Manual, *1846.*

That hope never came to fruition. Rather than blending into a unified whole, Ashkenazi culture came to dominate and swallow that of the Sephardim. We can see the shifts in the Ashkenazi–Sephardi balance of power by noting Shabbat stew recipes in subsequent cookbooks. Already in 1874, Estella Atrutel's *An Easy and Economical Book of Jewish Cookery* refers to its main Shabbat stew simply as "Peas and Beans" (even though it contains many more ingredients). It still has some Sephardi contents, but the Ashkenazi ones start to dominate—the recipe calls for a pound of white beans versus one pint of chickpeas. It also includes a sausage, described using the German word "worsht."[26] Over the next fifty years, Jewish cookbooks in Britain feature no Shabbat stew recipes, but the traditional recipes they do include skew largely Ashkenazi.* Once the Shabbat stew returns, in mid-twentieth-century cookbooks, it is usually Eastern European in style. The most common name we find is *cholent*, and the recipes feature such Ashkenazi elements as a *knaidel* (matzah ball in Yiddish) dumpling or schmaltz.

Around the approach of the twenty-first century, however, a swing back to the center slowly begins. One cookbook from the late 1990s features "Beef Cholent with Beans and Hamin Eggs," a return to the

* The lack of Shabbat stew recipes reflects a focus on the in-vogue French cuisine rather than traditional Jewish foods.

"Ashkephardi" style of Montefiore's book.[27] Subsequent offerings contain recipes for *cholent* side by side with those for a *hamin* that includes "a parcel of rice" (as in Moroccan *dafina*), or stews with other non-Ashkenazi ingredients such as lamb, wheat, chickpeas, *haminados*, turmeric, and cumin.[28] This reflects increased efforts by Britain's Sephardi population to gain recognition within Ashkenormative culture.*

South Africa's Jews, meanwhile, were much less diverse. The bulk have roots in Lithuania, after many Litvaks (Lithuanian Jews) immigrated in the early 1900s.[29] Not only does that mean fewer non-Ashkenazi Shabbat stews, but a purer Eastern European *cholent*. In the US, Jews from across Central and Eastern Europe lived side-by-side, and their cuisines melded into a generic pan-Ashkenazi cuisine. South African Jewish cuisine is largely unadulterated, featuring some old-fashioned foods that have become less popular in America and Britain. A great example is *teigelakh*, a dessert of dough balls fried in honey that remains popular in South Africa year-round, though it may only crop up on American Ashkenazi tables for Rosh Hashana, if at all.

Primarily in the second half of the twentieth century, South African Jews published a host of charity fundraising cookbooks.† While most recipes are of a general nature, many of the cookbooks featured a small, sequestered section of classic Jewish recipes. The same dishes show up repeatedly, turning them into an unofficial canon.[30] *Cholent* is not in these books, excluding it from that venerated "traditional" roster.

This may reflect the religious character of mid-century South African Jewry, often called "non-observant Orthodox."[31] They respected traditional Judaism in public, but less actively practiced it at home. In other words, the synagogue they *didn't* go to was an Orthodox one. Someone not observing the Sabbath would have less reason to prepare a Shabbat stew. Additionally, I suspect that in at least some cases, the lack of *cholent* recipes reflects a reality of apartheid-era South Africa. With a non-Jewish housekeeper doing much of the cooking, even a moderately observant Jew might have relied on her to cook on Shabbat.‡ Why leave a pot to cook overnight if your housekeeper would cook it fresh for you?

* Exemplifying this push, 2011 saw the establishment of Sephardi Voices UK, and in 2022 the British Sephardi community launched an internal census.

† *The South African Jewish Cookbook Project*, a digital archive, has many available at http://sajewishcookbooks.org.za.

‡ This wouldn't be acceptable to the most stringently Orthodox, but a less punctilious, still traditional Jew might accept this degree of leniency.

Not surprisingly, South African cookbooks changed when the community's religious culture did. Through the 1970s and '80s, there was an increase in *ba'alei teshuva*—Jews who grew up secular, but decided to become more traditionally observant. This started with the 1972 arrival of emissaries of Chabad-Lubavitch, a Hasidic group that focuses on encouraging deeper religiosity among less traditional Jews. Soon, other groups joined that movement.[32] Accordingly, we start seeing *cholent* recipes in cookbooks of the 1980s.*

Nothing identifies the South African stew as specifically Litvak, since *cholents* of Poland and Lithuania were not notably different. But as with South African Jewish cuisine overall, the Shabbat stews there remain a bit old-fashioned. We find much heavier use of schmaltz, long after cholesterol-phobic Americans had abandoned this classic Jewish ingredient. Similarly, some recipes feature the somewhat archaic Eastern European technique of cooking a *kugel* on top of the stew, to prevent the *cholent* from drying out.[33]

One final element of Shabbat stew innovation seems particularly prominent in Anglo-Jewish communities: recipes that feature iconic local ingredients, and/or adapt popular recipes from the non-Jewish population. As far back as Atrutel's 1874 book, we find a "Mock Turtle Soup," but one that is explicitly suggested as a Shabbat stew with overnight Friday cooking.[34] A more modern adaptation of a British classic is in a vegan "Great British Cholent," inspired by the Full English Breakfast (while leaving out that popular dish's non-vegan egg, sausage, and, of course, bacon). It includes such popular British ingredients as parsnips, button mushrooms, canned baked beans, and Worcestershire sauce.[35] Parsnips also appear, along with green cabbage, in a *cholent* recipe from the Shetland Isles of northern Scotland. Though the author's roots are Lithuanian, those two vegetables are much more British than Eastern European, especially in a *cholent*.[36]

As with the British stews, we find popular South African ingredients in *cholent* pots there. Many include samp, a local preparation of smashed, dried corn. Even with overnight cooking, it holds its shape without turning into mush, and has the added benefit (for those who need it) of being gluten-free. Similarly, some use mealie miel (a local cornmeal) for a *cholent* dumpling or *kugel*. Many flavor their stews with bottled South African "chutney" sauce, or local soup powders. I've even come

* One early outlier exception was 1970's *Arcadia Recipe and Household Guide*, 2nd edition, but no more until the 1980s.

## Great British Vegetarian Cholent

Helen Goldrein developed this on her blog, *Family Friends Food,* to be a distinctly British Shabbat stew. I tweaked it to add more elements of the Full English Breakfast. Changing it from vegan to vegetarian allowed me to include eggs. (They aren't fried as in the original, but, hey, they're still eggs.) I also added veggie sausage and tomatoes, important parts of the classic. Finally, while potatoes, carrots, and parsnips aren't in that breakfast, I kept them as solidly British ingredients that work great in a Shabbat stew. I'm positively chuffed by this Full English/*cholent* hybrid (in vegetarian form)!

***Ingredients***

4–6 tablespoons vegetable **oil**
3 medium **tomatoes**, sliced into quarters
4–8 vegetarian **sausages**
2 medium **onions**, sliced
3 large **carrots**, peeled and cut into 1-inch (2.5-cm) chunks
2 large **parsnips**, peeled and cut into 1-inch (2.5-cm) chunks
½ pound (250 g) small button **mushrooms**, cleaned but kept whole
2 (16-ounce/450 g) cans vegetarian **baked beans**
¾ cup (160 g) **pearl barley**
1½ quarts/1.5 liters vegetable or *pareve* (meat-free) "chicken" **stock**
2 teaspoons vegan **Worcestershire sauce**

across one version in which the meat was *boerwors*, an indigenous (and delicious, I might add) South African clove-and-coriander-flavored sausage.[37] These ingredients are little known outside South Africa, but few Jews there would bat an eye at finding them in a *cholent.*

Local stamps mark some Shabbat stews in Australia and New Zealand as well. One cookbook in Australia featured a classically Eastern European *cholent*, with one key difference: it called for lamb, rather than the traditional beef.[38] The recipe came from a Scottish-Jewish immigrant to Australia, and while both Australia and Scotland are well known for raising sheep, this choice most reflects Aussie tastes. Sheep in Scotland are raised for export, rather than consumed locally, with Scots eating *less* lamb than most other Brits.[39] Australia, however, sits among the world leaders in consumption.[40]

Finally, one recipe from New Zealand, created by the chef at Auckland's The Kosher Deli, features a unique "secret New Zealand ingredient"—a tablespoon of manuka honey.[41] The product of pollen from a local tree,

8 **eggs**, still in their shells
2 **bay leaves**

***Method***

Heat 4 tablespoons of **oil** in a large pot over medium heat. Fry the **tomatoes** lightly, turning to slightly brown each side. Remove to a plate. Next fry the **sausages**, turning regularly. After they start to brown, remove them as well.

If the **oil** is low, add up to two more tablespoons, as needed. Fry the **onions** for about 5 minutes, until they start to brown. Add the **carrots**, **parsnips**, and **mushrooms**. Continue cooking, stirring occasionally, for another 5 minutes.

Add the **baked beans**, **pearl barley**, **stock**, and **Worcestershire sauce**, and stir well to combine. Return the **tomatoes** and **sausages** to the pot. The liquid should completely cover the other ingredients. Place the **eggs** on top, at least partially submerged. Tuck in the **bay leaves**.

Cook overnight using any standard method (*see* pages 7–8).

***Notes***

Between the stock and the sausages, there should be enough salt in this, but if you like it saltier, add about 1 teaspoon while frying the vegetables.

Make sure to select a vegetarian sausage with a strong flavor, to stand up to the other ingredients.

this honey has a distinctive earthy flavor. Whether or not one tablespoon is enough to impact the flavor of the stew, including it instills pride in New Zealand's Jews, adding a Kiwi twist to their Jewish classic.

Of course, such local insertions are common worldwide. They reflect a core idea of this book: that in each place the Jews reached, they changed the stew with whatever ingredients were available or popular. But perhaps due to the relative recency of these changes in a stew with such a long history, the Anglo examples stand out and seem more ground-breaking.

## ¡Yo Quiero Cholent!

As mentioned in connection with the Spanish Expulsion, some Sephardim and *conversos* ended up in Latin America. However, most Shabbat stews found in Central and South America today are *not* Sephardi in style, highlighting a commonly-held fallacy. Since the primary languages of Latin America are Spanish and, to a lesser extent, Portuguese, many

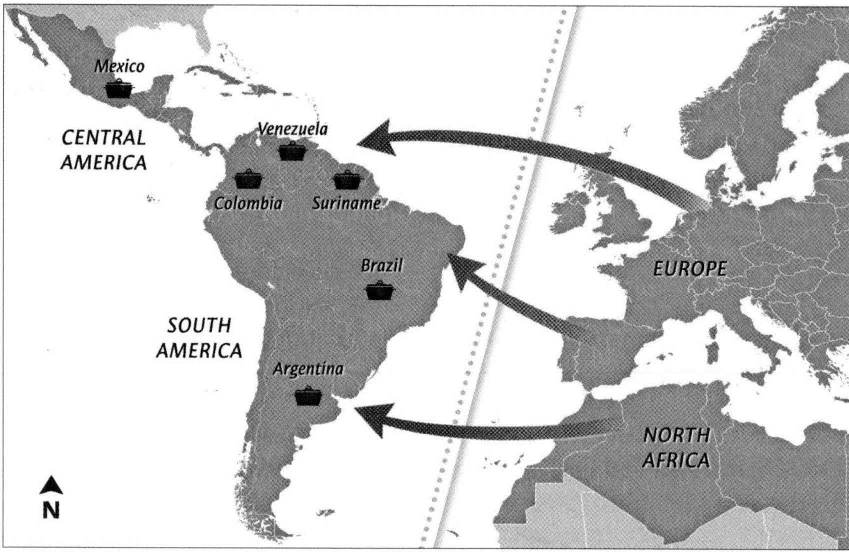


assume that the Jews there descend from the post-Expulsion refugees. Most, however, are actually of Ashkenazi heritage. And even among the non-Ashkenazi minority, most don't descend from colonial-era settlers. Latin American Jewry primarily arrived as immigrants during the late 1800s and early 1900s.[42] So, understandably, *cholent* of some sort is the predominant Shabbat stew there.

What happened to the early Latin American Jews of Sephardi origins? Why do we find so little influence of their cuisine around the region today? Brazilian Jewish history helps explain.

The country held one of the earliest *converso* settlements in the Americas. But, when the Dutch conquered the area around Recife (in northeastern Brazil), declaring religious tolerance in 1624, many Crypto-Jews came out of the religious closet, while others (already living openly) moved from Holland. Jewish life in Recife thrived beyond imagination . . . but only for thirty years. Then the Portuguese reconquered the area and reimposed Inquisition rules, so Recife's Jews rapidly dispersed. Some fled to the Netherlands or Dutch-controlled colonies around the Caribbean.[43] A small contingent even sailed for New Amsterdam (later to be known as New York)—the first Jewish community in the future United States. So even if a few Crypto-Jews remained in Brazil, they were too few, for too long a period, for their foodways to survive in any recognizable form.

Other South American countries had similarly small Crypto-Jewish populations. Only after these countries gained independence, during the first half of the nineteenth century, could open Jewish communities emerge. So, in the same waves of immigration that would inflate Jewish populations in the UK and US, others moved to Latin America. Later, small Sephardi and Mizrachi groups joined them.

Despite *cholent*'s continued dominance in South America, Sephardi and Mizrachi Jews have slowly increased their visibility in Jewish cuisine, as they have in the Britain. Their dishes became more prominent in Argentinian-Jewish cookbooks late in the twentieth century.[44] Similarly, an endearing Brazilian cookbook features recipes collected from non-Jewish housekeepers in the Jewish community. It contains recipes for both *adafina* and *cholent*.* And if placement and sequence say anything, the Moroccan-style stew appears much earlier in the book than the Ashkenazi one.[45]

No matter the specific type of Shabbat stew, they all express the integration of Jews into general Latin American society. As we saw in Hungary, this region's Jews established themselves just as their countries achieved independence. Therefore, Jewish eating habits largely mimic those of non-Jewish Latinos. This emerges via some local Shabbat stews. For example, Argentinian and Brazilian stews are made with a lot of meat, easily surpassing 50 percent of the stew's volume. Many versions include multiple cuts, or prepared meats such as sausage or meatballs. This reflects the regional love for beef, with Argentina and Brazil consistently ranked among the world leaders in consumption.[46]

More interesting are the ties between many Latin American Shabbat stews and generally popular South American dishes. Examples include unique non-Jewish foods adapted to *kashrut*, or stews that merely incorporate local ingredients. And in one case, we even encounter the opposite direction of influence, with a Shabbat stew becoming popular throughout its home country.

The "national dish" of Brazil is *feijoada*, comprised of black beans, sausage, and pig ears and tail, served with rice, and topped with *farofa*—crispy fried cassava crumbs. Some Brazilian Jews prepare a kosher *feijoada*, using beef in place of the pork. A beloved, fatty cut of beef—the back hump of the cow known locally as *cupim*—is paired with kosher sausage. It is not uncommon, however, for Jews in Brazil to repurpose this kosher *feijoada* into an overnight-cooked Shabbat stew.[47] In 2005, a rabbi in São Paulo even convinced a *treif* restaurant next to his synagogue to make a kosher *feijoada* that also met the chef's

* Though Moroccan, not Spanish, in style, it is called *adafina* rather than *dafina*.

exacting standards. After eight months of development, they held a one-off (kosher) event at the restaurant, then continued selling it in frozen portions for future Shabbats.[48] Kosher *feijoada* (especially as a Shabbat stew) reflects local Jews' embrace of their Brazilian side, which otherwise might conflict with their Jewish identity.[49]

Less prominently, but in a similar vein, one Venezuelan *adafina* recipe remains traditional to its Moroccan forebear, even including a *tamra* meatloaf. But it also features a very non-Moroccan element: corn on the cob, or *jojotas*, in the local parlance.[50] While Americans tend to eat their corn cobs on their own, finding them inside a stew is not abnormal in Venezuela. There is a type of *estofado* (stew) from the region that also contains *jojotas*. And guess what? Some local Jews also turn that into a Shabbat stew.[51] While not a national dish like *feijoada*, *estofado* is popular enough that it apparently inspired the author of that *adafina* recipe.

Finally, from the other end of the spectrum, a Surinamese Shabbat stew grew into that country's "national dish," much as *adafina* developed into *cocido* in Spain. This is particularly notable, since only about 200 Jews live in Suriname today.[52] But long before the US Jewish community rose in number and significance, Suriname's community in the 1600s was one of the most important in the Americas. Back then, the center of Jewry in the Western Hemisphere was around the Caribbean, and Dutch-controlled colonies absorbed large Jewish populations from Brazil and Holland, with many receiving free (albeit one-way) transportation.[53] Surinam (the spelling of the Dutch colony's name) had numerous Jewish sugar plantation owners, largely centered around the town of Jodensavanne—"Jewish Savannah." Many grew wealthy from this (significant for understanding the local Shabbat stew's origins).

The most adored celebratory food in Suriname is *pom*, named for its main ingredient *pomtajer*, also known as American taro.* The plant's root is grated and mixed with orange juice and sautéed chicken, then baked in the oven as a sort of casserole. Not only is *pom* commonly eaten in Suriname and Amsterdam (which has many Surinamese immigrants), but it is also popular among Jews as their overnight Shabbat stew. Indeed, most Surinamese people, and scholars of the country's food, recognize *pom* as Jewish in origin.[54]

*Pom* uses an indigenous ingredient, but in a unique manner. Most *pomtajer* dishes use the leaves or stem, while this is the only one to cook

* Botanical names may be confusing, and this plant is not related to actual taro. *Pomtajer*'s scientific name is *Xanthosoma sagittifolium*.

*Jodensavanne, painted in 1830 by Pierre Jacques Benoit.*

the root (grating it like potatoes for a *kugel*). Furthermore, it mixes that ingredient with two non-local foods: chicken and orange. Finally, it is baked in an oven, unlike most indigenous foods that are cooked over an open fire. Only wealthy people (such as Jewish plantation owners) had home ovens, and chicken has always been a popular Shabbat food. The theory, therefore, is that indigenous and slave cooks working in plantation kitchens created *pom* for Jewish landowners, mixing Jewish and African Creole influences.[55] While Brazilian Jews turned their national dish into a Shabbat stew, in Suriname it appears that a Shabbat stew became the national dish.

Finally, I would be remiss if I failed to note that this cultural crossover within the Shabbat stew is not universal in Latin America. In Mexico, the standard Ashkenazi *cholent* appears to be untouchable. Every recipe I have found could just as easily have been written in Poland or an ultra-Orthodox neighborhood of Brooklyn. This is odd, since Mexico's Jews have no apparent issue with mixing local ingredients into other classic Jewish foods. "Veracruz-Style Gefilte Fish" uses saltwater fish, such as red snapper, rather than the more common freshwater fish (like carp or pike), and serves it in a tomato sauce.[56] Other examples include *tacos al pastor* made of beef instead of pork,[57] challah stuffed with Oaxacan chocolate,[58] and *tzimmes* flavored with *panela* (whole cane sugar) and Mexican pumpkin.[59] Mexican-Jewish chef and TV personality Pati Jinich confirms that while community members are happy to take liberties with the foods they prepare, they *do not* do so with *cholent*.[60] I can only speculate that this reflects a specific element of Mexican-Jewish character. While many are not religiously observant, they remain insular and proud of their Judaism. Intermarriage with non-Jews remains extremely uncommon.[61] Since the Shabbat stew is so significant a Jewish food—more so than gefilte fish or challah—perhaps this highly traditional population refuses to adulterate its recipe with local ingredients. Some things must remain sacred!

## Arab Jews? In New York and Latin America?

As noteworthy as that Mexican exception to the Latin American trend is, even more intriguing is an exception *to* that exception. The Mexican-Jewish community actually comprises four distinct groups: Ashkenazi, Balkan, and Syrian from both Aleppo and Damascus.[62] And while the largest group (the Ashkenazim) don't adulterate their Shabbat stew with local elements, the Syrians do indeed add Mexican ingredients to theirs. Not only that, but the Shabbat stew which they infuse with Mexican flavors is a classically Ashkenazi *cholent*. So not only are the Syrian Jews (from both groups) cooking a dish that is not originally their own, but they are doing something to it that the Ashkenazim themselves don't do!

For starters, finding a unique custom among Syrian Jews is unsurprising. Around the Diaspora, Syrian Jews frequently separate themselves from other Jews nearby. Other than Hasidim, Syrian Jews may be the most insular of Jewish groups, while (unlike the Hasidim) remaining integrated into the secular world around them.[63] They achieve this by maintaining strong family and business ties with community members in different parts of the world, moving frequently between them. This gives Syrian Jewry a uniquely transnational nature.[64] To understand the Syrian-Jewish Shabbat stew, therefore, we must examine examples from each population center, rather than looking at a version from Syria itself.

Jews first came to Syria in antiquity from the neighboring Land of Israel, and lived there for thousands of years. After the Spanish Expulsion, the locals were joined by many new Sephardi immigrants. That blended community later dispersed following economic downturns and anti-Jewish discrimination during the nineteenth and twentieth centuries. In the 1800s, some Syrian Jews moved to such places as Egypt

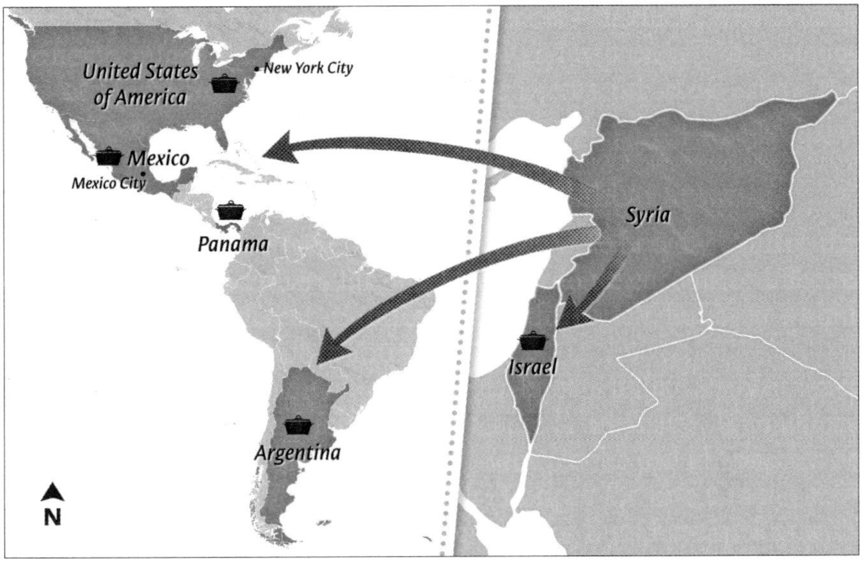


and Britain, though neither remains a major center for the community today. As tensions increased after Israel's 1948 establishment, many more fled the country.[65] Today, large Syrian-Jewish populations exist in Israel, New York, Argentina, and Mexico, with a smaller, but still significant group in Panama.* Each of these has a different attitude towards the Shabbat stew, highlighting its own character, but collectively explaining the character of Syrian Jews worldwide.

When I first began researching the Shabbat stew, I asked friends from the New York Syrian community what their family's version was like. I was surprised to hear that most don't eat one at all! Living in Ashkenazi-dominated America, they were familiar with *cholent* but felt it had no place in their community. Digging deeper, I posted in a Hebrew-language Facebook group dedicated to Syrian cooking in Israel. I asked if in fact the community had no Shabbat stews and received emotional pushback. Among the replies: "Of course we have!" and "Where did this crazy idea come from?" They described numerous *different* types of *hamin* that their population makes (*hamin* being the generic term in Israel). One respondent emphasized that, rather than a specific dish, *hamin* is a preparation method—slow cooking overnight.[66] So almost anything could be called *hamin*.†

* For the purposes of this exploration, I am treating the community of Deal, NJ, as the extension of the Brooklyn, NY, community. Many residents split their time between the two locations, and may even own a home in each.

† Compare this to Pomiane's comments on Polish *chulent*, in Chapter 6.

Meanwhile, in Mexico (as discussed) we find Syrians who prepare an Ashkenazi *cholent*, but add in such ingredients as apricots, tamarind, chili powder, cumin, and turmeric.[67] The Syrian Jews in Panama, by contrast, do not eat an Ashkenazi *cholent*, but *jamin* (the "j" in Spanish pronunciation being similar to the English "h"). It is often built around a Moroccan base, with a separate rice bag and each element dished up separately.[68] (I've been unable to learn much about the stew in Argentina's Syrian community, but I'll soon discuss them briefly.)

What we see in these four communities is that three have no distinctly Syrian stew, and that in the fourth—that of Israel—they have many different versions with no one type dominating. I believe this last case best helps us understand what's going on with Syrian Jews and their stews. Much as with Southern Europe (which you'll remember featured no dominant stew), Syria did not lie along the initial path that *harisa* took when it migrated from Mesopotamia to Iberia. So the dish couldn't make the impact there that it did in other parts of the world. Syrian Jews may have done what others did before *harisa* rose to prominence—slow-cooked whatever dish they felt like eating for Shabbat lunch. This explains why *none* of the communities had a singular, distinctively Syrian, Shabbat stew.

But this doesn't mean they are entirely un-Syrian either. Syrian culinary influences crop up regularly. One Panamanian version includes *kibbeh* dumplings* and stuffed baby eggplants, alongside the rice bag.[69] Reflecting the Sephardi community in Syria, *sofrito* is common, but Syrian Jews refer to it as *meudah* (from the Hebrew for "steamed.") An interesting example, which I'll discuss in the next chapter, buries chicken pieces in a mass of spaghetti overnight; its forebears might be Sephardi *or* Middle Eastern. One Facebook respondent told me about a dish of stuffed intestine, filled with chopped meat, rice, fried onion, and allspice, cooked with beans, potatoes, and more meat. The stuffing and allspice are classically Syrian Jewish, but reflecting the "Ashkephardi" mix of Israeli culture, she called it *hamin kishke*. Finally, one Israeli cookbook suggests that while no one Shabbat stew typifies Syrian-Jewish cooking, all of the different ones share a special technique: cooking everything separately before combining them in the pot.[70] If this is indeed a trademark of their stews (unclear, since I found no other mention of this), it may stem from *sofrito/meudah*, in which the potatoes are commonly pre-fried.

* *Kibbeh* is a Syrian pronunciation of *kubbeh*, described in Chapter 2. (See also "What is Kubbeh?", July 4, 2024. https://www.tasteofjew.com/what-is-kubbe, Haber, *Taste*.)

Many of these same dishes are known, and eaten, by Syrian Jews in America, just not as slow-cooked Sabbath lunch dishes. The popular cookbook *Aromas of Aleppo* includes recipes for *meudah*, the spaghetti-and-chicken dish, and even *huevos haminados*, though none are identified as overnight Shabbat foods.[71] This reflects the character of New York's Syrian Jews. They are even more insular than are their cousins in other regions, as a reaction to the dominant Ashkenazi culture there. Syrian Jews first settled in New York City neighborhoods that were full of Ashkenazi Jews. But the Ashkenazim discriminated against them, driving a wedge between the two groups. Also, with American antisemitism targeting Ashkenazim, Syrian Jews benefitted by remaining distinct.[72]

Thus, marriages between Syrian and Ashkenazi Jews in America are infrequent (though they are slowly becoming more common). But food also helps maintain their separation. Syrian Jews eat their traditional foods more frequently than do Jews of other backgrounds (though I certainly see creeping influence from Ashkenazi and general American cuisines).[73] But rejecting the idea of a Shabbat stew entirely might have helped distance Syrian Jews from the Ashkenazi community with which it (in the form of *cholent*) was most identified in America.

Why wouldn't Mexico's Syrian Jews similarly avoid eating Ashkenazi *cholent*? Because in some ways *they* are more culturally dominant. The first synagogue in Mexico City was built by Syrian Jews, and for some time they formed at least a third of the Jewish population.[74] So they have less need to place their Syrian identity in opposition to that of the Ashkenazim; eating *cholent* as a Syrian Jew in Mexico doesn't diminish their identity as it might in New York. Plus, taking liberties with *cholent* that Ashkenazi Jews do not suggests that the Syrians are less beholden to it. After all, it isn't *their* traditional food.

Similarly, in Panama, Syrian Jewish culture is not weakened by eating a different group's Shabbat stew, but there the dominant culture isn't Ashkenazi. In that way, adding Syrian twists to a Moroccan-inspired *jamin* (note the Sephardi name) is parallel to what their Mexican sisters and brothers do with *cholent*. And though I've uncovered less information on the Argentinian Syrian community, my suspicion is that I'd discover something similar to what has happened in Panama. While Ashkenazi culture dominates there, as in New York, the flexing of Sephardi-Mizrachi muscles (as detailed in the previous section) means that Syrian Jews can comfortably situate themselves within the sizable non-Ashkenazi minority. Furthermore, Syrian Jews in Argentina have increasingly disaffiliated from the Syrian (more religiously traditional)

## Blended-Origin Jamin

This recipe comes from Stefany Zakay, who credits her husband's grandmother, Selma. The recipe mixes many cultures—Syrian, Turkish, Israeli, and Moroccan–Panamanian. I've reduced quantities and simplified a few aspects. I hope Selma will forgive me! (If you still have trouble fitting everything in one pot, put the eggplants and *kibbeh* in their own pot, with extra water.)

### *Ingredients*

*For the kibbeh*

1 pound (450 g) **ground beef**
⅓ cup (50 g) **rice flour** or ground rice (see Notes)
2 tablespoons chopped **celery leaves** or **parsley**
1 teaspoon ground **allspice**
½ teaspoon ground **cinnamon**
½ teaspoon **salt**
A small bowl of **oil** mixed with a bit of lemon juice

*For the stuffed eggplants*

8 dried mini-eggplants, or fresh baby **eggplants** (see Notes)
⅔ pound (300 g) **ground beef**
¼ cup (50 g) **rice**
¼ cup (60 ml) **water**
1½ tablespoons vegetable **oil**
1 teaspoon ground **allspice**
½ teaspoon ground **cinnamon**
½ teaspoon **salt**

*For the jamin*

½ cup (120 ml) vegetable **oil**
2 small **potatoes**, quartered lengthwise
1 (15-ounce/425 g) can **chickpeas**
1 medium **onion**, sliced
6 cloves **garlic**, crushed
1 strip bone-in **beef** flanken (about 1½ pounds/700 g), or 1¼ pounds (550 g) brisket
1½ cups (300 g) **rice**
1 teaspoon ground **allspice**, divided
1 teaspoon ground **cinnamon**, divided
1 teaspoon ground black **pepper**, divided
2 teaspoons **salt**, divided
8 **eggs**, still in their shells
1 tablespoon **tomato paste**

*For serving*
2–3 small **radishes**, sliced thinly

### *Method*

*Make the kibbeh*: (May be made ahead and frozen until needed.) Mix ¾ of the **ground beef** with the **rice flour**. Mix the remaining **ground beef** with the **celery leaves**, **allspice**, **cinnamon**, and **salt**. Roll the meat and rice flour mixture into balls the size of ping-pong balls. Wet your thumb with the **oil** and lemon juice, and hollow a well in the middle of each ball. Fill the well with some of the spiced **ground beef** mixture, pinch the hole closed, and smooth over with your finger. Repeat with the remaining meat. Makes approximately 12 balls.

*Make the stuffed eggplants*: If using dried **eggplants**, rehydrate them by boiling in water for about 5 minutes, then transfer them to cold water for another 20 minutes. If using fresh, scoop out most of the eggplant pulp.

Mix the **ground beef**, **rice**, **water**, **oil**, **allspice**, **cinnamon**, and **salt**, then fill the eggplants with the stuffing.

*Make the jamin*: In a medium pot, heat about 2 tablespoons of the **oil** until shimmering, then fry the **potatoes** until they start to brown, about 5–8 minutes. Remove them to a plate. Add the rest of the **oil** to the pot and fry the *kibbeh* in it, until the outsides brown.

In a large pot (or slow cooker), scatter the **chickpeas**, **onion**, and **garlic**. Lay the **beef** and *kibbeh* on top.

In a bowl, mix the **rice** with half the **allspice**, **cinnamon**, **black pepper**, **salt**, and 3 tablespoons of water. Tie the mixture into a cheesecloth, leaving room for the rice to expand. Put the bag in the pot off to one side. In separate areas next to it, put the **eggplants**, **potatoes**, and **eggs** (don't break them).

Mix 2 cups (470 ml) water with the remaining **allspice**, **cinnamon**, **black pepper**, and **salt**, along with the **tomato paste**. Pour it over everything in the pot, then add enough water to cover. Cook overnight using any standard method (*see* pages 7–8).

*To serve*: Open the **rice** bag and peel the **eggs**. Put the **rice**, **eggs**, **kibbeh**, and **jamin** in different bowls, or in sections on a large platter. Garnish with the **radishes**.

### *Notes*

If you can't find rice flour, you can grind your own in a blender.

Baby eggplants are just miniature varieties. If you can't find them fresh, dried versions are sold in Middle Eastern groceries, or online.

population, further reducing the likelihood of finding distinctive iterations among Argentina's Syrian Jews.[75]

Thus, in each branch of the Syrian-Jewish world, we encounter a lack of any "Syrian" Shabbat stew. Each sub-community, however, responds differently. In New York, they avoid the overnight cooking method entirely, due to tensions with Ashkenazim. In Israel, they are part of a greater Israeli melting pot, and mix and match influences at will. Those who live in Latin America also draw from their non-Syrian neighbors, but with different versions based on the unique demographics in Mexico, Argentina, and Panama. Five different centers with five different responses, all because no singular version likely existed in Syria to begin with.

## The Silk-y Spice-y Stews of Asia

The final locations I'll look at in this chapter take a step beyond a previously explored area. In Chapter 2, I looked at the early versions of the stew in Iraq, and followed its spread to the edges of the Middle East. Persia (Iran of today) sits along the eastern and northern frontiers of that region, so it came into the most contact with neighboring cultures.* Persians are not Arabs, and their country was also not Muslim when *harisa* was becoming a popular Shabbat stew; only with the mid-seventh-century Arab conquest did the country begin Islamizing.[76] Arab and Persian cuisines then started influencing each other, but remained distinct, like dialects of the same culinary language. It is to areas within the Persian, non-Arab sphere of influence that I now turn.

In particular, I am referring to the Caucasus Peninsula to Iran's northwest, Central Asia to its northeast and east, and India only slightly further away to the southeast. All three of these areas interacted with Persia throughout history, and foods cross-pollinated between them.† One need only look at a map to understand why. Like the cork in a bottle of wine, Iran completely separates Iraq from East Asia. It forms a land bridge, sandwiched between the Persian Gulf and the Caspian Sea. Anyone traveling between the Middle East and India or China had to pass through Persia. So Persian culture absorbed culinary influences from both sides and disseminated their blended cuisine back out in every direction.

* For the distinction between the terms Iran and Persia, *see* Chapter 2.

† As part of this cultural exchange, the languages spoken in these areas are all part of one Indo-Iranian family of languages.

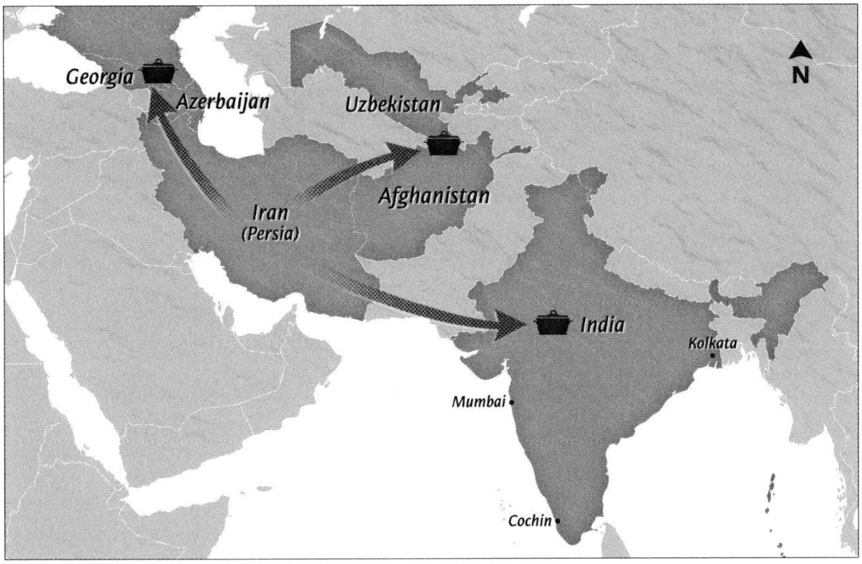


A major contribution to Persian cuisine came via the interlinked trade routes of the Silk and Spice Roads. To be clear, neither were actual roads, but loose networks of routes over both land and sea. The main spice-producing areas in southern India and Southeast Asia also connected to the Silk Road to their north.[77] Spices, grains, fruits, and vegetables all made their way across these trade networks, with Persia lying at the heart of the system.

Unlike the Anglo and Latin American Jews discussed earlier, these Asian-Jewish communities were very old. Despite their antiquity, however, they were fairly isolated from world Jewry, at best footnotes to the conversations of most Ashkenazi and Sephardi Jews. And if Jews in these areas learned about the Shabbat stew, it probably reached them by passing through Persia, along with other traded goods.

### *The Caucasus*

Two different Jewish groups come from the Caucasus Peninsula that sits between the Black and Caspian Seas—Georgian Jews and Mountain Jews. The main difference between the two communities is that the former (obviously from the country of that name) lived in a predominantly Christian country, while the latter lived under Muslim rule for most of the past millennium. Georgian and Mountain Jews were also separated geographically, on opposite sides of the 750-mile-long Caucasus range. Mountain Jews (also called "Kavkazi," from the word Caucasus) come from Azerbaijan, and six southern republics of the Russian Federation.[78]

Mountain Jews are diverse, scattered as they were across at least forty small mountain towns, with only a few larger urban communities in Derbent and Baku (both in Dagestan) and Quba in Azerbaijan.[79] Therefore, among Kavkazi Jews we sometimes find one dish may be called by different names in separate towns, or two separate dishes carry the same name. Furthermore, as in Russia itself, Soviet rule secularized many of the Jews there, so many of their religious traditions were lost. Even those who remained observant in the Soviet era often stopped making Shabbat stews overnight, instead having non-Jewish neighbors heat their food for Saturday lunch.[80] Despite these obstacles, however, we can still identify a few versions of the Shabbat stew within the Kavkazi Jewish community.

One goes by two different names: *normu* or *gendumedush*.* Its core is similar to an Ashkenazi *cholent*: beef, potatoes, onions, and barley (though sometimes wheat is also included). Conceivably, this Ashkenazi core only developed during the Russian occupation, but we can't know with certainty. The legumes differ by region; white beans in the Russian-influenced north and chickpeas in Azerbaijan, which absorbed more Middle Eastern culture. The dish also draws from communities further to the east. Dates, tomatoes, and a cherished local sour plum tie it closely to the Shabbat stew of Bukharian Jews, which I will come to shortly.† But the use of fruit in a meat dish is generally a hallmark of Persian cuisine (and those it influenced). More broadly, the tangy flavor this creates is popular in dishes from Afghanistan through Syria, derived from sour plums, pomegranate syrup or tamarind paste. Further highlighting the Spice Road influence of the Mountain Jewish–Persian connection, common flavorings in *normu/gendumedush* are turmeric, cumin, and pepper. Finally, this recipe includes two interesting ingredients: zucchini and rosemary.[81] I have only found zucchini in one other stew (versions of Kurdish *mebosa*), and I have not seen rosemary anywhere else. This stew therefore combines elements drawn from the many cultures that have influenced the area: Eastern Europe (via Russia), Central Asia, and Persia, alongside some local elements.

Other Mountain Jewish Shabbat stews also display this blended influence. One called *boro* is similar to *normu/gendumedush*, but with two main differences. First, the meat is lamb, making the stew less

* Confusingly, for others, *gendumedush* is not an overnight Shabbat stew, but a folk dish made of wheat and eaten when a child is getting his or her first tooth.

† Popular in Uzbekistan as well, these sour plums are known as *archa*, or *tursha elu* when they are dried.

Ashkenazi in style. Furthermore, rather than zucchini and rosemary, it includes leafy herbs: cilantro, parsley, and dill.[82] The herbs, as I'll soon show, connect the dish to one in nearby Georgia. A third stew, called *sholovo bogli*, includes a flour-filled intestine—clearly an Ashkenazi *kishke* without calling it that.[83]

All of these examples show some defining aspects of Mountain Jewish culture. Most significantly, they blend influences from both near and far, in every direction. While every Shabbat stew reflects its homeland, these show how the Caucasus itself is an intercontinental crossroads with many cultures leaving their mark. Secondly, the many different stews, and the confusion surrounding some names, indicates the variety within the Kavkazi community itself.

When we look at the Georgian Jews across the mountains, their greatest similarity to the Kavkazi community is the degree to which the Soviets secularized them. Most of the Georgians I spoke with do not make any version of overnight Sabbath dish, and couldn't think of any they'd even heard of. However, when I reached out to the Georgian-Jewish Center in the capital city of Tbilisi, I was told that the main food the community eats on Saturday is *khalia*, recognized as a genuinely Jewish dish.[84] Today's more secular Georgian Jews might eat it for Sabbath lunch *without* cooking it through the night. But since it is known as a Jewish food, and many of the best-known Jewish foods worldwide were created for Shabbat (and in keeping with the laws of that day), it is conceivable that *khalia* was previously made as an overnight Shabbat stew.

*Khalia* stews beef and onion together with tomatoes, pomegranate, walnuts, and fresh herbs (the connection with *boro* mentioned previously). As with *normu/gendumedush*, this stew mixes diverse influences. The herbs also tie it to *chakhokhbili*, a popular Georgian stew, while the pomegranate–walnut combination draws from the festive Persian dish called *fesenjan*. *Khalia* looks like a Jewish cross between those two popular dishes. And though these two dishes stew chicken or other poultry, *khalia* was also previously made with chicken.

### *Central Asia*

Central Asia, across the Caspian Sea, experienced strong influences from Persia when the Persian Empire expanded to its northeast. The region's countries are sometimes referred to collectively as "the -stans," since their names all end with that suffix, which also reflects Persian culture. It

## Normu/Gendumedush

Despite the many ingredients in this stew, no one flavor overpowers the others, and the whole remains a fairly subtle blend. If you like a more strongly flavored dish, feel free to increase the more boldly flavored ingredients, such as the garlic, sour plums, dates, or spices. You can do them all to maintain the balance, or if you prefer a specific flavor profile, choose which to increase.

***Ingredients***

3 tablespoons **olive oil**
1 (15-ounce/425 g) can **white beans**
1 (15-ounce/425 g) can **chickpeas**
½ cup (100 g) dried **brown** or **green lentils**
½ cup (100 g) **barley**
½ cup (100 g) **wheat berries**
1 large **onion**, cut into eighths
4 cloves **garlic**
3 medium **potatoes**, peeled and roughly chopped
2 medium **zucchini**, cut roughly into 2-inch (5-cm) chunks
2½ pounds (1.15 kg) **beef**, cubed
2 **marrow bones**
2 medium **tomatoes**, cut into chunks, or 1 (14½-ounce/400 g) can diced tomatoes
1 sprig **rosemary**
8 **dried sour plums** (see Notes for substitution option)

derives from Farsi for "land of," or a place with many of something.* The best-known Jews in the region are the Bukharians (or Bukharans), who come from Uzbekistan and Tajikistan, with major population centers in the cities of Bukhara, Samarkand, Tashkent, and Dushanbe.†

Bukharian Jews first arrived as fifth-century exiles from Persia, before the Persians themselves reached Central Asia.[85] Their language is a Persian dialect, underscoring their origins. So, naturally, Bukharian food also shows heavy Persian influence. The most popular food is *plov*, which is less a dish than a *type* of dish. The name comes from the Persian

* The suffix appeared in Chapter 2 when a Persian area with many Jews was called "Yahudistan."

† Few Bukharian Jews remain in Uzbekistan today. Most emigrated after the collapse of the USSR. The biggest concentrations are in the USA and Israel, with a smaller population in Britain.

3 **dates**, pitted
8 **eggs**, still in their shells
1 teaspoon **salt**
½ teaspoon ground **turmeric**
½ teaspoon ground **cumin**
½ teaspoon ground black **pepper**
½ teaspoon **sweet paprika**
½ teaspoon **hot paprika**

***Method***

Assemble all of the ingredients as follows. Pour **olive oil** into a large pot (or slow cooker). Scatter the **white beans, chickpeas, lentils, barley,** and **wheat berries** inside. On top of that, add the **onion** and **garlic.** Next, layer on the **potatoes** and **zucchini.** Put the **beef** and **marrow bones** on top of everything, then cover with the **tomatoes, rosemary, dried sour plums** and **dates.** Gently insert the **eggs** into the other ingredients. Over everything, sprinkle the **salt, turmeric, cumin, pepper, sweet paprika,** and **hot paprika.**

Add water to cover, and cook overnight using any standard method (*see* pages 7–8).

***Notes***

Dried sour plums come from Central Asia and are available in specialty groceries. If you can't find them, you can substitute regular prunes, plus 1 tablespoon tamarind paste or pomegranate syrup stirred into a glass of water.

*pilaf*, and includes different rice preparations, typically featuring meat and/or vegetables. But the key element is cooking the rice so that every grain stays separate.[86] The classic Bukharian Shabbat stew is a type of *plov*, called *osavo*, *oshi sabo*, or another variation (meaning "Sabbath dish").[87] In addition to the rice and meat, *osavo* includes tomatoes, shredded carrots, and fruits such as prunes, dried apricots, and green apples, creating a sweet-and-sour flavor.[88] This compares nicely with the Kavkazi *normu/gendumedush*, though the stews use different grains.

To Uzbekistan's south lies Afghanistan, formerly home to a separate, non-Bukharian Jewish population. Their Shabbat stew still reflects Persian impact, but differs from *osavo*. Known as *palau shabati* or *plov shabati*, it similarly contains beef and rice, with a particular Persian

## Palau Shabati

Key in this dish is properly preparing the rice, both the preliminary washing to keep grains separate, and cleaning/drying the pot to acquire a crispy *bunker* layer. Beef cheeks are wonderful in this dish, but other fatty cuts of meat work as well. When quinces are available, add some for a more luxurious flavor. If they have brown bits on the skin, clean them off thoroughly, or peel the skin.

### *Ingredients*

3 cups (600 g) long-grain **rice**, e.g. basmati
2¼ pounds (1 kg) **beef** (e.g. beef cheeks, boneless short ribs), cut into 1½-inch (4-cm) chunks
2 tablespoons **salt**
½ cup (120 ml) vegetable **oil**
1 **egg**, beaten
1 teaspoon ground **cardamom**
½ teaspoon ground **cinnamon**
½ teaspoon ground **cloves**
½ teaspoon ground black **pepper**
½ cup (75 g) black **raisins**
2 medium **quinces**, cored and cut into wedges (optional)

### *Method*

Rinse the **rice** well, until the water runs clear. Then put it in a bowl of water, and let it soak for 30–60 minutes.

aspect seen in the rice. The bottom of the pot is lined with a mix of rice, oil, and egg, turning into a crunchy layer.[89] Known as *bunker*, it is a clear parallel to the famed Persian crispy rice, *tahdig*. (*Tahdig*, literally "bottom of the pot," is created via its cooking technique rather than eggs and oil, but the two foods are obviously related.) The main distinction between *osavo* and *palau shabati* lies in their secondary flavors. Bukharians prefer sweet-and-sour while Afghani stews lean towards savory and aromatic spices such as cardamom, cinnamon, cloves, cumin, and black pepper. Sometimes a *palau shabati* may include quince or raisins, but they remain more subtle than *osavo*'s prunes or green apples. Ultimately, while both the Bukharian and Afghani Shabbat stews descend from Persian pilaf, the latter highlights spicing over fruitiness, potentially due to being closer to the southern Spice Road trade routes.

Add the **beef** to a large pot of boiling water. Return to a boil, then reduce heat to medium. Cook for 10 minutes, skimming off any scum that rises to the top. Remove from the heat.

Meanwhile, drain the **rice** and add it to a separate pot with 4 cups of water and the **salt**. Bring to a boil, then reduce heat to low. Cook for 5–7 minutes, until most but not all of the water is absorbed.

In a bowl, mix the **oil** with ¼ cup of the cooked **rice** and the **egg**. Add it to the pot you will cook the *palau* in overnight. (If using one of the pots already used, remove the contents, wash it, and dry it thoroughly.) Spread this layer evenly along the bottom.

Combine the **cardamom**, **cinnamon**, **cloves**, and **pepper** into a mixture.

From this point on, assemble the ingredients in layers. Start with **rice**, then sprinkle some spice mixture, then some **beef**, and then some **raisins**. Continue in layers, ending with rice on top. If using the **quinces**, add them as a final layer, skin side up.

Cook on a medium-low heat for 30 minutes, helping create the crispy bottom layer. Afterwards, if everything looks too dry, add another cup of water.

Put foil between the lid and the pot, and cook overnight in an oven at 210°F/100°C, or on a hotplate. (This recipe isn't as good in a slow cooker.)

*To serve*: Put the contents on a large platter, then scoop out the crispy *bunker* layer from the bottom. If you get it out whole, serve on its own plate. Otherwise, break it up and sprinkle over everything else!

## *India*

And it is to that southerly direction that I now turn, to close out this chapter. Though less so than in the Caucasus or Central Asia, the Indian subcontinent also received Persian food influences. At times, Persian rule extended across the Indus River into India's northern reaches. And when the Muslim Mughals ruled there (sixteenth to mid-nineteenth centuries), they maintained stronger connections with Persia. Culinary cross pollination appears via ingredients that traveled in both directions. Rice—that most precious Iranian staple grain—most likely reached Persia from India.[90] Saffron, on the other hand, notably moved from Persia to Kashmir, in northwestern India.[91]

Within the subcontinent, Indian Jews cannot accurately be described as a "community." To be accurate, there are Indian Jewish *communities*, in plural, since (depending on how you define your terms) there exist

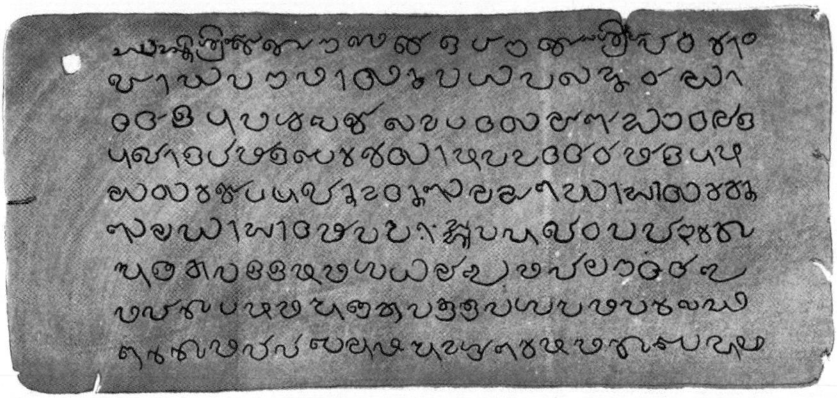

*This copper plate, belonging to the Cochini Jewish community, is the earliest physical evidence attesting to Jewish presence in the area. It is dated by scholars to* c. 1000 CE.

between three and seven separate Jewish groups. Due to India's massive size, with these Jewish groups distributed in different coastal corners, they developed almost entirely separately. I'll look here at the three most established groups: the ancient Cochini and Bene Israel Jews and the more modern Baghdadi Jews.*

The Cochini Jews† of the southwestern state of Kerala claim to have first arrived as sailor merchants during King Solomon's reign (*c.* 950 BCE), while the Bene Israel ("Children of Israel") of Mumbai, Ahmedabad, and the surrounding areas believe their ancestors arrived in the region via a second-century BCE shipwreck.[92] As with most communal origin stories, these two tales are unverifiable. But, whether or not the communities are as old as they claim to be, they are certainly ancient. With over 600 miles separating them, however, the two groups barely knew about each other until modern times.

The ancient Cochini Jews also absorbed Sephardi exiles in the Middle Ages.[93] They became known as *paradesi* ("foreign") Jews, as opposed to the *desi* ("local") ones. The Cochini Shabbat stew reflects the impact

* Two other groups—the Bnei Menashe and Bene Ephraim—are described as "emerging." They profess ancient Jewish roots, and are integrating with global Jewry, to varying degrees. Setting aside debates on origins, their practices aren't old, resurging only in modern times. So I leave their less entrenched food traditions out of this discussion.

† Cochin is their main modern city, though they are also called Malabar Jews, based on their home region.

## Cochini Hamin

In *Spice & Kosher: Exotic Cuisine of the Cochin Jews*, Essie Sassoon and her co-authors highlight the Spice Road influence on the community's food. I adapted this recipe from theirs, and while they say many members of the community don't include any legumes, I think adding lentils or split peas (which they say others did) gives it a more Indian character.

### *Ingredients*

4 tablespoons **oil**
3 medium **onions**, chopped
8 **cardamom** pods, or 1½ teaspoons ground cardamom
½ teaspoon ground **cloves**
1 teaspoon ground **turmeric**
1½ teaspoons **salt**
1 teaspoon ground black **pepper**
4 medium **carrots**, grated
4-inch (10 cm) piece of **ginger**, grated
4 medium **tomatoes**, chopped
3 medium **potatoes**, diced
8–12 dark meat **chicken** parts (legs and thighs)
2 cups (400 g) green or brown **lentils** or split **peas**
1 cup (200 g) long grain **rice**
8 **eggs**, still in their shells
6 cups (1.4 liters) boiling **water**

### *Method*

Heat the **oil** and fry the **onions** until they soften, but don't brown.

If using whole **cardamom** pods, remove the seeds from the husks, and chop/crush the seeds. Discard the husks.

Lower the heat to medium. Sprinkle the **cardamom**, **cloves**, **turmeric**, **salt**, and **pepper** over the **onions**. Stir and continue cooking for a few minutes. Next add all of the vegetables (**carrots**, **ginger**, **tomatoes**, and **potatoes**). Insert the **chicken** parts around the other ingredients. Cook for about 10 minutes, rotating the **chicken** pieces to brown all sides.

Rinse the **lentils** or **peas** and the **rice**. Add both to the pot. Slide the **eggs** into the top of the **rice**, submerging them part way. Pour the **water** over everything. Reduce the heat to low, and simmer for about 15 minutes.

Add up to 1 more cup of **water** if the stew looks dry. Cook overnight using any standard method (*see* pages 7–8).

## Baghdadi–Indian Hamin

London's Anita Elias lived in Kolkata and Israel at various points in her life. Her recipe here has been a massive favorite whenever I've served it to people. The chutney infuses the *hamin* with a thrilling brightness of color *and* flavor.

***Ingredients***

2 medium **onions**, sliced
1 tablespoon ground **cinnamon**
½ tablespoon ground **cardamom**
½ tablespoon ground **cloves**
2 tablespoons **tomato paste**
2 (14½-ounce/410 g) cans diced **tomatoes**
2 teaspoons **salt**
1 teaspoon ground black **pepper**
8–12 **chicken** pieces (whatever pieces you like)
4 cups (800 g) basmati **rice**
5 cups (1.2 liters) **water**
8 **eggs**, still in their shells (optional)

***For chutney***

2 bunches fresh **cilantro**
1 tablespoon ground **coconut**, or ground **almond**
2 cloves **garlic**
½-inch (1.25-cm) piece of fresh **ginger**, peeled
juice of 1 large **lemon**

of those *paradesis*. Its name, *hamin*, indicates Spanish origins, and it frequently contains *haminados* eggs, the Iberian Bonus Food.[94] With such prominent Sephardi fingerprints, we can surmise that Cochini Jews ate no Shabbat stew prior to the 1500s.

As usual, the Cochini *hamin* recipe is updated for local ingredients and tastes. Rice is the primary grain, as it is for a large majority of Indians. Some recipes include beans, lentils, or peas, but others include no legume at all. Chicken is the usual meat. The most noticeable local impact, however, comes through in the spicing, which features such regional favorites as ginger, cardamom, turmeric, cloves, and pepper.[95]

The Bene Israel Jews stand in sharp contrast to those of Cochin. The south Indian Jews lived on a maritime trade route, and thus had periodic contact with other Jews. The Bene Israel, however, were

¼–½ teaspoon ground black **pepper**
1 tablespoon **olive oil**

***Method***

Preheat oven to 325°F/160°C.

Put **onions**, spices (**cinnamon**, **cardamom**, and **cloves**), **tomato paste**, **tomatoes** and **chicken** in a pot over medium heat. Cook for about 10 minutes, stirring periodically.

Rinse the **rice** and add it to the pot along with the **water**. Insert the **eggs** gently, if using them. Bring to a boil.

Cover the pot tightly with foil, so steam does not escape. Place the lid on top and put in the oven for an hour.

Then lower the oven temperature to 210°F/100°C or transfer to the hotplate for overnight cooking.

*Prepare chutney*: Put all ingredients (**cilantro**, **coconut** or **almond**, **garlic**, **ginger**, **lemon juice**, **pepper**, and **olive oil**) in a blender and mix. Adjust for taste and texture. If too liquid, add more **coconut/almond**. If too dry, add more **lemon juice** or **oil**.

Serve the **chutney** alongside the hamin.

***Notes***

I like to remove the meat from the bones before serving, and mix it back into the rice along with a generous helping of chutney.

This works best in the oven, though the other standard methods (*see* pages 7–8) also work.

more isolated from other Jews, receiving no waves of immigrants. So, unsurprisingly, they have no Shabbat stew tradition.[96] A disconnected Jewish community with no Shabbat stew further highlights Jewish diversity. Even in antiquity we dispersed widely, so a group that was separated before this food tradition began would be unlikely to eat a Shabbat stew.

An interesting parallel may be found outside India among Ethiopian Jewry. Known as Beta Israel ("House of Israel"), they are another ancient group that was historically disconnected, and they too had no Shabbat stew tradition. For them, this also reflects religious differences that grew from that separation. In Ethiopia, the Beta Israel followed a literal interpretation of Exodus 35:3 and, like the Karaites, ate no hot food on Sabbath day. Thus, when I asked in an Israeli Facebook group about

Ethiopian Shabbat stews, I inadvertently stirred up some tensions. Some felt I was trying to discredit them rather than learn their customs.[97]

A reaction to anti-Ethiopian discrimination in Israel may also have played a role. Nowadays, some Ethiopians have begun overnight Shabbat cooking, applying it to such popular dishes as *doro wot* or *sega wot*, spicy stews made with chicken or beef, respectively. Others see this change as the demeaning impact of the Israeli Chief Rabbinate, who pushed Beta Israel to accept normative Jewish practices, rather than respecting their traditions.

Back in India, the third major Jewish community is a modern one, established in the late eighteenth century and into the nineteenth. As their name suggests, most Baghdadi Jews came from Iraq, though some were from Syria or Persia. Originally, most lived in Mumbai, integrated with the local Bene Israel Jews, but later moved to Kolkata. They famously traded internationally, forming networks across southeastern Asia. Like the Cochini Jews, they infuse their Shabbat stew with Indian elements, but theirs apply to a Middle Eastern base, rather than a Sephardi one. Even though Iraqi Jews are not Sephardi, they too call their stew *hamin*, and it clearly descends from Iraqi *t'bit*. It includes rice and chicken and the core spices of *baharat*. But garam masala, the Indian spice blend, also appears. Some cooks stuff the whole chicken, as in a traditional *t'bit*, though most just bury chicken parts in the rice.[98] One version showcases a particularly Indian angle: each diner stirs a chutney of cilantro, coconut, ginger, and lemon juice through their portion of *hamin*. Its bright flavors and color delightfully contrast with the savory and spicy tastes, and uniform beige of a standard *t'bit*.[99]

As a community that was heavily involved in international trade, the Baghdadi Jews were more cosmopolitan than the Cochinis or the Bene Israel. Thus, their foods also include culinary influences from a wider geographic array. In addition to the Iraqi/Indian blend, some serve it with *hilbeh*, a fenugreek dip of Yemenite origin.[100] Others create a Persian-inspired crispy rice layer, breaking it into pieces served as a garnish.[101]

But perhaps the best example to end on is a special version of the stew that some Baghdadi Jews prepare for the late spring holiday of Shavuot. It recalls the original Shabbat stew. *Harisi* stuffs a whole chicken, as in *t'bit*, but replaces rice with whole wheat, since the holiday commemorates the Israeli wheat harvest.[102] This dish combines old and new in a way I have not found elsewhere.

In Indian Jewry, and their Shabbat stews, we see many aspects that we met earlier in this chapter: migration, cosmopolitanism, and the blending of ancient and modern. But here they all combine in one location.

* * *

The dispersed groups examined in this chapter show modernity's impact on the Jewish nation. We've spread worldwide, frequently maintaining contact with our family members and traditions. Those who did *not* remain connected have noticeably different traditions. And still others never moved, but experienced upheaval due to changes around them. Each experience shines through in the Shabbat stew (or lack thereof).

## Chapter 9

# The Stew in (Red), White, and Blue

The two greatest triumphs in modern Jewish history unfolded in the twentieth century: the unrivaled achievements of American Jewry and the establishment of the State of Israel. And as we'll see once again, when Jewish fortunes thrive, so does the Shabbat stew. It is in these two countries where we encounter extraordinary innovations surrounding this beloved dish, leading to the contemporary trends that I'll explore in the final chapter.

In the US, Jews have fully integrated into society and risen to incredible heights in every cultural arena. With the exception of occupying the Oval Office, Jews in America have reached the pinnacles of success in virtually every field. Literature and the arts, business, politics, medicine, academia, and more—look at the leaders in twenty-first-century America, and you can find Jews there. (Okay, maybe not in sports—though even that's changing these days—but we're well represented by ownership and management in that area.)

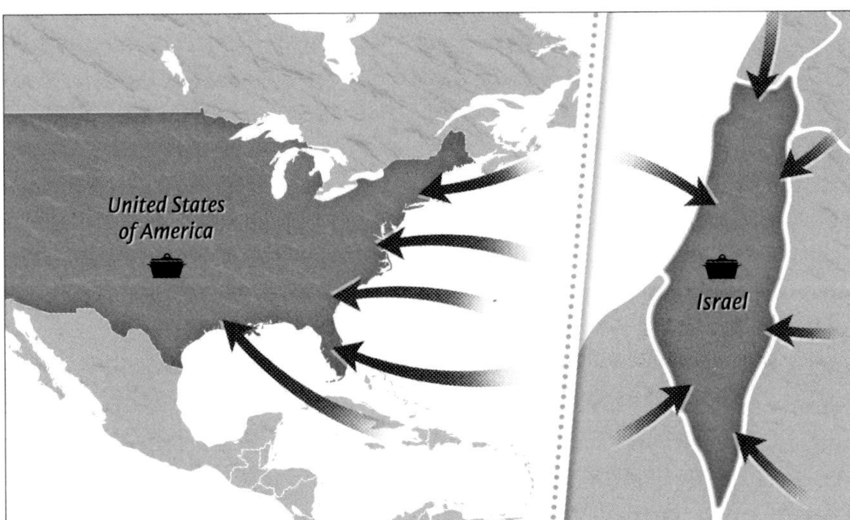

Jews have lived in what is today the United States since before independence, and were at least marginally involved in the revolutionary endeavor. About a century later, America truly began growing into a world power, and its Jews also grew noticeable both in numbers and in their prominence within society. Since religious and social equality defined American culture, such integration bore no stain of institutionalized discrimination.

Israel's Jewish story, meanwhile, is equally glorious, but in a different way. When the State of Israel was established in 1948, it returned Jewish self-rule in the nation's ancestral homeland for the first time in about 2,100 years. That alone would have been noteworthy. But with the massive influx of immigration from everywhere on earth, the Jewish people witnessed the fulfillment of the Biblical prophecy known as *kibbutz galuyot*, the "ingathering of the exiles."[1]

Now, Jews of numerous cultural backgrounds, speaking a plethora of languages, with widely distinct physical appearances—and cuisines—live side-by-side in Israel. And with a Jewish government, no less! As with their sisters and brothers in the United States, the Jews of Israel are living a life that their ancestors literally dreamed of. These two communities' stories are so incredible that it's no wonder that they've become by far the largest Jewish populations in the world today.

Perhaps that's why these two countries are also the ones that have produced cookbooks dedicated to the Jews' favorite dish. In America, Kay Kantor Pomerantz published two related books about Shabbat stews, while Israel saw glossy releases by Sherry Ansky and Osnat Lester. Personally, I bridge both countries, having grown up in the US and immigrated to Israel. And I, too, released an e-cookbook (smaller in scope than the previous four) through my website that promoted this work via twelve international recipes (and the book you're holding includes many more).

As you'd expect, since American and Israeli Jews are unique in Jewish history, each country's Shabbat stews are also unlike those that predated them. I turn now to these two communities, starting with each's development, then looking at their Shabbat stews.

## Land of Free Thought, Home of the Beef

Jews reached America during the colonial period, first as individual immigrants. In 1654, however, the first larger group landed in New Amsterdam (later to become New York). As mentioned in the last chapter, these twenty-three Jews were fleeing Portuguese rule in Recife,

Brazil. Scholars typically portray Jewish immigration to the US in three waves. This group characterized phase one—primarily Sephardim, often from *converso* families, during the colonial and post-colonial eras. What they ate for Sabbath is hard to uncover, but a few educated guesses are in order.

Based on their origins, their Shabbat stew was likely closer to a Spanish *adafina* than to the *cholents* that would later dominate in America. Even back then, cattle were widely available in America, so beef probably was the meat of choice, though undoubtedly some opted for lamb or chicken. Asser Levy, a member of that 1654 Recife group, was a butcher who probably also served as a *shochet*.[2] In time, more people learned ritual slaughter, so kosher meat (which there is every reason to believe they still desired) would have been fairly accessible.[3]

That being said, fresh beef could only have been available immediately after slaughter, due to hot summers, and no refrigeration. Much would therefore be preserved, in one of a few ways: brining (the main method in cold northern colonies), dry-salting (seen more in the south), and sometimes smoking (learned from Native Americans).[4] Salted beef was nicknamed "Jew beef," probably indicating their chosen method, so meat

*Gomez Mill House, Newburgh, NY, the earliest surviving Jewish residence in North America, built in 1714.*

of that sort presumably found its way into early American Shabbat stews.[5] Among vegetables, they may have included turnips, carrots, parsnips, onions, cabbage, pumpkin, and kidney or lima beans.

While at least some individual Ashkenazim were likely among the first wave of Jewish colonial settlers, the second wave (mid-1800s) brought nearly 150,000 from Germanic territories.[6] First-wave immigrants had settled mainly in Eastern cities such as Charleston, New York, Philadelphia, and Newport, but many who came in this second wave moved inland, to places like Cincinnati and Chicago, or even as far west as California.

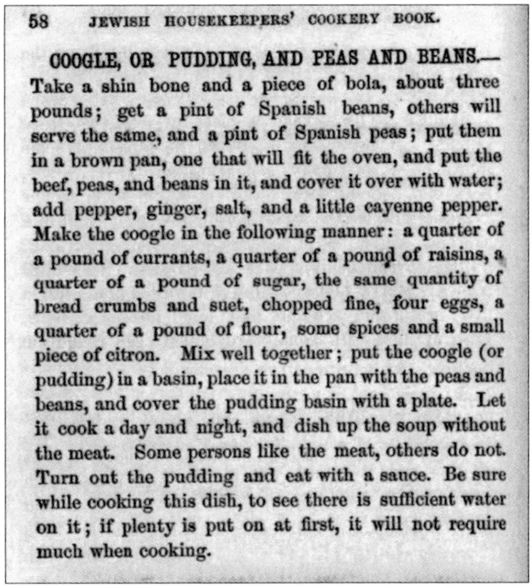

58 JEWISH HOUSEKEEPERS' COOKERY BOOK.

**COOGLE, OR PUDDING, AND PEAS AND BEANS.**—Take a shin bone and a piece of bola, about three pounds; get a pint of Spanish beans, others will serve the same, and a pint of Spanish peas; put them in a brown pan, one that will fit the oven, and put the beef, peas, and beans in it, and cover it over with water; add pepper, ginger, salt, and a little cayenne pepper. Make the coogle in the following manner: a quarter of a pound of currants, a quarter of a pound of raisins, a quarter of a pound of sugar, the same quantity of bread crumbs and suet, chopped fine, four eggs, a quarter of a pound of flour, some spices and a small piece of citron. Mix well together; put the coogle (or pudding) in a basin, place it in the pan with the peas and beans, and cover the pudding basin with a plate. Let it cook a day and night, and dish up the soup without the meat. Some persons like the meat, others do not. Turn out the pudding and eat with a sauce. Be sure while cooking this dish, to see there is sufficient water on it; if plenty is put on at first, it will not require much when cooking.

*Esther Levy's Shabbat stew, from 1871's* Jewish Cookery Book.

In the wake of this German immigration, we encounter the first American-Jewish cookbook. Esther Levy's *Jewish Cookery Book* was published in Philadelphia in 1871. Levy was likely German-Jewish, but her book (like Montefiore's in 1846 London) mixes recipes from Ashkenazi and Sephardi cultures, along with popular British and American dishes. Mentioned in Chapter 5, Levy's Shabbat stew recipe is titled "Coogle, or Pudding, and Peas and Beans."[7] Similar to Montefiore's "Kugel and Commean," it features a bread *kugel* cooked in a small container within the larger *cholent* pot. It also features a similar "Ashkephardi" mix. The stew itself is made of beef, marrow bones, beans, and chickpeas. But her preferred cut of meat is called "bola," a Spanish word for top sirloin. Furthermore, that is a cut that traditional Ashkenazi Jews avoid.*

Later that century, we can already see the Americanization of a Sephardi stew. Joan Nathan includes a recipe in her *Jewish Cooking in America* from the handwritten Gomez family recipe book. Dating to the nineteenth century, it came from a descendant of one of the Recife-to-New-Amsterdam settlers. Beyond its name, however, her *hamin* recipe features almost nothing that would betray its Sephardi origins.

* Eve Jochnowitz, "An Annotated Coogle," *KlezCamp*, 5. https://www.academia.edu/34227203/annotated_coogle_pdf. As mentioned in reference to Soviet Jews, Ashkenazim typically only eat meat from the front half of a cow.

Ingredients include a large beef brisket, onions, lima beans, garlic, cayenne pepper, and olive oil. It's finished with a flour-and-gravy slurry, as a thickener. Though olive oil hints at Sephardi ancestry, almost everything else in the dish is American. Not surprising, since this was written after the family had a century of American life behind it.[8]

Starting in the late 1800s, cookbooks grew increasingly popular, a trend that continues through today. American Jewry, for its part, has published innumerable cookbooks over the past 150 years. A representative sample, looking specifically at Shabbat stews, shows us the changes in American-Jewish religious norms, demographics, wealth, and eating habits.

A defining aspect of the Jewish-American story is an active and consistent effort to integrate into society. Rather than being seen as Jewish-Americans, they wished to be recognized as American Jews. This comes through in historical cookbooks. Many people are surprised when they first see American-Jewish cookbooks from the late 1800s or early 1900s. Two prominent examples, 1889's *Aunt Babette's Cook Book* and 1901's *The Settlement Cook Book*, featured recipes—even entire chapters—dedicated to such non-kosher foods as oysters, lobsters, and pork. This reflects the (largely German) Reform Jewish idea that *kashrut* was an archaic practice, and was no longer relevant or binding. Yet despite these *treif* recipes, the books remained unmistakably Jewish. *Aunt Babette's* featured a Star of David on the title page, and a whole section of Passover recipes (albeit called "Easter Dishes").* *The Settlement Cook Book*, meanwhile, raised money for a volunteer organization that provided support to new Jewish immigrants in Milwaukee.

Such unambiguously Jewish, overtly *treif* cookbooks reflect American-Jewish culture at the time. No longer observing *kashrut* helped them become more "American" by eating the same foods that the general public consumed. Understandably, then, such Jewish cookbooks also include no Shabbat stew recipes. They included other super-Jewy foods like *kugels*, but there is something particularly religious—apparently *too* religious—about a stew whose *raison d'être* is to allow the Sabbath-observant to honor the day with hot food.†

Notably, it was not only such secularizing cookbooks that omitted the Shabbat stew. The third major immigration wave, a millions-strong

* If anyone doubted this meant Passover, recipes include matzah, there are instructions for setting a Seder table, and the fruit-and-nut condiment *charoset* is named using only Hebrew letters.

† *Kugels* became more palatable to Americanized Jews by acquiring the name "pudding," a secular and popular English term (*see* Robinson, "Kugel").

tsunami of largely Eastern European Jews, also aimed to integrate into their new society. But more of them (particularly at first) remained traditionally observant. Aimed directly at that populace, Hinda Amchanitski published the first Yiddish-language cookbook in America, in 1901 New York City.[9] Her *Manual for Cooking and Baking* was not just Jewish, but strictly kosher, yet it still shows the pull of Americanization. She uses many English terms (transliterated into Yiddish), such as "stew," "steak," and "cheese cake." Even her *kugels* are referred to (in Hebrew letters) as "puddings." But her book also contains no Shabbat stew, perhaps for a different reason. Maybe it shows her focus on helping immigrants fit into their new homeland. But presumably, her readership still ate *cholent* as they had in Europe.*

*Cover of Hinda Amchanitski's Yiddish-language cookbook, 1901.*

As Amchanitski's cookbook heralded from the start of the century, by the 1920s, American-Jewish cookbooks began shifting away from the extremely secular. From then on, fewer contained overtly *treif* foods, whether they were aimed at religiously observant or secularized Jews. For example, in 1918 the publisher of *Aunt Babette's* replaced it with the kosher *The International Jewish Cook Book*. It contained a recipe for "Schalet or Tscholnt (Shabbas Soup)."[10] That change alone highlights the shifting attitude; that one recipe righted what many saw as a historic wrong. More Shabbat stew recipes appear in cookbooks from the 1940s and 1950s.

One expression of growing Americanization in Shabbat stew recipes is an increase in the quantity of beef. Eastern European immigrants regularly expressed amazement at Americans' daily consumption of meat (in sizable portions).[11] But beyond mere abundance, eating beef helped Jews

* Jane Ziegelman writes of Lower East Side Jews sending pots of *chulent* to each other by way of the clothesline between their buildings—so clearly they still ate it (Ziegelman, *97 Orchard*, 141).

integrate. Late nineteenth-century American beef consumption was the byproduct of creating modern America. Spreading west, settlers wiped out the Great Plains bison, simultaneously displacing Native American populations. In their place, they created massive cattle ranches. This meant that inexpensive beef was readily available, but also that whoever ate that meat (Jews among them) was helping to build the modern US.[12]

Beef proportions in American Shabbat stews parallel broader American consumption trends.* The earliest recipes (which also contained the fewest ingredients) present an outlier case, with meat typically ranging from about two-thirds to three-quarters of the dry ingredients by weight. However, the vague character of early recipes calls such figures into question. For example, Esther Levy's recipe implies that its huge, three-pound piece of meat may only be intended for flavoring. She writes, "Let [the stew] cook a day and night, and dish up the soup *without the meat.* Some persons like the meat, others do not."[13] What they would have done with that removed meat remains a mystery to me.

However, as recipes start appearing more regularly in the 1920s, the percentage of meat starts from a more reasonable 30 percent, steadily rising to a peak of nearly 50 percent on average in the late '60s and early '70s. From that point forward, this trend begins to reverse, presumably due (at least in part) to rising cholesterol-related fears. Nowadays, most recipes contain about 35 percent meat, despite a few quirky exceptions (in the 50–65 percent range). A popular American advertising slogan declared "Beef. It's what's for dinner." Well, no matter the percentages, we can say that in the US beef was also "what's for *cholent*."

Another American food trend found in Shabbat stew recipes comes from food's rapid mid-century industrialization. As processed foods transformed the American diet, Jewish food earnestly embraced them, creating what has been referred to as "industrial *kashrut*." Perhaps the most significant of kosher processed-food products was Crisco, a *pareve* (containing neither meat nor dairy) vegetable shortening. Its manufacturer, Procter & Gamble, proudly proclaimed "that the Hebrew Race had been waiting 4,000 years for Crisco." From the outset, their marketing targeted kosher consumers with ads, branded bilingual Yiddish-English cookbooks, and the like.[14]

While I haven't found any published Shabbat stew recipes containing Crisco, I did find it in an online forum for Orthodox women. The writer, "Barbara," mentioned her mother-in-law's *cholent* recipe (clearly from

* All calculations here are my estimates, based on average ingredient weights.

*Cover of a bilingual English–Yiddish cookbook, published to promote Crisco, 1933.*

years earlier) that included "1 can Crisco." Indicating generational shifts in taste and health consciousness, Barbara continued, "They tell me it was delicious, but I'm sure not trying to make it."[15] Another example of industrial *kashrut* in a Shabbat stew comes from a 1956 column in *The Indiana Jewish Post and Opinion*. It offered a "Quick Cholent" featuring canned lima bean soup. (Unsurprisingly, the soup's manufacturer provided the recipe.)[16]

One of the more visible changes in American Jewry took place at the end of the twentieth century, and into the twenty-first. After World War II, religious connection became stronger throughout the American populace in general, and Judaism boomed in particular.[17] As evidence of changes in American attitudes to religion, historian Jonathan D. Sarna points to congressional actions in the 1950s, adding "under God" to the Pledge of Allegiance and making "In God We Trust" the official national motto. He also highlights Will Herberg's 1955 book *Protestant–*

*Catholic-Jew* as indicative of Judaism's growing acceptance as America's "third faith." While the relatively small percentage of the Jewish population who were Orthodox remained stable, such observant Jews felt more comfortable openly expressing their religious identities. Their grandparents had to choose between Judaism and Americanism when they first arrived on US shores, but late-twentieth-century Jews saw an opportunity to live lives that were fully Orthodox *and* fully American. Pair that with the community's relatively high average incomes, and their cultural impact grew. Among other things, this brought new exposure to the Shabbat stew, eaten most frequently by the Orthodox each week.

One change in consumption habits among this largely upper-middle-class, openly Orthodox population is an embrace of international cuisines. Already in the 1960s Ruth and Bob Grossman put out three very tongue-in-cheek, pun-filled international kosher cookbooks (Italian, French, and Chinese)—none of which contained any Shabbat stew recipes. But by 1977's *The Spice and Spirit of Kosher-Jewish Cooking*, we find a recipe for a "Moroccan Cholent," alongside a "Basic Cholent" and a "Kasha Chicken Cholent" (both Ashkenazi in style).* That Moroccan recipe was a massive step towards cosmopolitanism in the American Shabbat stew, even though it lacked the tell-tale cooking bags of a *dafina/skhena*, and was sadly identified using an Ashkenazi name. ("Moroccan Cholent" makes no more sense than "Polish Dafina.") The cookbook's 1990 updated edition takes an even bigger step towards "cosmopolitan kosher." The original recipe was accompanied by, among others, Hungarian and Sephardi stews (alas, both still called "cholent"), as well as a "Tebeet" recipe.[18] (It wasn't called a "cholent," but was also misidentified as Sephardi, while Iraqis are Mizrachi Jews.)

Beyond cookbooks, a great illustration of cosmopolitan kosher tastes comes from my friend Steve Kay, who grew up in the catering business in New York City. As Kay Caterers, his family had been supplying the weekly *cholent* at a synagogue in Queens for years, until one day in the late 1960s, the main cook called in sick. Who would make the *cholent* that week? Steve's grandmother Fanny could do it, but she had too much else to do, and wasn't keen on preparing all that *cholent* as well. Then their dishwasher, Miguel "Mikey" Garcia, spoke up in his broken English, insisting that he could do it. He told them his family in Ponce, Puerto Rico, made a similar dish, just with pork instead of beef. But, if they

* The book, published by Lubavitch Women (a segment of the Chabad Hasidic movement), became very successful within the Orthodox world. It went through fourteen printings and sold 60,000 copies.

got him kosher meat, he'd make the *cholent*. Taking the chance, they let him have at it, and while his stew contained the same basic ingredients as a *cholent*, it featured a special spice blend that he created, giving the stew a deep red color. That Shabbat, everyone in synagogue loved the *cholent*, claiming it was the best they'd ever had! For years after, it became Garcia's weekly job.[19] While I've searched far and wide, I've been unable to identify the Puerto Rican stew on which he based his "*cholent*," but its popularity among these mainstream Orthodox New York Jews underscores their broadening tastes.

Moving forward, even more international Shabbat stews appear in Jewish-American cookbooks. Pomerantz gathered recipes from around the world, in addition to some that she created herself, for her two 1990s *cholent* cookbooks. Now in the twenty-first century, more and more examples of non-Ashkenazi Shabbat stews appear in American Jewish cookbooks. Peak cosmopolitan kosher shows up in Leah Koenig's *The Jewish Cookbook* (2019), which provides equal coverage for numerous stews of worldwide Jewish communities, including Ashkenazi, Sephardi, Syrian, Iraqi, Bukharian, and many more.[20]

Thus, a number of elements characterize the American Shabbat stew. First, it increased in popularity and recognition over time. Second, it features an abundance of beef, in most cases. And, finally, we see the influences of both industrial *kashrut* ingredients, and cosmopolitan kosher recipes.

## Stews of Zion

Unlike American Jewry, who reached critical mass just as their country began thriving, the Jews of modern Israel actually founded and built their country. Rather than integrating into a modernizing country, they had to integrate a land and its resources into their lifestyle. Biblically, the Land of Israel flowed with milk and honey and was blessed with agricultural bounty. But by the 1800s, neither Abraham nor King David would have recognized it. The Ottoman Empire's 400 years of rule brought a downward spiral that turned the land into a swampy, disease-filled backwater. At the end of the nineteenth century, Jews in Israel struggled under Third-World poverty while American Jews enjoyed the adolescence of a growing world power.

The fledgling modern Israeli community was a tiny fragment of world Jewry. But to be clear, there has never been a time, from antiquity until the present, when *no Jews* lived in the land.[21] Some Israeli Jews today trace their family trees in the land back to Temple times. The Shabbat stews they eat could reflect minor elements of what was eaten in Israel millennia ago, though we can't possibly know. Whether or not *harisa* became the go-to Shabbat stew in ancient Israel, as it did around the Middle East, remains an open question. None of its gastronomic grandchildren is particularly popular in Israel today. But just as the early stews eaten by South American Crypto-Jews disappeared over time, *harisa* might also have fallen out of popular usage in Israel, with so few Jews there through the Middle Ages.

There is, however, one specific Shabbat stew, still eaten in Israel today, whose roots go back at least a few hundred years. Known as *hamin macaroni*, it features chicken parts buried in a pot full of noodles.* Other ingredients include onions, turmeric, and cinnamon, and sometimes potato slices lining the pot bottom. Many associate *hamin macaroni* specifically with Jerusalem, which has one of the older Jewish communities in the land. During the 1800s, the city had many Sephardi and Mizrachi Jews, and few Ashkenazim, with whom this dish has no connection.

Syrian Jews, as mentioned last chapter, also eat a version, flavored with allspice. In *Aromas of Aleppo*, Poopa Dweck calls her recipe *djaj wa rishta*—"chicken with noodles" in Arabic.[22] As noted, however, hers was *not* intended as an overnight Shabbat stew. Claudia Roden also mentions the dish in *The Book of Jewish Food*. She refers to it as *treya*, presumably derived from the word *itriya*, a different Arabic word for noodle.[23] Roden's family lived in Egypt, where they ate this, but like so many other Egyptian Jews at the time, they were of Syrian descent. These two references suggest that *hamin macaroni* may have been brought to Israel by Syrian Jewish immigrants.

Tracing its roots further back remains challenging. Due to the pasta, and the fact that many Sephardi refugees moved from Italy to Syria, we might assume an Italian source. Furthermore, I noted a vaguely similar dish there, *ruota di Faraone*—"Pharaoh's wheel." In it, sausage not chicken was nestled in pasta. However, that dish wasn't typically cooked overnight and contained other unique ingredients (pine nuts and raisins). These differences suggest it is an unlikely ancestor. Remember, as well, that while people often think of pasta as Italian, it was widely eaten across the Middle East long before it was introduced in Italy. In fact, Roden mentions a similar recipe from a thirteenth-century Syrian

* Israelis frequently use "macaroni" as a generic term for pasta, rather than specifically small elbow noodles. In Italy, the term *maccheroni* also more broadly references pasta.

cookbook, suggesting potential Arab origins.* The slight similarities between *hamin macaroni* and Iraqi *t'bit*, with pasta replacing the rice, might offer mild support for Middle Eastern origins. Regardless of how it got to Syria, *hamin macaroni* was likely consumed in Israel at least a few centuries ago, while the Jewish community there was still rather small.

That tiny population, however, was destined for exponential growth. The Jewish people always yearned to return to their homeland, and finally could turn their dream into reality. By the 1700s, small groups were already making the arduous journey to the Holy Land, and changes in Ottoman land-ownership laws during the 1800s opened the door for more Jews to return to Israel. This became a significant flow late in the century, with successive waves of "*aliyot*" bringing half a million new Jewish residents between 1882 and 1948.† These *olim* laboriously worked and developed the land, and its cuisine.

From the outset, the diet of modern Israel mixed foods from various origins. As groups of *olim* arrived from countries around the world, their foods (and specifically their Shabbat stews) all became part of Israel's melting-pot cuisine. The Sephardim who made up most of the population between the Spanish expulsion and the arrival of the new *olim* probably ate some type of *hamin*. Later immigrants from Europe, Morocco, and Yemen brought *cholent*, *dafina*, and *marak regel*. All were likely tweaked slightly for local ingredients.

Cookbooks from the pre-State years give us some details of the foods consumed at the time. The first was *How to Cook in the Land of Israel* by Erna Meyer, published in 1936.[24] It includes no Shabbat stews, but stresses the need to cook with local ingredients, such as bulgur, eggplant, and olive oil. If she felt she had to encourage this practice, many must not have been doing so already. First-generation European immigrants (like most immigrants anywhere throughout history) held on to their old culinary habits. They might occasionally replace an ingredient with a local one, but as infrequently as possible.[25]

"The differences in climate and the necessary adjustments arising out of these differences," writes Meyer, "compel the European housewife to make many drastic changes, particularly in her cooking—a change not so easy to achieve as it would seem . . . [P]eople cling tenaciously to the eating and cooking habits acquired . . . in their respective countries."

* I have not been able to locate the specific recipe that she refers to.

† *Aliyah*, the Hebrew word for "ascent," describes Jewish immigration to Israel, referencing a spiritual rise. Those who "make *aliyah*" are called *olim* in plural, *oleh* or *olah* (male and female) in singular.

Meyer's lack of a Shabbat stew recipe reflects her book's focus: helping people cook what was suitable for the land. In support of this, she includes very few meat recipes overall, viewing a vegetarian diet as more healthful. No wonder a typically meat-based Shabbat stew is nowhere to be found.

In addition to health concerns, Meyer's focus on vegetables also reflects the scarcity of meat in Israel at her time. That dearth persisted through the next decades as Israel suffered economically during World War II (1939–45), its own War of Independence (1948–9), and the ensuing period of mass immigration. Thus, we also find no Shabbat stew recipe in Lilian Cornfeld's 1942 *How to Cook in the Time of War.*[26] A pioneer among Israeli cooks and food writers, Cornfeld addressed the shortage of meat at the time by including a four-page section on "Inexpensive Meat Dishes."[27] While a Shabbat stew could easily fit this category, Cornfeld probably felt it unnecessary to feature a recipe for such a common food, especially in a mere sixty-four page instructional pamphlet.

Immediately following the end of the War of Independence, with massive immigration, Israel lacked the infrastructure and finances to absorb so many people.* Israel entered an austerity period, known in Hebrew as the *tzena*, which included widespread food rationing. Many ingredients were in short supply, with meat and poultry the most sought-after foods in the early 1950s.[28] In 1949, Cornfeld responded with *What Will I Cook with the Austerity Rations?*[29] In it, she charges her readers to fulfill their patriotic duty, making do with what was available. The food would be less luxurious and more challenging to cook, she explains, but then pleads for their trust. "British citizens did this for many years; so we, too, can do this."[30]

She also highlights the frugal nature of cooking locally. Most meat in Israel came from overseas, meaning higher costs. To combat this, she reiterates an idea from prior Israeli cookbooks. "In the past, local people used meat primarily for flavor and in small quantities, accompanied by an abundance of vegetables and grains."[31] She follows her own advice in her *hamin* recipe, listing among the ingredients "a chunk of fatty beef with the bone."[32] Without a listed weight, it suggests a small piece used for taste alone. The stew's other ingredients—large quantities of beans and barley, an onion, and a dough dumpling—significantly outweigh the meat.

* In just eight years, the country gained a million new citizens, more than doubling its population. European Holocaust survivors were followed by hundreds of thousands forced to flee oppression and pogroms throughout the Arab world.

However, even those who wished to follow Cornfeld's suggestions for their *hamin* faced a problem during the *tzena*. Some of the available meat was not kosher, and rationing officials acted insensitively to the needs of religious citizens. The Minister of Agriculture declared, "If we offer . . . other kinds of food to those who cannot or do not wish to eat this [unkosher] meat, then that is just . . .. What is so terrible if some Israelis receive extra eggs and carp and others receive this meat?"[33]

In response, some chose to skirt the law—the *tzena* regulations, not *halacha*—to acquire meat. Smuggling and black-market sales (for many Israelis, not just religious ones) became rampant. One inspector found a "margarine transport" that was actually delivering thirty-five chickens. In another case, a live calf, six hens, and 200 eggs were hidden on a bus.[34] Soon, Tel Aviv's markets were overrun by vendors selling contraband poultry and meat, as well as eggs and harder-to-find vegetables. Observant Jews seeking meat for their Shabbat stews were no holier than their secular neighbors. One woman told me how she smuggled a live chicken from a *kibbutz*, hiding it under her bus seat the whole way to Jerusalem.

Alternatives to unavailable ingredients were one of the hallmarks of the austerity period, for Shabbat as with weekday meals. Fake soup powders worked their way into the cuisine, for instance. One of the most famous replacement foods is "Israeli couscous," known in Israel as *ptitim*.* Rice was extremely rare during the *tzena*, so Israeli Prime Minister David Ben-Gurion went to Osem, the country's major food manufacturer, and said something along the lines of, "Make me rice . . . just make it out of wheat!" The company developed *ptitim*, an extruded, toasted wheat pasta. Though produced as round balls today, they were originally rice-shaped, making them very similar to orzo. The replacement—known colloquially as "Ben-Gurion's rice"—remains one of the most popular comfort foods in Israel today.

During the *tzena*, *ptitim* may have found their way into some Shabbat stews. One Iraqi woman, at least, made her *t'bit* using "macaroni."[35] She might have meant actual pasta, as in *hamin macaroni*, but *ptitim* seems more likely since it needed to be stuffed into the chicken, and since they were specifically created to replace rice.† In her 2008 cookbook *Hamin*,

* *Ptitim* are not actually couscous, which is hand-rolled from semolina flour. The Hebrew word translates as "flakes," which is no more accurate a name.

† Alas, my attempts at making a *hamin* using *ptitim* failed. They largely became a mush, so I may be mistaken about their use during the *tzena*. Possibly, the formulation has also changed over the intervening decades.

Ansky includes a recipe that employs *ptitim* with chicken, so maybe it was done during the *tzena* as well.[36]

The multitude of immigrants from around the world who arrived during the *tzena* also poured their recipes into the Israeli melting pot. Therefore, numerous Shabbat stews from different countries around the Diaspora could be found cooking in neighboring homes in the Jewish state. This is already reflected in 1964's *The Israeli Cook Book* by Molly Lyons Bar-David. Throughout her book, Bar-David presents recipes from Jews around the world, but notably doesn't portray any as "exotic" or weird. On the contrary, she matter-of-factly explains how they combine into a singular cuisine. "As wave after wave of new immigrants arrived in Israel . . . dishes we had once considered foreign became familiar fare . . . They were adapted to Israeli products, seasoned to local tastes, and became distinctively Israeli."[37]

Bar-David includes recipes for a few variations on Ashkenazi *cholent* ("Alias Shalet or Sholet," as she writes), Egyptian *ferik*, Algerian *dafina* (with a *kukla* dumpling), Italian *hamin di fagiolo*, and *t'bit*. Her book also includes classic Shabbat stew Bonus Foods such as *haminados*, noodle *kugel*, and a *ganef* dumpling.[38] She even features a "Pharaoh's Wheel" that she indicates (unlike most Italian versions) "can be kept in a warming oven overnight (in plenty of sauce)."[39] Further normalizing these culturally diverse offerings as part of a general Israeli diet, these recipes are not sequestered in a Shabbat stew section. They are scattered among the general recipes. Most importantly, in contrast to many American cookbooks, Bar-David's book avoids using one generic term (such as *cholent* or *hamin*) for all of these stews. Each is called by its traditional name.

Ashkenazim only make up about 45 percent of the Israeli-Jewish population, in contrast to roughly 95 percent in the US, 85 percent in the UK, and 70 percent worldwide. Despite the presence of so many non-Ashkenazi Jews in Israel, however, Ashkenazim still dominated Israeli society through the initial decades of the State. This started shifting in the late 1960s and into the 1970s, due to activism and outspoken pride from Sephardi, Mizrachi, and other non-Ashkenazi Jews. These groups' foods rightfully began emerging from the kitchens of Israel's *savtot* ("grandmothers") and onto general Israeli tables.

Israeli cookbooks echo this shift in the culture. In 1975, Ruth Sirkis published *From the Kitchen With Love*, one of the most popular cookbooks in the country's history.[40] It had no Shabbat stews, but included both Sephardi *haminados* and Ashkenazi noodle *kugel*. But in her *Popular*

*Food From Israel*, a later English-language book aimed at foreign readers, "tcholent" appears among the newly added recipes.[41] Though the recipe, as the name suggests, is primarily Ashkenazi, it shows that cultural mixing was becoming commonplace by ending with a Moroccan-style option: "rice, loosely tied in a piece of muslin."

The trend against Ashkenazi hegemony strengthened in the twenty-first century. Janna Gur's internationally popular *The Book of New Israeli Food* (2007) uses *hamin* as its categoric term for the food, despite appealing to an international audience.[42] Latvian-born Gur is Ashkenazi, but her book refers to *cholent* as "Ashkenazi Hamin," the polar opposite of what many American cookbooks do to non-Ashkenazi stews. And T. Gila Levine's tourist-focused *Simply Israel* strikes a balanced tone, presenting both a "Cholent" and a "Chamin," neither taking precedence over the other.[43]

By now, international Shabbat stews are known and consumed in both the United States and Israel. But in the former, they are largely presented as foods of "other Jews" for an Ashkenazi to try, as novelty or to celebrate Jewish diversity. In Israel, they may be eaten by members of any community as a simple matter of course. They are recognized as different commonplace options, truly variations on the same dish.

## *Not* My Mother's Shabbat Stew

Jews venerate tradition, especially when it comes to food. We often aim to re-create the dishes of our mothers and grandmothers. Surprisingly, however, a distinct irreverence for their recipes marks the contemporary Shabbat stew, particularly in the US and Israel. (Quite the opposite of what I mentioned regarding Mexican Ashkenazim and their *cholent*.) Many people explicitly state that what they make is *not* the same as what their mothers prepared in the past.

To get a better handle on how people make their stews today, I ran an online survey that received 430 responses from around the world. In addition to asking about communal backgrounds, stew names, and ingredients, I also invited free-form comments. Many respondents wrote such comments as, "This is not the stew I grew up with," "I have added my own touches to this," or "We are Ashkenazi, but prefer to make *hamin*."

Multiple reasons explain this, I believe. First, on a broad scale this reflects the postmodern character of today's world. People now feel less bound by tradition-for-tradition's-sake. Previously, a cook might make her *cholent* as she did because "that's how my mother did it." Her

### Hamin Kharshuf

I invented this stew to highlight one of my favorite winter vegetables in Israel. Cardoon (*kharshuf* in Hebrew and Arabic) looks like a prehistoric celery. It is a relative of the artichoke (the taste is similar), and you must peel the whole thing to remove its thorns and tough exterior. But due to that toughness, it holds its form through long stewing, perfect for a Shabbat stew. I chose to combine it with other favorite Israeli flavors (though, after attempting a version with *techina* drizzled on top, I realized they don't *all* work).

***Ingredients***

1 medium **cardoon**, or 1¼ pounds (565 g) frozen artichoke bottoms (*see* Notes)
3 cups (600 g) **wheat** berries
1 (15-ounce/425 g) can **chickpeas**
1¼ pounds (565 g) **lamb** or fatty **beef**, cut into chunks
12 cloves of **garlic**
3 tablespoons **zaatar** spice blend (*see* Notes)
1 tablespoon ground **sumac**
2 teaspoons **salt**
1 teaspoon ground black **pepper**
8 **eggs**, still in their shells

***Method***

Carefully peel each **cardoon** stalk, removing the thorns, leaves and tough exterior. This will take a little while, but the effort is worth the result. Cut

son or daughter today might modify her recipe, explaining "I use my mom's recipe . . . but I changed the beef to lighter chicken, got rid of the gas-inducing beans, and added barbecue sauce for extra flavor." Some comments seemed apologetic, dripping in stereotypical Jewish guilt, while others were more matter of fact. Regardless of attitude, they indicate how common such alterations have become.

Of course, as I've repeated throughout this book, changing the Shabbat stew recipe has been commonplace for as long as we've cooked it. Otherwise, we'd all still be eating *harisa* for Saturday lunch. So why do I consider these changes "irreverent," rather than just another example of what has happened before? I'd argue that previously the adjustments were usually due to need. When olive oil was unavailable in France, they used schmaltz instead. Today's changes seem more like the peeled stalks into pieces about 3 inches (7.5 cm) long and put them into a large bowl of lightly acidulated water (water with a bit of lemon juice or vinegar added).

Mix the **wheat** and **chickpeas** together inside a large pot. Scatter the **lamb** or **beef** chunks around the pot so they are mixed in with the **wheat** and **chickpeas**. Remove the **cardoon** pieces from the water, and insert them all around. Distribute the **garlic** cloves in various places. Sprinkle the **zaatar**, **sumac**, **salt** and **pepper** over everything.

Add water to cover. Gently insert the **eggs** around the top of the pot. Bring to a boil, then simmer for about 20 minutes.

Cook overnight using any standard method (*see* pages 7–8).

***Notes***

If cardoon is not in season (or you have no idea where to find it), frozen artichoke bottoms work as a great substitute. Do not use marinated bottoms in jars, just plain, unflavored frozen ones. Cut them into smaller pieces before using.

Zaatar is usually sold as a blend, mixing hyssop (the actual zaatar), sesame seeds, salt, and sometimes sumac.

I like serving this with some extra virgin olive oil and a bit of lemon juice drizzled on top.

Another option, for those who like their food spicy, is to stir some *schug* or *harissa* through your portion. The flavors work perfectly.

choices. (Some relate to medical restrictions, but those are the minority.) Some homemakers throughout history tweaked recipes for personal tastes alone, but it happens frequently enough today to suggest the true motivating factor is novelty.

The first area in which most people take liberties is in the minor flavorings. They might retain the meat, grain, and vegetables, but have no issue with adding soy sauce, cola, beer, or an exotic spice. In a discussion I facilitated in Britain, one participant confessed to flavoring her *cholent* with a very British condiment: Marmite. Rather than being shocked, others said they'd done it too, or would try it for their next *cholent*.

Similarly, it is not uncommon to find someone including a Bonus Food from a different culture; many Ashkenazi Jews cook *haminados* in their stews, and a Moroccan couple I know happily add a Yemenite *jachnun* into their *skhena* "because our kids like it." Like spices or condiments, these are less central to the stew itself, which can explain why they are among the first to be altered.

Interestingly, today's Shabbat stew irreverence manifests differently in the US and Israel. In America, after the addition of unorthodox minor ingredients into a familiar stew, the liberties move on to core elements. It is not uncommon to find salami, hot dogs, or pastrami in an American *cholent*. Others might use chicken or lamb instead of the traditional beef. The result is a recognizable Shabbat stew that has been enriched and modernized.

Israel's Shabbat stews contain fewer "non-traditional" ingredients, but remain no less iconoclastic. There, many people cook stews that originate in a community other than their own. We even find many cross-cultural examples, mixing elements from different communities into a single stew. This goes beyond just adding a *kugel* to an otherwise Sephardi *hamin*. Reflecting Israeli diversity, many blend stews from places as diverse as Tunisia, Yemen, Persia, Kurdistan, and France. This type of hybrid stew seamlessly becomes a unified whole where nothing is out of bounds. In Israeli cookbooks, the first that I've found was Sirkis's Ashkenazi-style *cholent*, accented by an optional Moroccan-ish rice bag. A better example, however, appears in Janna Gur's 2014 *Jewish Soul Food*. She provides a recipe for an "Exiles Cholent," containing the core ingredients of an Ashkenazi *cholent*, infused with Moroccan and Iraqi spices. Other international ingredients include celery and parsley roots, dates and *silan* (date honey), cayenne pepper, rice, and *hamin* eggs.[44]

These cross-cultural examples also reflect a second explanation for today's Shabbat stew irreverence. With widespread population shifts, many more Jews marry those who come from different parts of the world. This happens a bit in the US, but much more in Israel where a greater array of Jews live. So the mixing of cultures in the Shabbat stew pot there comes about organically. Some have described Israel's culturally blended cuisine as "the world in a pita," but on Shabbat that world hops into the *hamin* pot!

Finally, a third reason for increased experimentation in Shabbat stews today is the large number of Jews who make them but ate no specific version growing up. I'm referring both to *ba'alei teshuva* (as described in connection to South African Jews) and converts to Judaism.* These

* In Israel, *ba'alei teshuva* (which translates to "masters of repentance") are more commonly called *chozrim beteshuva* ("returners in repentance").

people have no specific recipe drawing their loyalty, so their unique choices aren't irreverent. They choose based on taste alone. But as they integrate into observant communities, their foods influence new friends and neighbors.[45]

Today's attitude of innovation is only one shift in the contemporary Shabbat stew. In the final chapter I'll explore other trends that have taken it to places it had never been before. These new elements helped the Shabbat stew reach its pinnacle as the most Jewish food on Earth.

# Chapter 10

# What's New with the Shabbat Stew?

Over the preceding chapters, I've followed the Shabbat stew as it spread around the world. After all that, you might think it's gotten everywhere. But wait for the grand finale, because you ain't seen *nothing* yet. Today's Shabbat stew has boldly gone where none has gone before. For most of history, it was eaten at a specific time (Saturday lunch) by a specific group of people (Sabbath-observant Jews). But now, it is no longer eaten *only* on Shabbat, nor solely by the religiously observant. In fact, it is not even only for Jews any more! The Shabbat stew has become the Jewish food par excellence, loved and consumed by people of all types in any number of different contexts.

So, go ahead and pop a bowl of *cholent* into the microwave. (What, am I the only one who freezes Shabbat stew leftovers to use as a starter the following week?) Relax, as I unravel the astonishing climax to this story of a dish like no other.

## Every Stew, Everywhere, All at Once

Historically, the Shabbat stew was always eaten at home. During the week, people might have eaten street foods of some sort, but Shabbat meals were for the house, with family and invited guests. Restaurants, as we think of them today, are a relatively modern innovation, and kosher ones are even newer. But, by the early twentieth century, enough American Jews were eating enough meals outside the home that the Yiddish-language *Forverts* ("Forward") newspaper coined a new word: *oyesessen* ("eating out").[1] And those who were *oyesessen*-ing didn't only do so on weekdays. They ate out on Shabbat, too, for presumably the first time in history. This pioneering shift in the Shabbat dining venue took the Shabbat stew away from its traditional setting, opening the door for the many further changes I'm about to discuss.

A December 1920 advertisement in the *Hebrew Standard* newspaper for Garfein's Kosher Family Restaurant (on New York's Lower East Side)

*Garfein's ad for Saturday cholent,* The Hebrew Standard, *Dec. 24, 1920.*

promotes the "same home-cooked meals which you imagine can only be obtained in a private home." It continues, "Saturday 'Chulent' is served all day, and all as strictly Kosher as is possible."[2] This innovation is particularly notable, since a year earlier, ads promoting the restaurant's Grand Opening stressed that they would remain closed the entire Shabbat.[3] Considering that observant Jews do not handle money on the Sabbath, it's unclear how customers paid for their *cholent.* (In advance?) But clearly Rabbi Guth of Clinton Street Synagogue approved, since the ads highlighted his *kashrut* supervision. Throughout the century, there have been other restaurants which dished up Saturday *cholents* in New York, Chicago, and as far away as Sydney, Australia.[4] (It is absolutely correct to use the word *cholent* here, as they were all Ashkenazi in style.)

While restaurant *cholents* first broadened the Shabbat stew's reach, they were only the "gateway drug" for changing how it was eaten. Soon, the Shabbat stew ceased to be for Shabbat lunch alone. First, *cholents* show up in other Jewish contexts. In 1955, for example, a Chicago club served the stew as part of its Purim Masquerade Ball.[5] While that holiday forefronts silliness and levity, nothing suggests this *cholent* was anything beyond a normal Jewish celebration food. The following year, at Melbourne's Summer Olympics, the caterers served it to the Israeli delegation.[6] In this case they simply served *cholent* because what could be more appropriate to feed to the Jewish state's athletes?

These, however, were one-off events. A 1957 advertisement reveals a time change that happened regularly. Hartman's Strictly Kosher Restaurant in Los Angeles served *cholent* weekly . . . on Friday nights.[7] The restaurant wasn't even open on Saturdays! True, Friday night was still Shabbat, but it was never the traditional time for eating a Shabbat stew.

And if you don't find the Saturday-to-Friday-night shift notable, soon Shabbat stews were regularly eaten on a day that was not Shabbat at all. In what I consider a true contemporary phenomenon, "Thursday night *cholent*" has become a weekly habit for many people. Particularly in heavily Orthodox areas, one finds pop-up eateries serving steaming bowls of *cholent* every Thursday night. I use the term "phenomenon" because, when you think about it, eating *cholent* on Thursday is actually *really* weird. I can understand the aroma of a bubbling stew tempting you to sneak a bowlful on a Friday night (and more on that later). But to sell the Shabbat stew on Thursday, someone needs to start cooking the dish an *entire day* early! How and why did *that* happen?

The earliest examples appear to have targeted *yeshiva* (Talmudic academy) students, who traditionally stay up late on Thursday studying Torah. That tradition probably began as a way to combat the negative influences of what otherwise might be a night out on the town. With so many young men sitting around late at night, this "captive audience" would no doubt crave a genuinely Jewish (and strictly kosher) midnight snack. The oldest Thursday night *cholent* venues can, in fact, be found near *yeshivot*, in heavily Orthodox Israeli cities such as Bnai Brak (a Tel Aviv suburb) and Jerusalem.

Bnai Brak's *Hamakom Shel Hillel* ("Hillel's place"), self-proclaimed as the first to sell Thursday night *cholent*, sits very close to one of the largest *yeshivot* in the country. Another early innovator, Rabbi Pinchas Berger, sold *cholent* to students of that same *yeshiva*, but with one major difference. In what may have been the first (only?) ultra-Orthodox version of a Good Humor ice cream truck, he sold his Thursday night stew out of the back of a bright yellow van. In time, he expanded his business, traveling to other Israeli cities to hawk his *cholent*, on different weeknights, too. Now any time could be *cholent*-time!

Still, hungry *yeshiva* students alone could hardly have made Thursday night *cholent* the full-blown sensation it has become. They're not a large

*Cholent Yericho. Inset: a bowl of their cholent.*

enough market. A sociological change probably contributed at least as much. With more dual-income Jewish families, less time remained for cooking. People increasingly purchased pre-cooked takeaway foods, even for Shabbat. Stores therefore needed to make food early, to have it ready for sale on Friday morning, or even Thursday. Once they were already making *cholent* for Shabbat takeaway, why not *also* make enough to sell to those craving it on Thursday night?

After decades of Thursday night *cholents*, no one even thinks they're remotely strange any more. Pop-up eateries exist throughout Israel, in Jewish areas of America from Los Angeles to Miami, and in the heavily Orthodox areas of northwest London. It has even grown so popular that it created a spin-off sub-trend: gas station *cholent*. I know that sounds like some kind of off-color Dad joke, but it's actually a thing. In both northern New Jersey and in Monroe, NY, nestled between a number of Orthodox suburbs, you can buy a bowl of your favorite Shabbat stew from a local gas station convenience store. It's like a kosher 7-Eleven, selling *cholent* instead of chili dogs.[8] (Hey . . . *cholent* dogs, anyone?)

*Bnai Brak cholent vending machine.*

---

Eateries at Israeli service stations are legendary, with some ranking among the most popular restaurants in the country,[9] so finding something similar there shouldn't surprise us. In fact, one called The Greenhouse existed for a short time in Jerusalem, at a gas station near the capital's Botanical Garden, and a few others *almost* fit the bill. Bobes & Beer has two branches, both located in industrial parks. Beyond their standard *cholent* (which they call "*chunt*"), they also offer a lamb version and *yapchik*—a cherished combo food that sandwiches beef between layers of potato *kugel*.

Even more distinctively Israeli, desert pop-up Cholent Yericho sits at Almog Junction, near the Dead Sea and right outside the Palestinian city of Jericho. Though not technically a "gas station" *cholent*, it sits at a roadside strip-mall opposite a gas station/rest area. The owners are Orthodox Jews, but most workers are Palestinian Arabs, and the atmosphere is very much of its surroundings. Low seating surrounds outdoor tables, and *nargileh* (hookah) water pipes wait to be smoked as you devour *cholent* or *yapchik*. A local camel oversees it all, in case you want to ride off your meal—for an extra fee, of course. With such a cross-cultural atmosphere, Cholent Yericho has been called "the first Arab *cholent*."[10]

The next sub-trend may have launched in Bnai Brak. A small, unstaffed store is loaded with food vending machines. But on Thursday nights and

*A* pashkevil *public notice, calling for a protest against a Jerusalem cholentia deemed a den of delinquency.*

Fridays, straight out of a 1930s automat, one machine has compartments from which you can buy individual portions of hot *cholent*.

And that may take off soon, as some feel that Thursday night *cholent* has gotten out of hand. In June 2024, ultra-Orthodox residents in Jerusalem's Geula neighborhood protested a popular *cholentia* (*cholent* eatery).[11] A posted notice declared that the restaurant was a hotbed of immoral behavior, trapping innocent *yeshiva* boys in a web of iniquity.[12] More *cholent* vending machines, however, may help get those boys their fix, while keeping them safe from the alleged negative influence.

On a similar note, Orthodox Jews worldwide were shocked in July 2025 when Rabbi Yitzchok Zilberstein issued a *halachic* ruling stating that Thursday night *cholent* was forbidden. He declared eating it on a weekday could be dangerous to one's health, and certainly decreased the food's ability to honor the Shabbat. Following significant backlash and many follow-up questions, the rabbi's grandson clarified that R. Zilberstein had moderately walked back his ruling. While it was still not ideal to eat *cholent* outside of Shabbat, there were limited circumstances in which it might be permissible. The rabbi presumably believes honestly that Shabbat food should remain exceptional, but it would not surprise me if he was also motivated by combatting the full-on Thursday night social scene.

That scene, however, is the culmination of a century-plus that saw unprecedented changes to the Shabbat stew. The single shift of eating Shabbat meals in a restaurant led, in stages, to the stew being eaten for other Jewish occasions, and on other days, one of which even became a popular phenomenon. That last is now near-obligatory for some, and birthed many innovative business ventures, from a mobile food truck to a *cholent* vending machine. With those developments, the stage was set for the Shabbat stew's rise to the top of Jewish popular culture.

## Famous Beyond Fifteen Minutes

Jews everywhere felt a jolt of pride in October 2021 when *cholent* appeared in an episode of the popular TV game show *Jeopardy!* Even though none of the three contestants answered correctly, those playing at home hit the Daily Double that night via such public representation.[13] While that might have been the most prominent example, today's Shabbat stew pervades pop culture.

In 2023, children's musician Joanie Leeds released the song "Cholent Time," celebrating the popular dish (despite never having eaten it herself).[14] It was part of her album "Freadom," highlighting banned children's books. In this case, the song was based on Mara Rockliff's *Chik Chak Shabbat*, which highlights the food's appeal to a multicultural collection of neighbors. And Rockliff's is not the only children's book focused on Shabbat stews. Others include Michael Herman's *The Cholent Brigade* and Danny Zeldin's *The Cholent Man* (aimed more at Orthodox children). Recently, we've even seen non-Ashkenazi Shabbat stews exposed to kids. Sarah Sassoon's *This is Not a Cholent* describes a young girl of Iraqi descent winning over her Ashkenazi community with her grandmother's delicious *t'bit*.

For those kids who'd rather play than read on Saturday afternoon, they can enjoy 2010's *Cholent: The Game*. Players compete to purchase ingredients in a "Shuk" (market) and become the first to assemble their secret recipe. Along the way, they encounter various community members (called "Chevra"), such as the "Rebbe" (rabbi), "Bubby" (grandmother), "Matchmaker," "Big Macher" (big shot), and even a "Golem" or a "Ganef" (not the dumpling kind). A 2018 Expansion adds "Mazel" (luck) cards to enliven game play.[15]

These days, whoever won that game might trumpet their triumph on social media. And there are at least three *cholent* influencer/critic accounts. Instagrammer @thecholent_connoisseur features weekly profiles of the scene in Manchester, UK (and beyond), while @cholent.and.chill offers a similar take in Israel, from an apparently American transplant. And if you're of the Hebrew-speaking persuasion, you can also check out the Twitter/X account of ultra-Orthodox reviewer @mevaker_chunt.

Meanwhile, from a different side of the pop culture map, *cholent* appeared in a one-off line from 2014's *Cannon Fodder*—Israel's first-ever zombie movie.[16] While many feel like zombies after overstuffing their bellies with *cholent*, this brought the stew somewhere that no Talmudic sage could have even imagined.

Another pop culture phenomenon is the *cholent* club. Unlike the antisemitic country clubs of the past, *cholent* clubs welcome everyone. New York City boasts one such grassroots (dis)organization that grew from a group of misfit friends who'd hang out in Brooklyn every Thursday night. Nowadays, "Cholent" (as it is simply known) has become a sizable weekly gathering, drawing many who slip through the proverbial cracks of organized Judaism. Like the ingredients of any Shabbat stew, they are a mixed bag of characters: current and formerly ultra-Orthodox Jews, neo-Hasidic hippies, curious Modern Orthodox explorers, *ba'alei teshuva*, and more. They chill out, play music, flirt, debate philosophy,

*Former Choolant Society president Jonathan Webber, wearing the official necktie.*

or argue about the mundane . . . and of course eat *cholent*. The welcoming atmosphere that founder Isaac Schonfeld created (first in Brooklyn and later in Manhattan) draws men and women, old and young alike.[17]

A *cholent* club of a different sort met for decades in Britain: Oxford University's Choolant [*sic*] Society. Founded in 1956, the club joined other Oxford "dining clubs" which today include such colorfully-named groups as The Assassins, The Myrmaids, and The Faeries. Each such club features costumes, often secret rules, and a set gathering schedule. The all-male Choolant Society met on the seventh Tuesday of each semester, and had neckties and *kippot* (skullcaps) brandishing the society logo.[18] Why on a Tuesday? Former president Jonathan Webber says it grew out of a Jewish Oxford-ism. If someone did something particularly ridiculous, the response would be, "That's like eating *cholent* on Tuesday!"[19] Thus, the Choolant Society fully embraced a very British style of tongue-in-cheek and self-deprecating humor.

The society lasted about forty years, until the late 1990s. Webber feels a male-centric club may have grown passé amidst increasingly egalitarian attitudes. But perhaps the club also outlived its original purpose. For some, a Jewish dining society at Oxford was a step toward Jewish integration at the venerable English university. The Jews who established the society stated loudly and proudly that they belonged at Oxford, just like anyone else.[20]

In 2004, a different group of university students formed a more activist *cholent* club. In Kraków, Poland, they gathered at first to share traditional foods, exploring their remote Jewish backgrounds.[21] Though by now the club has transformed into a social advocacy organization, the Czulent Jewish Association (using a Polish spelling) still operates today.[22] Despite little remaining connection to food, the name is deemed so indicative of Jewish culture that it works for this political organization.

While clubs share the Shabbat stew with fans, *cholent* festivals bring the admired food to the masses. As mentioned, Hungary's non-Jews are very familiar (even obsessed) with this Jewish soul food. So it is there that one can attend *Sóletfesztivál*, an annual event in downtown Budapest since 2015. You won't find a pork-filled *sólet* there, however, since this event is strictly kosher, organized by the Orthodox Chabad-Lubavitch-affiliated Association of Hungarian Jewish Communities.[23] In addition to four types of *sólet*, other Hungarian-Jewish favorites appear as well.[24] In a country whose Jewish population was among the hardest hit during the Holocaust, and which still faces significant amounts of antisemitism, this festival helps Hungarian Jews embrace Jewish pride, while exposing their culture to non-Jews.

Israel has hosted many one-off Shabbat stew festivals. One of the more interesting examples took place in early 2020 in an underused shopping mall on the outskirts of Tel Aviv. What made this *hamin* festival unique was that it reflected the diversity of Israel's "tossed salad" mix of Jews. In addition to a few *cholents*, other stands offered *t'fina pkaila*, *t'bit*, *dafina*, and more.[25] This alone set it apart from the other Ashkecentric festivals and pop-up restaurants around the world. Nowhere is the Jewish people's diversity on display as effectively (or appropriately) as in our national homeland.

On a smaller scale, many synagogues and groups of friends run *cholent* cookoffs. The combination of good-natured competition and a meal of multiple courses (all of the same primary food) warms Jewish hearts while filling our bellies. I've judged such contests a few times. Even kids are getting in the game. In 2023 a private Jewish middle school in Long Island, NY, set students against each other in the ultimate Jewish "Master Chef." Teams battled it out to claim best *cholent*, impressing a panel of judges that included Jewish food media personality Naomi Nachman.[26] But to be completely honest, I'm waiting for some competitive Jews to throw down in Texas; the food world will be a better place with a *cholent*-chili hybrid contest in it.

## The Stew of Life, and Law & Order

While pop-culture references are fun, the Shabbat stew has also been involved in some more serious events. The first we'll look at helped counterbalance a historic tragedy. You'll recall that, during the Spanish Inquisition, eating *adafina* could get a Jew killed. Nowadays, the not-just-for-Shabbat stew has turned 180 degrees into a dish that actually *saves* lives.

During the COVID-19 pandemic, amid Israel's rapid vaccine rollout, many of the country's cities fought low vaccination rates via free food giveaways. The foods matched the demographics in each location. Petah Tikva, for example, attracted its Russian immigrants with *blintzes* and *piroshki*. Hummus and *knafeh* drew Jaffa's Arab-Israelis, while a few miles away in north Tel Aviv, espresso shots targeted hipster residents. Bnai Brak was among the worst-hit municipalities. Despite high rates of infection, only 17 percent of the city's residents had been vaccinated. So, on a 2021 Thursday, the Orthodox and largely Ashkenazi city opted for an appropriate lure: free bowls of hot *cholent* to those who got inoculated. Over 2,000 people received jabs that night, many of whom had otherwise not planned to get vaccinated.[27] How fitting for a city that may have been the birthplace of the Thursday night *cholent* phenomenon itself.

While some retrospectively debate the efficacy of the COVID-19 vaccines, another event in the Israeli town of Elad indubitably exemplifies the life-saving power of Shabbat stews. In May 2022, two friends, David and Elchanan sat in their car for a Thursday night *cholent* chow-down. Just then, two axe-wielding terrorists spotted and attacked them. Luckily, needing room to eat comfortably, the two friends had moved their seats back. So, one terrorist made contact, but not with either man. Tragically, his axe hit David's bowl of *cholent*! No doubt enraged, David struggled to disarm his assailant. The terrorist, realizing he'd bitten off more than he could chew, bolted. Meanwhile, the other attacker missed both Elchanan *and* his stew. Thinking on his seat, Elchanan weaponized his dinner, hurling his bubbling *cholent* in the terrorist's face. Singed by steaming stew, he fled too. The friends gave chase briefly, then returned to call the police, and seek medical attention. That night, *cholent* truly became the Stew of Life. One can only hope these heroes received free bowls to replace their edible shield and weapon.[28]

One of the most moving, and sad, Shabbat stew stories I know happened in the wake of the October 7th Hamas terror attacks in Israel. One of the many people taken into Gaza as a hostage was a young man from Kibbutz Kfar Azza named Alon Shimriz. A short while later, TV food personality Ruthie Rousso interviewed his friends, who told her of their weekly Saturday ritual at Alon's house, hanging out and eating his mom's *hamin*. The story left a deep impression on Rousso. A few months after, in one of the more dreadful events from the war that followed, Alon was among three hostages mistakenly killed by the IDF. When Rousso heard, her heart was shattered. Without even thinking, she went onto social media and suggested that the following Shabbat, "instead of mourning, let's all celebrate Alon Shimriz" by cooking and eating *hamin* with family and friends. The response was viral, with people from all over the world participating, posting pictures, and virtually hugging each other through this Shabbat ritual. This time, the stew couldn't save a life, but it helped the living stay strong and gave tribute to one of the war's tragic victims.[29]

While these stories deal with matters of life and death, others relate to a different type of crime—thievery. In British Mandate Palestine (1920–48), David Tidhar served as a Jerusalem police investigator, then private detective. A locally born Jew, Tidhar wrote a True Crime memoir in 1924, *Criminals and Crime in the Land of Israel.** One such tale, written in flowery, Biblically-tinged Hebrew, tells of an appalling theft in the upscale Bukharian Quarter of Jerusalem. One Shabbat morning, the neighborhood woke to screams of agony echoing through its wide streets. Someone had robbed the locals the night before, not of their jewelry, but their Shabbat stew. The culprits had snuck into the communal oven, and torn into the *osavo*. Audaciously, they didn't take the stew and run, but sat on an overturned pot and ate it right there! Tidhar led the investigation team, eventually discovering that the midnight misdemeaning munchers were poverty-stricken Persian immigrants, recently arrived in Israel. These thieves were not heartless, just hungry. Tidhar doesn't report the aftermath, but one of Jerusalem's many charities presumably helped feed these immigrants, also protecting the Bukharians' *osavo* each week thereafter.

This was certainly not the only time someone stole from the weekly stewpot. Most often, such thefts lean towards the mischievous more than the malicious. Sneaking an early helping from your community's Shabbat stewpot is very different than stealing from a stranger. A 1957 article tells of some Cleveland *yeshiva* students pilfering from the pot of tempting *cholent* one Friday, many years earlier. One student climbed through an unlocked window while others debated the *halachically* permissible way to remove food from a pot still on the fire. (Apparently they didn't debate the *halacha* of "Thou shalt not steal.") After their midnight snack, they "washed up the plates and spoons, and left no trace." That is, until the author published his confession in a newspaper.[30] Similar nefarious activities have taken place on religious *kibbutzim* in Israel as well. I know of one case in which *cholent* theft had become so problematic that the

* The book was translated into English as *Crime and Criminals in Palestine*, but the following story does not appear in the English version.

*kibbutz* metal shop welded brackets onto the lid of their oversized cooking pot, to padlock it shut every Friday night.

And on a happy note, how about the time that *cholent* actually saved a Detroit family from getting robbed. A 2013 article tells of an event from years earlier, when crime was rampant in the city. The family was eating *cholent* on a chilly Friday night, outside in their *sukkah* (an open-air booth used on the Sukkot holiday). Two gunmen entered, demanding money from the flabbergasted family (they had no money, as it was Shabbat). One would-be thief said to the other, "I don't think these people have anything. They're sitting in a hut eating beans! They've got less than we do!" With that, they left the family to continue enjoying their warming—and theft-preventing—*cholent*.[31]

## *Cholent*'s Ch-Ch-Ch-Chaaanngesss ...

After crossing its prior time and space boundaries, and popping up across Jewish culture as the preeminent Jewish food, the Shabbat stew is now breaking new ground in its own substance. Both the stew itself and the manner in which it is prepared have changed drastically, taking it one step closer to fully embodying the Jewish nation.

One increasingly widespread change alters the fundamental recipe. As I've described throughout this book, most versions historically combined a grain with a meat, developing from the original *harisa* recipe. However, many people today omit half of that duo, opting for a vegetarian stew. Vegetarian Shabbat stew recipes appear in cookbooks from the 1970s until today, often alongside meaty ones. Some people just leave out meat, while others use vegetarian replacements such as mushrooms, tofu, seitan, plant-based sausages, or jackfruit. But despite the novel faux-meats, vegetarian Shabbat stews themselves are not brand new.

Some Jews must have eaten meatless Shabbat stews in the past, but more likely due to poverty than to dietary choice. But starting in the 1800s, vegetarianism as a movement began, attracting many Jews for health or ethical reasons. Between the world wars, Fania Lewando ran a vegetarian Jewish restaurant in Vilnius (now in Lithuania, but then Wilno in Poland), and in 1938 she published a Yiddish-language cookbook. Translated to English for its re-release in 2015, *The Vilna Vegetarian Cookbook* includes three different *cholent* recipes. Interestingly, though all of them contain butter (which could not be included in a kosher meat-based stew), Lewando only refers to one of the three as a "*Milkhik* [dairy] Cholent."* Perhaps once was enough to make the point that an additional benefit to a vegetarian *cholent* is that it *can*, in fact, contain dairy.[32]

Tel Aviv-based American-Israeli chef and cookbook author Adeena Sussman invented her own creative vegan Shabbat stew. Her book *Shabbat* features classic and updated recipes, all for the Shabbat table, and this Shabbat stew features an entire head of cauliflower. This plays off Israeli chef Eyal Shani's famous roasted cauliflower.[33]

Other groups today are changing the Shabbat stew for social activist reasons. Jews of Color often struggle with dual prejudice: racism from broader society *and* from White Jews, who (consciously or subconsciously) treat them differently. This latter discrimination can hurt even more, coming from their own people. One response forefronts their hybrid identities, eating foods that represent both Judaism and their race. We see this most among the relatively sizable population of Black Jews.

Holiday and Sabbath meals offer a great opportunity for this type of fusion. One Shabbat dinner celebrating Black-Jewish culture included "Black-Eyed Pea Hummus" and "Blewish [Black-Jewish] Chicken Soup with Collard Greens."[34] Similarly, Orthodox African-American rabbi Shais Rishon, using his pen name MaNishtana, has written about a *charoset* that "consists of the slave crops of pecans, cocoa powder, figs, and sugarcane."[35] These examples show racially relevant foods being eaten at religiously appropriate times.

Some similarly blend different sides of their identity within a Shabbat stew. One prominent figure doing this is Michael W. Twitty, an African-American, gay, Jewish, Southern chef and food historian.† In 2022's *Koshersoul*, Twitty includes a recipe for *cachopa*, a stew from Cape Verde, the former Portuguese colony off Africa's western coast. "Today's Cape Verdean diaspora is rediscovering its many Jewish roots . . . Cachopa, one of the island's signature dishes, scaled down here, makes an excellent Shabbat stew or replacement for cholent." Twitty adds a very Jewish cooking method to a classic African dish. His recipe includes chicken, kosher sausage and bacon, cabbage or kale, plantains, and hominy.[36]

Some Jews of Latin descent look to old-school Sephardi stews, recognizing their shared Spanish heritage. Rachel Figueroa de Zimmerman, a Puerto Rican Jew, has written about her admiration for *sofrito*, the popular Sephardi stew seen a few times already. She says it "ties together

* Not having seen the Yiddish original, I don't know if they were identified that way originally, or only in the English translation.

† I list all of these descriptors since Twitty himself highlights each one in his work.

### Vegetarian Hamin

Flavors from around the Sephardi diaspora combine here, while avoiding meat. It works even better as a base for experimentation. I include some potential changes in the Notes. I believe the key when trying new variations is thinking about whether a possible ingredient will hold up to overnight cooking. Also, make sure something provides a meaty consistency.

***Ingredients***

3 tablespoons **olive oil**
2–3 medium **onions**, chopped roughly
2–4 cloves of **garlic**, sliced
1 large or 2 small green **chilies**, seeds and membranes removed, diced
3 tablespoons **tomato paste**
1 tablespoon ground **cumin**
1 tablespoon ground **turmeric**
1 teaspoon ground **cardamom**
1 teaspoon **salt**
1 teaspoon ground black **pepper**
2 (15-ounce/425 g) cans mixed **beans** (red or white kidney, lima, chickpeas, or other)
1 cup (200 g) green or brown **lentils**
1½ cups (300 g) **wheat** berries
1 large handful dried **mushrooms**, rehydrated in hot water
4 medium **potatoes**, cut into chunks
1 large **sweet potato**, cut into chunks
8 **eggs**, still in their shells

kitchens all throughout the Sephardic Diaspora," including in her own Puerto Rican Jewish home.[37]

Asian Jews sometimes act similarly. In the "Israeli Foodies" Facebook group, a Chinese Jew described adapting a Cantonese-style brisket as her Shabbat stew. Among the uncommon ingredients were star anise, cloves, and soy sauce. Extended Shabbat cooking was not the only modification she made to her recipe. Unable to source Chinese turnip, she replaced it with the locally available kohlrabi. Perhaps most interestingly, one substitution seemed purely motivated by flavor: she replaced rice wine with arak, a Middle Eastern anise liquor that she said "makes it taste even better." Notably, despite her alterations, she insisted the dish remained "authentic."[38]

### *Method*

In a large pot, heat the **olive oil** over medium-high heat. Fry the **onions** until they start to soften and turn brown, but not until they turn dark brown or black, approximately 5–7 minutes. Add the **garlic** and **chilies** and continue frying for 1–2 minutes.

Add the **tomato paste, cumin, turmeric, cardamom, salt**, and **pepper**. Mix well. Next, add the **beans, lentils, wheat**, and **mushrooms** (with the water they soaked in). Scatter the **potatoes** and **sweet potato** on top. Then add enough water to cover the contents by about a half inch (1.25 cm). Tuck the **eggs** gently around the top of the stew ingredients, making sure they are at least partially submerged.

Cook overnight using any standard method (*see* pages 7–8).

### *Options*

Add one large carrot, or one large turnip, peeled and chopped.

Add seitan strips or vegetarian sausages.

In place of, or in addition to the dried mushrooms, use chopped fresh oyster or portobello mushrooms.

Swap in thoroughly-rinsed long grain white or brown rice, or pearl barley, instead of the wheat.

For a spicier flavor, leave in some of the chili seeds and membranes, and/or add 1 teaspoon of cayenne.

For a different flavor profile, leave out the cumin, turmeric, and cardamom, replacing them with 1 teaspoon each of ground cinnamon, allspice, nutmeg, and cloves.

Contemporary chefs are also reimagining what can be done with a Shabbat stew, not to express identity but to inventively broaden its appeal. For example, at Abe Fisher, a Jewish but non-kosher Philadelphia eatery, chef Yehuda Sichel tapped into his traditional upbringing to make a *cholent* pot pie. The restaurant already offered such Ashkenazi classics as *kugel* and *kishke*. But Sichel knew his Shabbat stew would require some upscaling, rather than just being ladled into a bowl. "I don't think we could get away with that," he said. But he couldn't ignore it either since *cholent*, as he puts it, is "like *really* Jewish." Sichel pre-cooked the stew, cooled it overnight, then baked it covered in puff pastry. "This is not only my connection to Judaism," says Sichel. "This is my contribution to Judaism."[39]

## Mole Cholent

So, here's me taking *cholent* somewhere new, in the spirit of novelty and creativity. Mole (MOE-lay) is one of the supreme sauces of the world. Or more accurately, it is a class of supreme sauces, all native to Mexico. Layered with numerous types of flavor (spicy, nutty, fruity, sweet, etc.), it typically includes lots of ingredients, and the most complex versions can take hours, or even days, to prepare.

Since this will cook overnight, and since rather than the sauce coating a single item (like chicken) the recipe incorporates a host of stew ingredients, I've opted for a tremendously simplified version. (Don't worry, this won't take hours to prep.) But it still includes a host of different items, in order to create the layers of flavor. This is neither a genuine mole, nor a traditional *cholent* of Mexican Jews, but it is *muy delicioso.*

### *Ingredients*

*For mole sauce*

1 cup (160 g) blanched **almonds**
5 dried **chili peppers** (ideally a mix of varieties), or fewer to taste
2 medium **tomatoes**, cut in quarters
2 medium yellow **onions**, cut in quarters
8 cloves **garlic**
1 cup (150 g) black **raisins**
1 cup (150 g) roasted **peanuts**, or 3 rounded tablespoons natural **peanut butter**
1 small (2.5-ounce/70 g) bag plain **tortilla chips**
3 tablespoons dried **oregano**
2 teaspoons **salt**
1 teaspoon dried **chili flakes** (optional)
1 tablespoon ground **cinnamon**
½ teaspoon ground **cloves**
3.5 ounces (100 g) dark **chocolate** (ideally at least 75–85 percent chocolate)

*For cholent*

2¼ pounds (1 kg) boneless fatty **beef**, cut into 2-inch (5-cm) cubes
2 medium **potatoes**, diced to 1-inch (2.5-cm) cubes
2 red bell **peppers**, diced
2 **red onions**, diced
2 (15-ounce/425 g) cans **corn kernels**
2 (15-ounce/425 g) cans red **kidney beans**

***For serving***
1 **avocado**, sliced

### *Method*

*Make the mole sauce*: If the **almonds** are unroasted, put them in a dry frying pan over medium-high heat and toast them for a few minutes. Make sure they do not burn, and when they begin to give off an aroma, remove them from the heat and pour into a heat-proof bowl.

Put the **chili peppers**, **tomatoes**, **onions**, **garlic**, **raisins, peanuts**, and **almonds** in a blender. Add about ½ cup of water to ease the blending. Blend on high until all is beginning to become a purée. Add in the **tortilla chips**, **oregano**, **salt**, **chili flakes** (if using), and **cinnamon**. Continue blending until everything is smooth, uniform, and moderately thick. Add extra water as needed, a small amount at a time.

Transfer the purée to a pot over medium heat. Break the **chocolate** into smaller pieces, and put into the pot to melt. Once the **mole sauce** starts to bubble, reduce heat to low, cover most of the way (leave the lid slightly off the edge), and let simmer for about 15 minutes, stirring periodically.

*Assemble the cholent*: In the pot you will be cooking the *cholent* in, put the **beef**, **potatoes**, **peppers**, **red onions**, **corn**, and **beans**. Mix everything together. Pour enough **mole sauce** over it to barely cover all of the ingredients. (If you have leftover sauce, *see* Notes, below.) Add enough water to raise the level another half-inch (2 cm) above. Ideally, rather than the classic thick sauce, this should be a slightly liquid cover, but still not soupy. It will thicken somewhat as it cooks.

Cook overnight using any standard method (*see* pages 7–8).

Serve with sliced **avocado** to garnish.

### *Notes*

You may end up with more sauce than you need. I've used these quantities to make it easier to get the right balance, but also, when putting in the effort, it is always better to make more to have for other dishes. Mole sauce can easily be frozen for later use.

This recipe has some noticeable, though not overpowering heat. Reduce the chilies in the sauce if you require less.

Perhaps the most imaginative take was a short-lived creation in Queens, New York: *cholent* ice cream. Mark and Bruce Becker, brother co-owners of Max and Mina's Homemade Ice Cream, are known for creating bizarre flavors. But even for them, *cholent* ice cream may be the strangest, considering they are a kosher establishment, even if no actual meat was used in the creation of this unique flavor. On the other hand, once they'd already made such Jewish ice cream flavors as lox, *etrog* (the citron used on Sukkot), and hamantaschen (a popular Purim cookie), how could they *not* make an ice cream out of the Jews' favorite food, too?[40]

A final example of a chef-imagined Shabbat stew transformation comes from a non-kosher Jewish-style restaurant in Budapest. At Fülemüle Étterem, they rolled balls of *sólet* in breadcrumbs, then deep-fried them to create *rántott sólet gombóc*—breaded *sólet* dumplings.* Created in 2018 for a food festival, the name could confuse some diners, for whom a *sólet* dumpling means a *kugel*-inspired *ganef*!

Beyond new ingredients and versions, the stew today is also being cooked using new devices. I discussed the development of the slow cooker, and how it became a go-to cooking device. While it actually grew out of the food's history, other newfangled devices did not. But with every trendy new kitchen gadget, it seems someone wants to use it for their *cholent* or *hamin*. One peculiar example is the Instant Pot, a multicooker that includes a pressure cooker function. I call it peculiar because the whole point of a Shabbat stew is that it cooks *slowly*, not instantly. Nonetheless, one can find Instant Pot *cholent* recipes online. One blogger used the pressure cooker setting, then switched to the warming function until Shabbat lunch. His results were distinctly underwhelming.[41] Admittedly, many of the other Instant Pot *cholent* recipes seem designed for weekday meals, yet another example of the Shabbat stew breaking out of its traditional bounds.[42]

Conversely, a fashionable kitchen device that seems tailor-made for a Shabbat stew is a sous vide cooker. Using it, vacuum-sealed food is immersed in warm but not hot water, and kept at a constant temperature for an extended time. The result is extremely tender, but fully cooked. After decades of growing popularity, some adventurous Jews thought of making Shabbat stews in their sous vide cookers.[43] Alas, the method doesn't appear to have a future for Orthodox foodies; rabbinic opinions

* The restaurant appears to have closed during the COVID-19 pandemic, but pictures of the dish still exist online.

on the method forbid its use on Shabbat for a number of technical *halachic* reasons.[44] Still, some will probably try it anyway, either out of ignorance of this rabbinic opinion, or because they aren't strictly Orthodox.

## The Final Frontier of Stew-biquity

So far, I've looked at how the Shabbat stew has transcended the bounds of time, space, formula, and cooking method. All that remains is to show how it broke out of its originally limited dining community. In passing, I've mentioned a few examples of non-Orthodox Jews eating the dish, and even its presence in non-kosher restaurants. But what kind of appeal can a Shabbat stew find among the non-observant, or non-Jewish population? The answer, apparently, is quite a bit. By now, it has reached its rightful iconic status as the quintessential Jewish food, made and consumed by secular and religious Jews alike . . . and by plenty of non-Jews, as well.

For starters, Israel's vibrant Thursday night *cholent* eateries attract a much wider audience than *yeshiva* students alone. Many less religiously observant Israelis visit too, nurturing the traditional side of their identities while feeding their culinary cravings. (This may have contributed to the ultra-Orthodox backlash mentioned earlier.)

Indeed, one Israeli chef spiced up her *cholent* with a gimmick that appealed to an exclusively non-religious audience. She was working at the time on an ostrich farm near Eilat, and wanted to attract visitors on Saturdays.

> I cooked *cholent* in a pot the size of a dining room table, over an open fire . . . Since we had plenty of ostrich eggs, we figured we'd use them instead of regular eggs. We placed an ad in the local paper inviting people to eat *cholent* with ostrich eggs. The night before the opening, we emptied one of the eggs, and five minutes before we started serving, we put a small pigeon in it. When we "cracked" the egg shell, the pigeon flew out of the pot. It was the talk of the town and people kept coming every Saturday.[45]

How do I know this attracted specifically non-observant Jews? The dish included the eggs of an ostrich, a bird that is explicitly unkosher according to the Torah.[46]

We also now find the Shabbat stew in more restaurants around the world, many not even aimed at a Jewish audience. Kazimierz, the old Jewish quarter of Kraków, Poland, features many "Jewish-style" restaurants that are neither kosher, nor run by Jews. The menus feature canonical Ashkenazi fare, including *cholent* (all week long, of course). But as with much else in Kazimierz, the food is just a Vegas-style caricature, designed to attract tourist dollars more than preserve the area's authentic traditions. Diners imagine they're experiencing a lost world, despite the lack of continuity with those who ate these foods in the past.

But even in restaurants that *are* genuinely Jewish, the Shabbat stew has attracted non-Jewish devotees. One such (not strictly kosher) eatery in Melbourne, Australia, served *cholent* every Saturday. A Chinese-Australian local loved it so much that he'd return weekly for a helping. When he married, he brought his wife to the restaurant so she could learn how to make *cholent* at home.[47]

The Shabbat stew is clearly no longer just for Jews, just as it is no longer eaten only on Saturday at home. If traveling alongside us throughout our Diasporic wanderings wasn't enough to cement the Shabbat stew as the most Jewish food on Earth, the degree of ubiquity it has currently achieved certainly should.

## The Stew of Every Jew

The Shabbat stew is not just a popular Jewish food. It actually embodies our character. Jews are a truly unique nation; there is literally no other people in the world like us. And as I've shown throughout this book, the Shabbat stew is like no other dish, expressing the distinctiveness of the people who invented it, and who adore and eat it on a weekly basis.

Over the past few thousand years, Jews have spread everywhere on Earth, and more frequently than not the stew has traveled with us. Living in Diaspora for so long in so many places has also turned our people into the most diverse. By following the evolution of this one food, I've traced the major (and some minor) routes of our travels. In each location I examined, we saw different angles on the Jewish nation's multifaceted history.

I must note that as many places as I've covered in this book, even I didn't cover all Jewish communities. There were many I left out, either because I couldn't uncover much information about their food, or because what I did find was not distinct from what I found in other areas. I have said nothing, for example, about the Jews of Northern Europe, in such places as Holland and Scandinavia. Also in Europe, I unearthed no unique versions to write about from within the Balkan territories. While there were certainly historic (and important) Jewish communities in the Caribbean, they have largely been overrun by Ashkenazim, and prior food traditions are hard to research. Finally, some of the furthest-flung Jews may be found in the Far East. Chinese Jews and those of southeast Asia (for example in Singapore, Thailand, the Philippines, and Indonesia) provide some of the most intriguing stories of the Jewish Diaspora, but their historical gastronomies are particularly tough to dig up.*

Jewish diversity goes beyond place, to defined categories as well. Historically, Jews have been clustered into three major groups: Ashkenazim and Sephardim, connected with the medieval hubs of France/Germany and Iberia, and Mizrachim, in the orbit of the earlier center in Mesopotamia. But just as many Jewish communities do not fit neatly into any of those categories. Similarly, while three meat-and-grain pairs lined up neatly with the three hubs, many exceptions exist there as well. Beef often replaces lamb in contemporary North African stews. Central Asian stews frequently use beef, not chicken. Many other stews use versions of prepared meats: sausages, *kubbeh* dumplings, or the cured meats in *choucroute garnie*. On the grain side, as well, we sometimes encounter unique grains, such as freekeh, spelt, *Grünkern*, or couscous. A few even replace the grain entirely with a parallel ingredient (as in Surinamese *pom* or Turkish chestnut *hamin*).

"Funny, you don't look Jewish" has turned into a punchline. But really, Jews are represented in every race and bear every shade of skin. We speak in different languages and with numerous accents. Similarly, the Shabbat stew includes an array of secondary ingredients and flavoring agents. It may be sweet, spicy, savory, fruity, sweet-and-sour, or herby. It may be richly flavored or subtle, bright or bland. Vegetables and fruits are only limited by their ability to hold up under overnight cooking conditions (and even, sometimes, are used despite their inability to do so).

The names by which Jews refer to this stew are almost as numerous as the places in which we have lived. Yet, these are also less disparate than they appear at first, with repeated themes tying most together. Some translate to "hot" (*hamin*, *schalet*, *sólet*, *cholent*, *skhena*). Others connect with the cooking method: *adafina* for "buried," *harisa* for "pounded," and *meudah* or *sofrito* for "steamed" or "fried." Other names highlight a central ingredient (*ferik*, *Grünkernsuppe*, *soupa de avikas*) or

* I did find Jewish cookbooks from some of these areas, such as Curaçao, the Netherlands, Denmark, or Singapore. All, for different reasons, offered Shabbat stews that were familiar from other related communities.

just describe it as Sabbath lunch (*osavo* or *palau shabati*). The many languages of the Jewish world divide us, but only at first glance. Jewish connections remain, hidden just beneath the surface.

We are both an ancient and modern people, tied to our roots but continually evolving. We still eat a Shabbat stew today, developed from one first eaten over 1,500 years ago. The telltale slow-cooking technique, created to solve a Biblically-created conundrum, connects the Shabbat stew even further back than *harisa*'s adaptation by Middle Eastern Jews. But the stew is constantly reinvented and updated. A whole second class of overnight dishes—Bonus Foods—grew out of the Shabbat stew. Later, modern innovations such as industrial food ingredients or newfangled kitchen devices further updated the dish. And the irreverence with which we now approach the Shabbat stew has created new versions, or combinations of older ones that never existed in the history of this ancient food.

The Shabbat stew's endless diversity and malleability may be its most impressive aspect, paralleling the Jewish people's developments. But more dazzling than Jewish diversity are the throughlines that tie all Jews together. It is truly incredible that a Jew from Los Angeles reads the same Torah as a Jew from Mumbai. How much more so that kosher food in Hong Kong, is also kosher in Paris or Cape Town. It is equally surprising (and gratifying) to encounter one Shabbat stew, prepared in the same way, and consumed at the same time each week by Jews in every corner of the world, despite the countless different ingredients that have been added on to the original core.

When it comes to the Shabbat stew, and to the Jewish nation itself, more impressive than our differences is the unity *within* our diversity. No food embodies this better than the Shabbat stew. Just as no dish better exemplifies the full historical scope of the Jewish experience.

Jewish legend valorizes our special relationship with this dish. A folktale relates that a special angel has the task of watching over the pots of Shabbat stew each week, ensuring the food doesn't burn.* But elevating this task to something more spiritual, we are told that this angel has one other, very holy responsibility: he is in charge of the shofar blasts on Rosh Hashana. We know it is the same angel, since when Rosh Hashana falls on Sabbath, we do not blow the shofar, freeing him to keep watching over our *cholents* and *hamins*![48] We love our stew and honor God with it, so God pays us back with an angelic assistant.

* Traditionally, Jews believe that angels can only perform one task at a time.

Zionist essayist Ahad Ha'am famously said, "More than the Jew has kept Shabbat, Shabbat has kept the Jew." I'd add that as much as Shabbat has kept the Jew, the Jew has kept the Shabbat stew.

Without a doubt, the Shabbat stew truly is the most Jewish food on Earth.

Appendix

# Food and Cookery Terms in the US and UK

| US | UK |
|---|---|
| Canola oil | Rapeseed oil |
| Cilantro | Coriander leaves |
| Coriander | Coriander seeds |
| Corn | Sweetcorn, maize |
| Corn flour/corn meal | Maize flour |
| Corned beef | Salt beef |
| Beet | Beetroot |
| Bell pepper | Sweet pepper, capsicum |
| Broth | Stock |
| Cheesecloth | Muslin |
| Collard greens | Spring greens |
| Eggplant | Aubergine |
| Fava beans | Broad beans |
| Flanken | Short ribs |
| Green beans | French beans |
| Green onions/scallions | Spring onions |
| Ground beef | Mince |
| Lima beans | Butter beans |
| Navy/kidney beans | Haricot beans |
| Parchment paper | Baking paper |
| Pickle | Gherkin |
| Skillet | Frying pan |
| Stove top | Hob |
| Strain(er) | Sieve |
| String beans | Runner beans, French beans |
| Tomato paste | Tomato purée |
| Tomato sauce | Passata |
| Zucchini | Courgette |

# Notes

## *Introduction*: The Stew with a Thousand Flavors

1. For a few examples, see Roden, *Jewish Food*, 9; Gil Marks, *Encyclopedia*, ix; Koenig, *Jewish Cookbook*, 12.
2. Sassoon, et al., *Spice*, xiii.
3. Guetta, *Cooking*, 49–52.

## *Chapter 1*: The Shabbat Stew: A Prehistory

1. Isaiah 58:13.
2. BT Shabbat 119a.
3. BT Shabbat 117b. A minority opinion there even requires four meals for the day!
4. Shabbat 7:2
5. Exodus 16:23 [emphasis added].
6. BT Shabbat 119a.
7. Shabbat 2:7. To be fair, it seems that the word *hamin* here may apply specifically to hot water, not to food, but in the next Mishnah (Shabbat 3:1), two rabbis debate whether one may place a *tavshil* (a cooked dish) or only water. So clearly there was an early desire to keep food hot on Shabbat.
8. Juvenal, *Satires* 3.12–16 and 6.542–7. For one example of interpreting this reference as a Shabbat hay box insulator, see Gil Marks, *Encyclopedia*, 513. A similar contraption, called a *Kochkiste*, was later used to keep the Shabbat stew warm in Germany (Cooper, *Eat*, 186).
9. For example, see BT Shabbat 36b–38a.
10. Davidson, *Oxford*, 681–3.
11. Ibid., 63–4.
12. Gil Marks, *Encyclopedia*, 39–41.
13. Cooper, *Eat*, 3.
14. Coulthard, *Fowl Play*, 203.
15. Gil Marks, *Encyclopedia*, 116–19.
16. B. Tyr Fothergill and Martin Sterry. "Poulíography and 'Poultrymen': Chickens in North Africa". In *L'Homme et l'Animal au Maghreb, de la Préhistoire au Moyen Âge*, edited by Véronique Blanc-Bijon, et al. Aix-en-Provence: Presses universitaires de Provence, 2021. https://doi.org/10.4000/books.pup.62607.
17. Ibid., 44–5.

## *Chapter 2*: Babylon and On: The Original Stew

1. Nasrallah, *Annals*, 256–60.
2. S. D. Goitein, "Jewish Subject Matter in 'Ansab al-Ashraf' of al-Baladhuri," *Zion* no. 1 (1935): 75–81. http://www.jstor.org/stable/23541428.
3. Numbers 11:4–5.
4. Jordan D. Rosenblum, "A Brief History of Jews and Garlic," in Gross, et al., *Feasting*, 147–56.

5. See Gil Marks, *Encyclopedia*, 428; Cooper, *Eat*, 127–8.
6. Muḥammad, *Baghdad*, 72; Nasrallah, *Smorgasbords*; Nasrallah, *Delectable Foods*.
7. Jean Bottéro, "The Most Ancient Recipes of All," in Waines, *Patterns*, 242–3.
8. Larkey, *Bone Soup*, 236.
9. Tzabar, *Yemenite*, 27
10. Gil Marks, *Encyclopedia*, 258–9.
11. Larkey, *Bone Soup*, 236. Gil Marks, *Encyclopedia*, 498–9.
12. Roden, *Jewish Food*, 277.
13. Gil Hovav, "Gil Hovav sameach l'eadam" [Gol Hovav is happy for *eadam*], *Foodspy*. https://foodspy.co.il/%D7%9E%D7%AA%D7%9B%D7%95%D7%A0%D7%99%D7%9D/%d7%92%d7%99%d7%9c-%d7%97%d7%95%d7%91%d7%91-%d7%a9%d7%9e%d7%97-%d7%9c%d7%90%d7%99%d7%93%d7%9d.
14. Larkey, *Bone Soup*, 236.
15. Hovav, "Gil Hovav sameach."
16. Brauer, *Jews of Kurdistan*, 92.
17. Shilo, *Habishul hakurdi*, 124.
18. Brauer, *Kurdistan*, 100.
19. Shilo, *Habishul hakurdi*, 131.
20. Shilo, *Habishul hakurdi*; Luzon, *Mah basimah*.
21. Brauer, *Kurdistan*, 96–7.
22. Ibid., 95.
23. Shilo, *Habishul hakurdi*, 130; Luzon, *Mah basimah*, 23.
24. Brauer, *Kurdistan*, 420.
25. Haber, *Taste of Jewish*, "The Freaky Ancient Grain Still Prepared Today and Connected with the Season," May 4, 2021. https://www.tasteofjew.com/freaky-ancient-grain-still-prepared-seasonal.
26. Abdennour, *Egyptian Cooking*, 85.
27. Roden, *Jewish Food*, 376–7.
28. Rubin, *Ha'ochel shel mama*, 52; Zamir, *Matamei mitzraim*, 85.
29. Goitein, *Mediterranean*, Vol. IV, 250.
30. Davidson, *Oxford*, 752–3.
31. Loeb, *Outcaste*, 279. The suffix "-stan" today colloquially references Muslim-dominated areas, but it actually means a place with a lot of something. Thus, "Yahudistan" means somewhere with a lot of *yahudim*, or Jews.
32. Shoaib Daniyal, "The haleem debate: Why some Indian Muslims are renaming the Ramzan delicacy 'daleem,'" *Scroll*, June 3, 2019. https://scroll.in/magazine/925615/why-are-some-indian-muslims-renaming-ramzan-favourite-haleem-as-daleem.
33. Hekmat, *Persian Cooking*, 88.
34. Liberzon, *Mitbach parsi*, 76.
35. Rejwan, *Jews of Iraq*, 136.
36. Perry, *Scents and Flavors*, 28–30; Nasrallah, *Smorgasbords*, 160.
37. Nawal Nasrallah, email to author, July 11, 2021.
38. Beattie, *Recipes*, 116; Nasrallah, email, July 11, 2021. The Arabic book is called *Daleel al-Tabkh wal-Aghdhiya*, by Nazeeha Adeeb and Firdaws al-Khateeb.
39. Nawal Nasrallah, email to author, July 10, 2021.
40. Roden, *Jewish Food*, 378–9.
41. Exodus 23:19; Exodus 34:26; Deuteronomy 14:21.
42. Daniel J. Lasker, "Rabbanism and Karaism: The Contest for Supremacy," in Jospe, *Great Schisms*, 62.
43. Marina Rustow, "The Qaraites as Sect: The Tyranny of a Construct," in Stern, *Sects*, 149; Moshe Gil, "The Origins of the Karaites," in Polliack, *Karaite Judaism*, 73 ff.

44. Goitein, *Mediterranean: An Abridgment*, 76.
45. Gil, *Jews in Islamic Countries*, 267.
46. Rustow, "The Qaraites," 168, 176–8.
47. Elinoar Bareket, "Karaite Communities in the Middle East During the Tenth to Fifteenth Centuries" in Polliack, *Karaite Judaism*, 239.
48. Baron, *Jewish Community*, 168.
49. Gil Marks, *Encyclopedia*, 513–16.
50. Zerachiah ben Isaac HaLevi, *Sefer HaMaor*, Shabbat 36b.
51. Lasker, "Rabbanism and Karaism," 62.
52. Daniel J. Lasker, "Karaite Languages and Karaite History," *Studia Hebraica*, 8 (2008): 32.
53. Daniel Frank, "May Karaites Eat Chicken? Indeterminacy in Sectarian Halakhic Exegesis," in Dohrmann, *Jewish*, 128–35
54. Ibid., 138. There were some who accepted the kosher status of chickens even in the earliest days of Karaism.

## *Chapter 3*: The Golden Age of Spanish Stewery

1. Josephus, *Wars*, 6.9.2–4; Graetz, *History*, 3:42–4; Assis, *Jews of Spain*, 9; Richard Gottheil, Meyer Kayserling, and Joseph Jacobs, "Spain," *Jewish Encyclopedia*. https://jewishencyclopedia.com/articles/13940-spain.
2. A few examples: Ṭāhā, *Muslim Conquest*, 63, 92, 95; Kennedy, *Great Arab Conquests*, 96–7.
3. Nahum M. Sarna, "Hebrew and Bible Studies in Medieval Spain," in Barnett, *Sephardi Heritage*, 324.
4. Assis, *Jews of Spain*, 11, 44–5; Sachar, *Farewell*, 4; Stillman, *Jews of Arab Lands*, 24; Baron, *Economic History*, 108.
5. Ashtor, *Jews of Moslem Spain*, 8.
6. Mac Con Iomaire, M., and P. Gallagher, "Irish Corned Beef: A Culinary History." *Journal of Culinary Science and Technology*, 9, no. 1 (2011). doi: 10.21427/d7b179.
7. Davidson, *Oxford*, 762–4.
8. Nasrallah, *Smorgasbords*, 425.
9. Ibid., 426–7.
10. Gitlitz, *Drizzle*, 29, 36; Piñer, *Jews, Food*, 117. These were later listed among other foods as signifiers of Jewish practice during the Inquisition.
11. Piñer, *Jews, Food*, 123.
12. Gitlitz, *Drizzle*, 180.
13. Roden, *Jewish Food*, 377.
14. Cooper, *Eat*, 104; Wexler, "'The Term 'Sabbath Food,'" 462.
15. Assis, *Jews of Spain*, 16.
16. Gil Marks, *Encyclopedia*, 250.
17. Assis, *Jews of Spain*, 19.
18. Ibid., 17.
19. Gottheil, "Spain."
20. Piñer, *Jews, Food*, 44.
21. Assis, *Jews of Spain*, 29.
22. Henry Charles Lea, "Ferrand Martinez and the Massacres of 1391," *American Historical Review*, 1, no. 2 (Jan. 1896): 209–19. http://www.jstor.com/stable/1833647; Gottheil, "Spain."
23. Assis, *Jews of Spain*, 30.
24. Gitlitz, *Drizzle*, 99.
25. Piñer, *Jews, Food*, 177.

26. Gil Marks, *Encyclopedia*, 1. Emphasis added.
27. Gitlitz, *Drizzle*, 3–4.
28. Schama, *Story of the Jews*, 43; Theodora Sutcliffe, "The Unlikely Sausage that Saved Lives," *BBC*, Sept. 12, 2017. http://www.bbc.com/travel/story/20170929-the-unlikely-sausage-that-saved-lives.
29. Davidson, *Oxford*, 200; Piñer, *Jews, Food*, 161.
30. Shabbat 38a
31. Roden, *Jewish Food*, 213. *See* Chapter 2 for more on *jachnun, kubaneh*, and *t'bit*.
32. Koerner, *Jewish Cuisine*, 58. Though such eggs are much more prevalent in Sephardi cooking, they do, at times, crop up in the Ashkenazi world, as this example indicates.
33. Gil Marks, *Encyclopedia*, 253.
34. Gitlitz, *Drizzle*, 74.
35. Sachar, *Farewell*, 72.
36. Ibid., 71.
37. Ibid., 51–2.
38. Abarbanel, *Commentary on I Kings*, Introduction.
39. Sachar, *Farewell*, 72.
40. Ibid., 169–70.
41. Ibid., 333–6. It has long been debated whether Columbus himself was a Crypto-Jew. Though much circumstantial evidence exists, and recent aggrandizing news stories notwithstanding, claiming that he was should be considered pure speculation.
42. Ibid., 336.
43. Scott Sessions, "Inquisition, The: The Inquisition in the New World," *Encyclopedia of Religion*, 2005. https://www.encyclopedia.com/environment/encyclopedias-almanacs-transcripts-and-maps/inquisition-inquisition-new-world.
44. Gitlitz, *Drizzle*, 169–70.
45. Crosby, *Columbian*, 170; Davidson, *Oxford*, 211.
46. Crosby, *Columbian*, 172.
47. Davidson, *Oxford*, 825–6; Crosby, *Columbian*, 183–4.
48. Jody Myers, "Food in the Modern Era," in Gross, *Feasting*, 112.

## *Chapter 4*: Le Cordon Stew

1. Obadiah 1:20; I Kings 17:9; Genesis 10:30; Jeremiah 51:27
2. Benjamin, *Itinerary*, 80.
3. Tori Avey, "Cholent," *Tori Avey*, May 8, 2023. https://toriavey.com/toris-kitchen/cholent.
4. Mordecai Kosover, "Gleanings from the Vocabulary of a 15th Century Yiddish Manuscript Collection of Customs," in Dawidowicz, *For Max Weinreich*, 356–7. The last two possibilities, unique to his research, still relate the name to the Shabbat stew. The rest align with other scholars' suggestions.
5. Cooper, *Eat*, 106.
6. Weinreich, *History*, 400.
7. Wexler, "Sabbath Food," 461.
8. Benbassa, *Jews of France*, 12.
9. Gil Marks, *Encyclopedia*, 127–9.
10. Cooper, *Eat* 103–4.
11. Davidson, *Oxford*, 332. The name itself derives from a Latin word for grain.
12. Bertholle, *French Cuisine*, 121–3; Gay, *Illustrated History*, 181.
13. Courtine, *Larousse*, 203–4.
14. Cooper, *Eat*, 107. Presumably, he was thinking of this when he wrote that *frumenty* was not the only ancestor of the Ashkenazi stew.

15. "Castelnaudary cassoulet," *Castelnaudary Tourist Office*. https://www.castelnaudary-tourisme.com/en/gastronomie/le-cassoulet-de-castelnaudary.
16. I am indebted to Dr. Wendy Pfeffer, Professor of French (Emerita) at University of Louisville, for her assistance in finding and translating these sources. They are the works of Pierre-Augustin Boissier de Sauvages (1756) and Maximin d'Hombres (1870).
17. Gil Marks, *Encyclopedia*, 128–9.
18. Nathan, *Quiches*, 196.
19. Gil Marks, *Encyclopedia*, 128. Unfortunately, he does not explain why he believes this.
20. Albala, *Beans*, 116.
21. Gil Marks, *Encyclopedia*, 128.
22. Benbassa, *Jews of France*, 4; Ivan G. Marcus, *Jewish Culture*, 151. Benbassa says fourth century, Marcus says fifth.
23. Benbassa, *Jews of France*, 4; Ivan G. Marcus, *Jewish Culture*, 150.
24. Grossman, *Chachmei tzarfat*, 555.
25. Ibid.
26. Rabinowitz, *Jewish Merchant Adventurers*, 11–14.
27. Ephraim Kanarfogel, email to author, Oct. 8, 2020.
28. Benbassa, *Jews of France*, 25, 49.
29. Ibid., 43, 64, 71.
30. Davidson, *Oxford*, 716.
31. Nathan, *Quiches*, 216; Gil Marks, *Encyclopedia*, 129–31. Additionally, both point out the history of Alsatian Jews' involvement in making charcuterie—preserved meats.
32. "Alsatian Baeckeoffe," *French Cooking Academy*. https://www.thefrenchcookingacademy.com/recipes/alsatian-baecheoffe.
33. "Community in France," *World Jewish Congress*. https://www.worldjewishcongress.org/en/about/communities/FR.
34. Ibid.

## *Chapter 5*: **Stuck in the Middle (of Europe) with Stew**

1. Eva Haverkamp, "Jews in Christian Europe: Ashkenaz in the Middle Ages," in Levenson, *Wiley-Blackwell*, 192–5.
2. Gropman, *German-Jewish*, 97–8.
3. Gay, *Jews of Germany*, 9.
4. Ibid., 12.
5. Ram, *Jews in Germany*; Gotthard Deutsch and S. Mannheimer, "Rindfleisch," *Jewish Encyclopedia*. https://jewishencyclopedia.com/articles/12765-rindfleisch.
6. Jacob R. Marcus, *Jew in the Medieval World*, 44.
7. Ibid., 47.
8. Gay, *Jews of Germany*, 28.
9. Ibid., 28.
10. Ibid., 70.
11. Marjorie Ingall, "Meet the Jewish Inventor of the Slow Cooker," *Tablet*, August 3, 2017. https://www.tabletmag.com/sections/food/articles/jewish-inventor-of-slow-cooker-irving-naxon.
12. Gil Marks, *Encyclopedia*, 338–41.
13. Ibid., 338.
14. Robinson, "Kugel," 15.
15. Gil Marks, *Encyclopedia*, 529–30.
16. Gay, *Jews of Germany*, 127.
17. Walter Grab, "The German Way of Jewish Emancipation," in Ram, *Jews in Germany*.

18. Marion Kaplan, "From the Comfort of Home to Exile: German Jews and Their Foodways," in Diner, *Global Jewish*, 244.
19. Translations taken from Michael A. Meyer, "The Imagined Jew: Heinrich Heine's 'Prinzessin Sabbath,'" in William, *History*, 209–22. doi: 10.2307/j.ctvzpv540.23.
20. Koerner, *Jewish Cuisine*, 58.
21. Belovari, "Viennese Cuisine."
22. Stessel, *Wine and Thorns*, 38–9.
23. Lederer, *Israelitische*, 9–10.
24. Koerner, *Jewish Cuisine*, 82.
25. Ibid., 340.
26. Jacob Katz, "Before the Holocaust," in Ram, *Jews in Hungary*.
27. McCagg, *Habsburg Jews*, 190.
28. Stessel, *Wine and Thorns*, 60.
29. Ibid., 91.
30. Koerner, *Jewish Cuisine*, 155.
31. Yaakov Schwartz, "Why Budapest is the (Treif) Cholent Capital of the World," *The Times of Israel*, Feb. 8, 2018. https://www.timesofisrael.com/why-budapest-is-the-treif-cholent-capital-of-the-world.
32. Katalin Franciska Rac, "How Shabbat Cholent Became a Secular Hungarian Favorite," in Gross, *Feasting*, 244.
33. Koerner, *Jewish Cuisine*, 154.
34. Rac, "Shabbat Cholent," 236
35. Koerner, *Jewish Cuisine*, 154.

## *Chapter 6*: A Geshmakte Yiddisher Shabbes Stew

1. Bar-Itzhak, *Jewish Poland*, 34.
2. Weinryb, *Jews of Poland*, 24.
3. Dembińska, *Food and Drink*, 44.
4. Davidson, *Oxford*, 523; Dembińska, *Food and Drink*, 107.
5. Dembińska, *Food and Drink*, 112.
6. William Woys Weaver, email to author, Jan. 17, 2022.
7. Dembińska, *Food and Drink*, 74 ff.
8. Weinryb, *Jews of Poland*, vii; Polonsky, *Poland and Russia*, 11.
9. Dembińska, *Food and Drink*, 10 ff.
10. Weinryb, *Jews of Poland*, 115; Polonsky, *Poland and Russia*, 13.
11. Weinryb, *Jews of Poland*, 116.
12. Polonsky, *Poland and Russia*, 14.
13. Josh Tapper, "Q&A: Glenn Dynner on Yankel's Tavern: Jews, Liquor, and Life in the Kingdom of Poland," *Moment*, March 10, 2014. https://momentmag.com/qa-glenn-dynner-yankels-tavern-jews-liquor-life-kingdom-poland.
14. Petrovsky-Shtern, *Golden Age*.
15. Holland, *Schmaltz*, 152.
16. Gil Marks, *Encyclopedia*, 483.
17. Ibid., 483.
18. Davidson, *Oxford*, 646.
19. Stutchkoff, *Der Oytser*, 222.
20. Levy, *First Jewish-American*, 58.
21. Steinberg, *Jewish Heartland*, 116.
22. Wirkowski, *Cooking*, 55–6. Of the last three, one has barley with the beans, one uses kasha (buckwheat groats), and one has no grain at all.
23. [Krasilnikova], *Алеф бейт*.

24. Meisels, *Shabbes*, 291.
25. Holland, *Schmaltz*, 155.
26. Engle, *Jewish Festival*, 36.
27. Wirkowski, *Cooking*, 54; Ansky, *Hamin*, 14. Wirkowski features a recipe for *kishke* inside a potato *kugel*, and Ansky writes of Israeli Hasidim who put it inside their special *Yerushalmi* [Jerusalem] *kugel*.
28. For examples see: Shosteck, *Lexicon*, 99–101; Lester, *Tavshilei hamin*, 50–1; Leonard, *Jewish Cookery*, 231.
29. Jacob Joseph, *Toldos Yaakov Yosef*, Parshat Naso, Se'if 236.
30. Lamm, *Religious Thought*, 323.
31. Louis Jacobs, "Eating as an Act of Worship in Hasidic Thought," in Stein, *Jewish Religious*, 158.
32. Shneur Zalman of Liady, *Tanya, Likkutei Amarim*, ch. 7, quoted in Lamm, *Religious Thought*, 329.
33. Zevi Elimelekh of Dinov, *Maamarei ha-Shabbatot* 10:5, quoted in Lamm, *Religious Thought*, 332.
34. Shalom of Koidonov, *Mishmeres Shalom*, 40b.
35. Bacon, *Atlas*, 110.
36. Daniel Pipes, "The Impact of World War I and the Russian Revolution on the World of Russian and East European Jewry," *YIVO Institute for Jewish Research*, June 16, 2014. https://youtu.be/ua7whC_Mafo.
37. Pomiane, *Jews of Poland*, xiv.
38. Ibid., 59.
39. Ibid., 42.
40. Ibid., 43.
41. Ibid., 42, 67, 115, 140, 147, 149, 202.
42. "Murder of the Jews of Poland," *Yad Vashem*. https://www.yadvashem.org/holocaust/about/fate-of-jews/poland.html#narrative info.
43. Nino Shaye Weiss, "Freud and his Cholent: The Austrian Origins of the Jewish Bean Stew," Jewish Viennese Food, January 31, 2019. https://jewishviennesefood.com/freud-and-his-cholent-the-austrian-origins-of-the-jewish-bean-stew-scholet.
44. Nino Shaye Weiss, interview by author, Dec. 23, 2020.
45. De Silva, *Memory's Kitchen*, xxix.
46. Sternberg, *Recipes*, 3–4.
47. De Silva, *Memory's Kitchen*.
48. Sternberg, *Recipes*, 183–4.
49. Margaret Littman, "Star chef Alon Shaya helped a Holocaust survivor recreate recipes from his prewar youth," *JTA*, March 3, 2021. https://www.jta.org/2021/03/03/food/star-chef-alon-shaya-helped-a-holocaust-survivor-re-create-recipes-from-his-prewar-youth.

## *Chapter 7*: **The Stew That Circled the Sea**

1. Beinart, *Atlas*, 85–6.
2. Chouraqui, *East and West*, 10–11.
3. Perez-Rubin, *Matamim*, 100. This example does not, in fact, contain potatoes, but others do.
4. Zeitoun, *250 Recettes*, 197.
5. Lewi, *La Cuisine*, 66.
6. Castiel, *I Thought*, 74.
7. Chouraqui, *East and West*, 57.
8. Ansky, *Hamin*, 136–8; Zana-Murat, *De Mére*, 222–3.

9. Bahloul, *La Culte*, 273–4.
10. Cohen-Levran, *Ya Amna*, 148.
11. Algeria: Clabrough, *Pied Noir*, 84. Libya: Perez-Rubin, *Matamim*, 120.
12. Choroquai, *East and West*, 90.
13. A few examples: Craig, *Grandma Elmaleh's*, 213; Danan, *La Nouvelle Cuisine*, 102–5.
14. Piñer, *Jews, Food*, 205.
15. Vitali-Norsa, *La Cucina*.
16. Pintar, *Rebelot*.
17. Stavroulakis, *Cookbook*, 24–5.
18. Fleming, *Greece*, 6–8.
19. Camerini, *Ricette*, 33–7.
20. Goldstein, *Cucina Ebraica*, 56.
21. Davidson, *Oxford*, 169.
22. Caroline Eden, "The magic and mystery of Turkey's chestnuts," *Financial Times*, November 26, 2021. https://www.ft.com/content/118b31e6-ce91-43c6-97e8-c063f0044f36.
23. "Fresh/Dried Chestnuts," OEC. https://oec.world/en/profile/hs/freshdried-chestnuts.
24. Davidson, *Oxford*, 169.
25. Elazar, *Other Jews*, 102.
26. Nimrod Etsion-Koren, "The Livornese Jews in Tunis: Experiences of the Diasporic Community in the Unification of Italy and Beyond, 1830s–1939," *Journal of Education, Society and Behavioural Science* 26, no. 2 (2018): 1–10.
27. Choroquai, *East and West*, 92–5.
28. Riley, *Sufferings*.
29. Davidson, *Oxford*, 188–9.

## *Chapter 8*: The Stew that Grew With the World of the Jew

1. Nathans, *Beyond the Pale*, 25.
2. Ibid., 3.
3. Baron, *The Russian Jew*, 13.
4. Ibid., 14.
5. "Modern Jewish History: The Pale of Settlement," *Jewish Virtual Library*. https://www.jewishvirtuallibrary.org/the-pale-of-settlement.
6. Baron, *The Russian Jew*, 40.
7. Weintraub, *Поваренная*, 176–7.
8. Shternshis, *Soviet and Kosher*, 153–4.
9. Nakhimovsky, "You Are," 63–77.
10. Zvi Gitelman, "Thinking about Being Jewish in Russia and Ukraine," in Gitelman, *Jewish Life*, 49.
11. Veidlinger, *Shadow*, xiv, 134 ff; Anna Shternshis, email to author, July 26, 2023.
12. Rosa Zaks Feldman, "Cholent—The Twenty-Four-Hour Dish," in Sogolow, *Memories*, 192.
13. Veidlinger, *Shadow*; and Feldman, "Cholent."
14. Veidlinger, *Shadow* (italics added).
15. Nakhimovsky, "You Are," 67.
16. Shternshis, *Soviet and Kosher*, 1.
17. Gennady Estraikh, "Soviet Jewish Foodways: Transformation through Detabooization," in Diner, *Global*, 129.
18. Anna Shternshis, "Salo on Challah: Soviet Jews' Experience of Food in the 1920s–1950s," in Helman, *Jews*, 14, 18.
19. Ibid., 20.

20. Nakhimovsky, "You Are," 72–3.
21. Project Kesher, *A Woman's Place*, 37, 48.
22. Grace Kirschenbaum, "This Cookbook Was Banned in Russia," *Los Angeles Times*, Sept. 13, 1990. https://www.latimes.com/archives/la-xpm-1990-09-13-fo-255-story.html.
23. [Krasilnikova], *Aleph-Bet*.
24. [Krasilnikova], *Алеф бейт*.
25. [Montefiore], *Jewish Manual*, 55.
26. Atrutel, *Easy and Economical*, 57.
27. Jackson, *Jewish*, 38.
28. Spieler, *Best-Ever*, 19; Spitzer, *Fress*, 94.
29. Beinart-Smollan, "Community cookbooks," 86.
30. Ibid., 89–91.
31. Gavin Beinart-Smollan, email to author, January 1, 2024.
32. Beinart-Smollan, "Community cookbooks," 101.
33. Braude, *Kosher Cuisine*, 117–18.
34. Atrutel, *Easy and Economical*, 7.
35. Helen Goldrein, "Easy Vegan Cholent – With a British Twist!" *Family Friends Food*. https://family-friends-food.com/easy-vegetarian-cholent.
36. Hofman, *Everyday Cooking*, 132.
37. *Kosher Cuisine*, 250; Lurie, *Cooking*, 82; Sharon Lurie, email to author, January 7, 2024.
38. Koval, *Jewish Cooking*, 73–7.
39. "Sheep and lamb processing: assessment," Scottish Government, November 14, 2019. https://www.gov.scot/publications/assessment-opportunities-retain-increase-sheep-lamb-processing-scotland/pages/4.
40. "Lamb Consumption by Country 2024," *World Population Review*, 2024. https://worldpopulation review.com/country-rankings/lamb-consumption-by-country.
41. Sam Lewis, "New Zealand Cholent Recipe." Author is proprietor of "The Kosher Deli." Recipe sent by Gavin Beinart-Smollan, email to author, January 7, 2024.
42. Beker, *Jewish Communities*, 54–79.
43. Arbell, *Jewish Nation*, 13–18.
44. Adriana Brodsky, "The Battle Against Guefilte Fish: Asserting Sephardi Culinary Repertoires among Argentine Jews in the Second Half of the Twentieth Century," in Diner, *Global*, 181–206.
45. Lessa, *Cozinha Judaica*, 85, 236.
46. "Beef Consumption by Country 2024," *World Population Review*, 2024. https://worldpopulation review.com/country-rankings/beef-consumption-by-country.
47. Esther Weyl, interview by author, December, 6, 2023.
48. Bill Hinchberger, "Brazil's national dish goes kosher," *Jewish Telegraphic Agency*, August 11, 2005. https://www.jta.org/2005/08/11/lifestyle/brazils-national-dish-goes-kosher.
49. Klein, *Kosher Feijoada*, 87–92.
50. *Nuestras Mejores*, 171. The corn cobs are broken in half before they are put into the pot.
51. Andrés Gonzalez, interview by author, February 13, 2023.
52. "Community in Suriname," World Jewish Congress. https://www.worldjewishcongress.org/en/about/communities/SR.
53. Sarna, *American Judaism*, 7–8.
54. Vaneker, "Cooking Pom."
55. Ibid.
56. Pati Jinich, interview by author, January 15, 2024.
57. Paulette Kershenovic Schuster, "A Tapestry of Tastes: Jewish Women of Syrian Descent and Their Cooking in Mexico and Israel," in Helman, *Jews*, 166.

58. Mel Romero, "This Oaxacan Chocolate Stuffed Challah is the Ultimate Taste of My Family's Jewish Journey," *The Nosher*, November 22, 2022. https://www.myjewishlearning.com/the-nosher/this-oaxacan-chocolate-stuffed-challah-recipe-is-the-ultimate-taste-of-my-familys-jewish-journey/.
59. Stavans, *Sabor*, 80–1.
60. Jinich, interview. Jinich now lives in the United States.
61. Beker, *Jewish Communities*, 68.
62. Ibid., 69.
63. Zenner, *Global Community*, 156.
64. Ibid., 27–28.
65. Persoff, *Jews in Syria*; Zenner, *Global Community*.
66. Joel Haber, post on *Ochel rak suri levanoni neto* [Only Syrian and Lebanese Food, Period], *Facebook*, September 10, 2019. https://www.facebook.com/groups/216400638720074/posts/928560050837459.
67. Schuster, "Tapestry," 175, fn 35.
68. *El Sabor*, 44–5.
69. Stefanie Zakay, email to author, August 5, 2020.
70. Gindi, *Mishulchana*, 181.
71. Dweck, *Aromas*, 173, 192, 232.
72. Zenner, *Global Community*, 138.
73. Ibid., 136–7.
74. Ibid., 107–19.
75. Susana Brauner and Rayen Torres, "Orthodoxy and Disaffiliation among Argentine Jews of Syrian Origin in Buenos Aires, from the 60s until today," *Hamsa*, 8 (2022). https://doi.org/10.4000/hamsa.2824.
76. Spengler, *Fruit*, 54.
77. Ibid., 8, 42.
78. Mikdash-Shamilov, *Mountain Jews*, 8.
79. Ibid., 18, 20, 65.
80. Sarah (orig. from Quba, Azerbaijan), interview by author, December 5, 2023.
81. *Recipes of Mountain*, 40–3.
82. Lester, *Tavshilei Hamin*, 80–1. No one else I spoke to recognized the name *boro*, nor could they guess its meaning.
83. Alona Eisenberg, email to author, October 11, 2020.
84. "Kalia," *Georgia Travel*. https://georgia.travel/kalia.
85. Beker, *Jewish Communities*, 186.
86. Davidson, *Oxford*, 624.
87. Kimyagarov, *Classic Central Asian*, 126.
88. Cordell, *Miriam's*, 80.
89. Kort, *Hamitbach*, 50–1; Gil Marks, *Encyclopedia*, 434–5.
90. Davidson, *Oxford*, 681–2.
91. Ibid., 699.
92. David, *Bene Appétit*, 6; Sassoon, *Spice*, 3.
93. Sassoon, *Spice*, 6.
94. Ibid., 101.
95. Ibid., 102.
96. Golda Rohekar, comment on Joel Haber, "My next Jewish Food history primer," December 25, 2023, *Facebook*. https://www.facebook.com/FunJoel/posts/pfbid0Ttzq1wiAXU3vLse1XQTd9BGGA CQbAe 4ZMgePNS4UKocktsTkLLH8 NvdmeYwHMMjql.

97. Zenbeshe Or-Neshama Pakado, et al., comments on Joel Haber, "Shalom uvracha. Ba'avar sha'alti kan . . . [Hello and greetings. In the past I asked here . . .]," December 23, 2023, *Facebook*. https://www.facebook.com/groups/Ethiopiankitchen/posts/2888281044646061.
98. David, *Bene Appétit*, 100, 105; Copeland Marks, *Varied Kitchens*, 56–7; Hyman, *Indian-Jewish*, 96.
99. Anita Elias, interview by Joel Haber, August 31, 2020.
100. David, *Bene Appétit*, 116.
101. Marks, Copeland, *Varied Kitchens*, 56–7.
102. Ibid., 58.

### *Chapter 9*: **The Stew in (Red), White, and Blue**

1. Deuteronomy 30:1–5.
2. Cyrus Adler and L. Hühner, "Levy, Asser (Asser Levy van Swellem)," *Jewish Encyclopedia*. https://www.jewishencyclopedia.com/articles/9876-levy-asser-asser-levy-van-swellem.
3. Nathan, *Jewish Cooking*, 10.
4. D. M. Kinsman, "Meat Preparation and Preservation in Colonial America," *American Meat Science Association*, 1976. https://meatscience.org/docs/default-source/publications-resources/rmc/1976/meat-preparation-and-preservation-in-colonial-america.pdf.
5. Nathan, *Jewish Cooking*, 11.
6. Hasia R. Diner, "German Immigrant Period in the United States," *Shalvi/Hyman*. https://jwa.org/encyclopedia/article/german-immigrant-period-in-united-states.
7. Levy, *First Jewish-American*, 58.
8. Nathan, *Jewish Cooking*, 163.
9. Amchanitski, *Lehr-buch*.
10. Greenbaum, *International Jewish*, 14.
11. Diner, *Hungering*, 180 ff.
12. Specht, *Red Meat*.
13. Levy, *First Jewish-American*, 58. Italics added.
14. Rachel B. Gross, "Jews, Schmaltz, and Crisco in the Age of Industrial Food," in Gross, *Feasting*, 189–211.
15. Barbara, "In the opposite direction . . ." April 8, 2015, comment on Penguin, "Spin-off – Bubbies' recipe expressions," *Imamother*, April 8, 2015. https://www.imamother.com/forum/viewtopic.php?t= 268206#3284805.
16. Sarah Lieber, "What Foods These Morsels Be: Canned Soups, Rice, Dried Peas Handy if You Hate to Brave Weather," *The Indiana Jewish Post and Opinion*, Dec. 14, 1956.
17. Sarna, *American Judaism*, 274–7.
18. *Spice and Spirit*, 207–10.
19. Steve Kay, interview by author, May 29, 2023.
20. Koenig, *Jewish Cookbook*.
21. Bahat, *Twenty Centuries*.
22. Dweck, *Aromas*, 192.
23. Roden, *Jewish Food*, 308–9.
24. Meyer, *Eich levashel*.
25. Ofra Tene, "'The New Immigrant Must Not Only Learn, He Must Also Forget': The Making of Eretz Israeli Ashkenazi Cuisine," in Hellman, *Jews*, 50.
26. Cornfeld, *Keitzad*.
27. Ibid., 26–9.

28. Orit Rozin, "Austerity Tel-Aviv: Everyday Life, Supervision, Compliance, and Respectability," in Azaryahu, *Tel-Aviv*, 170.
29. Cornfeld, *Mah Evashel.*
30. Ibid., 8.
31. Ibid., 43.
32. Ibid., 53.
33. Orit Rozin, "Craving Meat during Israel's Austerity Period, 1947–1953," in Hellman, *Jews*, 79.
34. Segev, *1949*, 308.
35. Liora Gvion, "Hummus – couscous – sushi: ochel v'etniut b'chevrah haYisraelit" [Hummus, couscous, sushi: food and ethnicity in Israeli society], in Kleinberg, *Beten m'leah*, 48.
36. Ansky, *Hamin*, 122.
37. Bar-David, *Israeli*, v.
38. Ibid., 130–4, 153, 166. Though her *t'bit* is only called "Iraqi Hamim," it is described using the old-school method of removing the chicken from its skin before restuffing it with the rice mixture, leaving no doubt as to what the dish is.
39. Ibid., 107.
40. Sirkis, *Meihamitbach.*
41. Sirkis, *Popular Food.*
42. Gur, *New Israeli.*
43. Levine, *Simply Israel.*
44. Gur, *Soul Food*, 146–7.
45. Benor, *Becoming Frum*, 19, 61–2.

## *Chapter 10*: What's New with the Shabbat Stew?

1. Diner, *Hungering*, 200.
2. *Hebrew Standard*, December 24, 1920.
3. *Hebrew Standard*, December 19, 1919.
4. *Sentinel*, July 7, 1938; *Der Tog*, December 24, 1944 (English section); *Forverts*, November, 24, 1945; *Sydney Jewish News*, August 22, 1952; Claire R. Aronson, "Key to New York," *Indiana Jewish Post and Opinion*, December 7, 1956.
5. "Covenant Club members will Take Part in Gala Purim Masquerade Ball," *Sentinel* March 3, 1955.
6. "By The Way . . .," *Australian Jewish Herald*, Oct. 14, 1955.
7. *B'nai Brith Messenger*, October 25, 1957.
8. JLNJ Staff, "Gas Grub," *Jewish Link*, October 21, 2021. https://jewishlink.news/gas-grub.
9. Abigail Klein Leichman, "Israel's 10 Best Gas-Station Eateries," *Israel 21c*, February 17, 2016. https://www.israel21c.org/israels-10-best-gas-station-eateries.
10. Noam Ler, "B'ikvot tziutz . . ." [Following a tweet . . .] *Twitter*, August 19, 2022. https://twitter.com/Mevaker_chunt/status/1560373079850852356.
11. Shilo Fried, "Chareidim kitzoni'im nisu lifrotz l'misada b'Yerushalayim, shemocheret hamin acharei 23:00" [Ultra-Orthodox extremists try to shut down a restaurant in Jerusalem that sells hamin after 11:00 p.m.], *Ynet*, June 21, 2024. https://www.ynet.co.il/judaism/article/h1uom7mlc.
12. From a public notice, known as a *pashkevil.*
13. Shira Hanau, "'Sabbath for $400': Cholent stumps '*Jeopardy!*' contestants in question about Shabbat restrictions," *Jewish Telegraphic Agency*, October 14, 2021. https://www.jta.org/2021/10/14/culture/sabbath-for-400-chulent-stumps-jeopardy-contestants-in-question-about-shabbat-restrictions.

14. Lior Zaltzman, "Beloved Children's Musician Joanie Leeds Has a New Song About Cholent," *Kveller*, September 27, 2023. https://www.kveller.com/beloved-childrens-musician-joanie-leeds-has-a-new-song-about-cholent.
15. Cholent the Game. http://www.cholentthegame.com.
16. Liel Leibovitz, "Israel's First-Ever Zombie Movie Kills It With Cholent Joke," *Tablet*, February 21, 2014. https://www.tabletmag.com/sections/news/articles/israels-first-ever-zombie-movie-kills-it-with-cholent-joke.
17. Boyarin, "Cholent," 82–91.
18. Pomerantz, *Cholent Again*, 11–12.
19. Jonathan Webber, interview by author, May 17, 2023.
20. Nahma Sandrow, "The Jewish Traveler: Oxford," *Hadassah Magazine*, April 2005. https://www. hadassahmagazine.org/2005/04/09/jewish-traveler-oxford.
21. Sax, *Save the Deli*, 260.
22. https://czulent.pl.
23. Eliana Rudee, "'Cholent Festival' brings Jewish culture to Hungary via food, music, traditions," September 12, 2021. https://www.jns.org/cholent-festival-brings-jewish-culture-to-hungary-via-food-music-traditions.
24. https://www.budapest.com/things_to_do/budapest_events/gastronomy/cholent_festival.en.html.
25. Jessica Steinberg, "It's a melting pot of cholent, hamin and tbit at Tel Aviv bean fest," *Times of Israel*, December 16, 2019. https://www.timesofisrael.com/its-a-melting-pot-of-cholent-hamin-and-tbit-at-tel-aviv-bean-fest.
26. Hernesto Galdamez, "Cooking, tasting and judging the chulent at Brandeis in Lawrence," *LIHerald*, January 23, 2023. https://www.liherald.com/fivetowns/stories/cooking-tasting-and-judging-the-chulent-at-brandeis,159880.
27. "Bnei Brak to distribute cholent at Thursday night vaccine drive," *Times of Israel*, February 11, 2021. https://www.timesofisrael.com/bnei-brak-to-distribute-cholent-at-thursday-night-vaccine-drive; Haviv Rettig Gur, "To encourage vaccination, Israeli cities serve free food with a side of comfort," *Times of Israel*, February 19, 2021. https://www.timesofisrael.com/to-encourage-vaccination-cities-serve-up-free-food-with-a-side-of-comfort.
28. Yaakov Farber and Yossi Reiner, "Hanitzolim meshachzerim et hanes bamakom hapigua: 'Hamechabel nechaveh meihachulent'" [The Survivors Recreate the Miracle at the Scene of the Attack: 'The Terrorist was Burned by the *Chulent*'], *B'Chadrei Chareidim*, May 8, 2022. https://www.bhol.co.il/news/1382435.
29. Joel Haber, "Chulent/Hamin: The Dish that Embodies Jewish Culture," *18 Jewish Foods* (podcast), March 27, 2024, https://www.tasteofjew.com/ep3-chulent-hamin.
30. Samuel Gorr, "Operation X: The Fate of the Shabbos Cholent," *Australian Jewish Herald*, October 4, 1957.
31. Devorah Klein Lev-Tov, "Saved by Cholent," *Tablet*, January 30, 2013. https://www.tabletmag.com/sections/food/articles/saved-by-cholent.
32. Lewando, *Vilna Vegetarian*.
33. Sussman, *Shabbat*, 294.
34. Shoshana Isaacson, "A Soulful Shabbat," *Unorthoboxed Magazine*, Feb 1, 2022. https://unorthoboxed.com/2022/02/01/a-soulful-shabbat. Accessed May 14, 2023.
35. MaNishtana [Shais Rishon], "Charoset," in Newhouse, *100 Most Jewish*, 64.
36. Twitty, *Koshersoul*, 272.
37. Rachel Figueroa de Zimmerman, "Sofrito," in Newhouse, *100 Most Jewish*, 245.
38. Chaya Rus Alexandra Kong-Hazan, "My favorite (yearly?) Cantonese brisket," "Israeli Foodies" group, *Facebook*, January 18, 2022. https://www.facebook.com/groups/israelifoodies/posts/3035066506760740/.

39. Yehuda Sichel, "Finding Meaning in a Cholent Potpie," *Jewish Food Society*, December 14, 2018. https://www.jewishfoodsociety.org/stories/finding-meaning-in-a-cholent-potpie.
40. Erica Chernofsky, "Here's the Scoop," *Jerusalem Post*, November 17, 2005. https://www.jpost.com/jewish-world/jewish-features/heres-the-scoop.
41. Rob Eshman, "Instant Pot Cholent v. Le Creuset Cholent," *Foodaism*, March 2, 2018. http://foodaism.com/instant-pot-cholent-v-le-creuset-cholent.
42. Examples include https://www.kosher.com/recipe/parve-cholent-in-the-instant-pot-15304 and https://www.corriecooks.com/instant-pot-cholent.
43. One person asked in an online forum in 2020: https://community.anovaculinary.com/t/cholent/27648.
44. Mordechai Frankel, "Sous-vide Cookers on Shabbos," *Star-K*. https://www.star-k.org/articles/kashrus-kurrents/6469/sous-vide-cookers-on-shabbos.
45. Liora Gvion, "Two Narratives of Israeli Food: 'Jewish' versus 'Ethnic,'" in Hellman, *Jews*, 134.
46. Leviticus 11:16.
47. "Recipe for Friendship," *Australian Jewish News*, November 5, 1982.
48. Pintel-Ginsberg, *The Angel*, 160–4.

# Bibliography


Abdennour, Samia. *Egyptian Cooking and Other Middle Eastern Recipes, New and Revised Edition*. Cairo: American University in Cairo, 2005.

Albala, Ken. *Beans: A History*. Oxford: Berg, 2007.

Amchanitski, Hinda. *Lehr-buch vi azoy tsu kuken un baken* [Manual for cooking and baking]. New York: Avraham Farneburg, 1901.

Ansky, Sherry. *Hamin* [Tscholent]. Jerusalem: Keter, 2008.

Arbell, Mordechai. *The Jewish Nation of the Caribbean: The Spanish-Portuguese Jewish Settlements in the Caribbean and the Guianas*. Jerusalem: Gefen, 2002.

Ashtor, Eliyahu. *The Jews of Moslem Spain*, Vol. 2. trans. Aaron Klein and Jenny Machlowitz Klein. Philadelphia: Jewish Publication Society of America, 1979.

Assis, Yom Tov. *The Jews of Spain: From Settlement to Expulsion*. Jerusalem: The Rothberg School for Overseas Students and Dor Hemshech, 1988.

Atrutel, J. (Estella). *An Easy and Economical Book of Jewish Cookery Upon Strictly Orthodox Principles*. London: Alabaster & Passmore, 1874.

Azaryahu, Maoz and S. Ilan Troen, eds. *Tel-Aviv, The First Century: Visions, Designs, Actualities*. Bloomington, IN: Indiana University, 2012.

Azuelos, Evelyne. *La Table Juive Marocaine* [The Moroccan Jewish Table]. Bordeaux: Aviva, 1996.

Bacon, Josephine. *The Illustrated Atlas of Jewish Civilization: 3000 Years of History*. London: André Deutsch, 1990.

Bacri, Mélanie. *100 Recettes de Cuisine Familiale Juive d'Algerie* [100 recipes of the familial cuisine of the Jews of Algeria]. Paris: Grancher, 2001.

Bahat, Dan, ed. *Twenty Centuries of Jewish Life in the Holy Land: The Forgotten Centuries, Second Edition*. Jerusalem: The Israel Economist, 1976.

Bahloul, Joëlle. *La Culte de la Table Dressée: Rites et Traditions de la Table Juive Algérienne* [The cult of the set table: Rites and traditions of the Algerian Jewish table]. Paris: A.-M. Métailié, 1983.

Bar-David, Molly Lyons. *The Israeli Cook Book*. New York: Crown, 1964.

Bar-Itzhak, Haya. *Jewish Poland—Legends of Origin: Ethnopoetics and Legendary Chronicles*. Detroit: Wayne State University, 2001.

Barnett, R. D., ed. *The Sephardi Heritage: Essays on the history and cultural contribution of the Jews of Spain and Portugal*, Vol. 1. New York: Ktav, 1971.

Baron, Salo Wittmayer. *The Jewish Community: Its History and Structure to the American Revolution*, Vol. 1. Philadelphia: Jewish Publication Society of America, 1942.

———. *The Russian Jew Under Tsars and Soviets*. New York: Macmillan, 1976. (Reprinted New York: Schocken, 1987.)

———, Arcadius Kahan, et al. *Economic History of the Jews*. Nachum Gross, ed. New York: Schocken, 1975.

Beattie, May H., ed. *Recipes from Baghdad*. Baghdad: Iraqi Red Crescent Society (Women's Branch), 1961.

Beinart, Haim. *Atlas of Medieval Jewish History*. Jerusalem: Carta, 1992.
Beinart-Smollan, Gavin. "Community cookbooks: a new lens on postwar South African Jewish culture." *Jewish Historical Studies*, 55: no. 1 (2023).
Beker, Avi, ed. *Jewish Communities of the World*. Jerusalem: Institute of the World Jewish Congress, 1996.
Belovari, Susanne. "The Viennese Cuisine before Hitler—'One Cuisine in the Use of Two Nations." *The Sophie Coe Prize*, 2020. https://sophiecoeprize.files.wordpress.com/2020/07/belovari-the-viennese-cuisine-before-hitler-e28093-e28098one-cuisine-in-the-use-of-two-nationse28099.pdf.
Ben Simhon, Rina. *Ochel Morokai* [Moroccan Cooking]. Tel Aviv: Kineret, 1982.
Benbassa, Esther. *The Jews of France: A History from Antiquity to the Present*. M.B. DeBevoise, trans. Princeton: Princeton University, 1999.
Benedetti, Ines de. *Poesia nascosta: le ricette della cucina tradizionale ebraica italiana* [Hidden poetry: recipes from traditional Italian Jewish cuisine]. Palermo: Edizioni La Zisa, 2013.
Benjamin of Tudela. *The Itinerary of Benjamin of Tudela*. Marcus Nathan Adler, trans. London, 1907. (Reprinted New York: Philipp Feldheim, n.d.) https://www.gutenberg.org/files/14981/14981-h/14981-h.htm.
Benor, Sarah Bunin. *Becoming Frum: How Newcomers Learn the Language and Culture of Orthodox Judaism*. New Brunswick, NJ: Rutgers University, 2012.
Bertholle, Louisette. *French Cuisine for All*. New York: Doubleday, 1980.
Boyarin, Jonah Sampson. "Cholent: Post-Hasidic Explorations and Jewish Modernities," unpublished undergraduate thesis. Middletown, CT: Wesleyan University, 2008.
Braude, Dulcie. *Kosher Cuisine with Dulcie Braude*. Sandton, SA: Dulcie Braude, 2001.
Brauer, Erich. *The Jews of Kurdistan*. Raphael Patai, ed. Detroit: Wayne State Univ., 1993.

Camerini, Miriam. *Ricette e precetti* [Recipes and precepts], Florence: Giuntina, 2019.
Castiel, Mercedes. *I Thought I'd Never Taste This Again: Cuisine of Spanish Morocco, Second Edition*. New York: Joshua Morgan, 2021.
Chouraqui, André N. *Between East and West: A History of the Jews of North Africa*. Michael M. Bernet, trans. Philadelphia: Jewish Publication Society of America, 1968.
Clabrough, Chantal. *A Pied Noir Cookbook: French Sephardic Cuisine from Algeria*. New York: Hippocrene, 2005.
Cohen-Levran, Shoshana. *Ya Amna: From Djerba to Israel: A Tunisian Family Kitchen*. Tel Aviv-Yafo: LunchBox, 2020.
Cooper, John. *Eat and Be Satisfied: A Social History of Jewish Food*. Northvale, NJ: Jason Aronson, 1993.
Cordell, Lilian. *Miriam's Table*. Peterborough, England: FastPrint, 2017.
Cornfeld, Lilian. *Keitzad mevashlim bimei milchama?* [How to cook in the time of war]. Tel Aviv: Olam HaIsha, 1942.
——. *Mah evashel b'manot tzena?* [What to cook with austerity rations]. Tel Aviv: Hotza'at HaMechaberet, 1949.
Coulthard, Sally. *Fowl Play: A History of the Chicken from Dinosaur to Dinner Plate*. London: Head of Zeus, 2022.
Counihan, Carole, Penny Van Esterik, Alice Julier, eds. *Food and Culture: A Reader*, 4th edn. New York: Routledge, 2017.
Courtine, Robert J., ed, *Larousse Gastronomique*. New York: E.P. Dutton, 1984.
Craig, Lisa Elmaleh. *Grandma Elmaleh's Moroccan Cookbook*. London: Hesperus, 2012.
Crosby, Alfred W. *The Columbian Exchange: Biological and Cultural Consequences of 1492*. Westport, CT: Greenwood Press, 1972.

Danan, Simy and Jacques Denarnaud. *La Nouvelle Cuisine Judéo-Marocaine* [New Judeo-Moroccan Cuisine]. Paris: ACR, 1994.
David, Esther. *Bene Appétit: The Cuisine of Indian Jews*. Noida, India: HarperCollins, 2021.
Davidson, Alan. *The Oxford Companion to Food*, 3rd edn. Tom Jaine, ed. Oxford: Oxford University, 2014.
Dawidowicz, Lucy, et al., organizing committee. *For Max Weinreich on his Seventieth Birthday, Studies in Jewish Languages, Literature and Society*. The Hague: Mouton, 1964.
De Silva, Cara, ed. *In Memory's Kitchen: A Legacy from the Women of Terezín*. Bianca Steiner Brown, trans. Northvale, NJ: Jason Aronson, 1996.
Dembińska, Maria. *Food and Drink in Medieval Poland: Rediscovering a Cuisine of the Past*. Magdalena Thomas, trans., revised and adapted by William Woys Weaver. Philadelphia: University of Pennsylvania, 1999.
Diner, Hasia R. *Hungering for America: Italian, Irish, & Jewish Foodways in the Age of Migration*. Cambridge, MA: Harvard University, 2001.
———. & Simone Cinotto, eds. *Global Jewish Foodways: A History*. Lincoln: University of Nebraska, 2018.
Dohrmann, Natalie B. and David Stern, eds. *Jewish Biblical and Cultural Exchange: Comparative Exegesis in Context*. Philadelphia: University of Pennsylvania, 2008.
Dweck, Poopa. *Aromas of Aleppo: The Legendary Cuisine of Syrian Jews*. New York: Ecco, 2007.

Elazar, Daniel J. *The Other Jews: The Sephardim Today*. New York: Basic, 1989.
*Encyclopedia of Religion, Encyclopedia.com*, 2005. https://www.encyclopedia.com.
Engle, Fannie and Gertrude Blair. *The Jewish Festival Cookbook: According to the Dietary Laws*. New York: David McKay, 1954.

Fleming, K. E. *Greece: A Jewish History*. Princeton: Princeton University, 2008.

Gay, Christian. *An Illustrated History of French Cuisine: From Charlemagne to Charles de Gaulle*. Elisabeth Abbott, trans. New York: Orion, 1962
Gay, Ruth. *The Jews of Germany: A Historical Portrait*. New Haven, CT: Yale University Press, 1992.
Gil, Moshe. *Jews in Islamic Countries in the Middle Ages*. David Strassler, trans. Leiden, Netherlands: Brill, 2014.
Gindi, Tova. *Mishulchana shel Esther hamalka: minhagim umatamim mehamitbach hachalabi hamasorti* [From Queen Esther's table: customs and flavors from the traditional Aleppan kitchen]. Israel, 2014.
Gitelman, Zvi with Musya Glants and Marshall I. Goldman, eds. *Jewish Life After the USSR*. Bloomington, IN: Indiana University, 2003.
Gitlitz, David M. and Linda Kay Davidson. *A Drizzle of Honey: The Lives and Recipes of Spain's Secret Jews*. New York: St. Martin's Griffin, 1999.
Goitein, S. D. *A Mediterranean Society: The Jewish Communities of the Arab World as Portrayed in the Documents of the Cairo Geniza*, Vol. IV: *Daily Life*. Berkeley, CA: University of California, 1983.
———. *A Mediterranean Society: An Abridgment in One Volume*. Jacob Lassner, ed. Berkeley, CA: University of California, 1999.
Goldstein, Joyce. *Cucina Ebraica: Flavors of the Italian Jewish Kitchen*. San Francisco: Chronicle, 1998.
Graetz, Heinrich. *History of the Jews*. Philadelphia: Jewish Publication Society of America, 1894
Greenbaum, Florence Kreisler. *The International Jewish Cookbook*. New York: Bloch, 1918.

Greenspoon, Leonard J., Ronald A. Simkins, and Gerald Shapiro, eds. *Food and Judaism: A Special Issue of Studies in Jewish Civilization*, Vol. 15. Omaha: Creighton University, 2005.

Gropman, Gabrielle Rossmer and Sonya Gropman. *The German-Jewish Cookbook: Recipes & History of a Cuisine*. Waltham, MA: Brandeis University, 2017.

Gross, Aaron S., Jody Myers, and Jordan D. Rosenblum, eds. *Feasting and Fasting: The History and Ethics of Jewish Food*. New York: New York University, 2019.

Grossman, Avraham. *Chachmei tzarfat harishonim: koroteihem, darkam b'hanhagat hatzibur, yetziratam haruchanit* [Early French sages: their lives, methods of communal leadership, religious writings]. Jerusalem: Magnes, Hebrew University, 1995.

Guetta, Benedetta Jasmine. *Cooking alla Giudia*. New York: Artisan, 2022.

Gur, Janna. *The Book of New Israeli Food: A Culinary Journey*. Tel Aviv: Al Hashulchan Gastronomic, 2007.

———, with Nirit Yadin and Ruth Oliver. *Jewish Soul Food: From Minsk to Marrakesh*. Tel Aviv: Al Hashulchan Gastronomic, 2014.

Haber, Joel. *The Taste of Jewish Culture*. https://www.tasteofjew.com.

Hekmat, Forough-es-Saltaneh. *The Art of Persian Cooking*. Garden City, NY: Doubleday, 1961.

Helman, Anat, ed. *Jews and Their Foodways: Studies in Contemporary Jewry, an Annual, XXVIII*. Oxford: Oxford University Press, 2015.

Hess, O. and A., *Viennese Cooking*, ed. and trans. Carla Schlesinger (New York: Crown, 1952).

Hirschberg, H. Z. (J. W.). *A History of the Jews in North Africa*, Vol. 1: *Antiquity to the Sixteenth Century*. Leiden, Netherlands: E. J. Brill, 1974.

Hofman, Ethel G. *Everyday Cooking for the Jewish Home: More than 350 Delectable Recipes*. New York: John Boswell and King Hill, 1997.

Holland, Shmil. *Schmaltz*. Moshav Ben-Shemen, Israel: Toad/Modan, 2011.

Hyman, Mavis. *Indian-Jewish Cooking*. London: Hyman, 1992.

Jackson, Judy. *Jewish: Traditional Recipes from a Rich Culinary Heritage*. London: Lorenz, 1998/1999.

Jacob Joseph of Polonne. *Toldos Yaakov Yosef*, Eichen edition. Jerusalem, 2011. Creative commons license from National Library of Israel. https://www.sefaria.org.il/Toldot_Yaakov_Yosef%2C_Nasso.236?vhe=Eichen_edition._Jerusalem,_2011&lang=bi.

Jaffin, Leone. *150 Recettes et Mille et un Souvenirs d'Une Juive d'Algerie* [150 recipes and a thousand-and-one memories of a Jewish woman from Algeria]. [Paris]: Encre, 1987.

*Jewish Encyclopedia* (1901–1906). https://www.jewishencyclopedia.com.

*Jewish Virtual Library: A Project of AICE*. https://www.jewishvirtuallibrary.org.

Jospe, Raphael and Stanley M. Wagner, eds. *Great Schisms in Jewish History*. New York: Ktav, 1981.

Kanarfogel, Ephraim and Moshe Sokolow, eds. *Between Rashi and Maimonides: Themes in Medieval Jewish Thought, Literature and Exegesis*. New York: Michael Scharf Publication Trust of Yeshiva University, 2010.

Keinan, Rachel. *Habishul hamorokai shel ima* [Mother's Moroccan Cooking]. Kiryat Gat, Israel: Korim, 2008.

Kennedy, Hugh. *The Great Arab Conquests: How the Spread of Islam Changed the World We Live In*. Philadelphia: Da Capo, 2007.

Kimyagarov, Amnun. *Classic Central Asian (Bukharian) Jewish Cuisine and Customs*. New York: Alpha, 2010.

Klein, Misha. *Kosher Feijoada and Other Paradoxes of Jewish Life in São Paulo.* Gainesville, FL: University of Florida, 2012.
Kleinberg, Aviad, ed. *Beten m'leah: mabat acher al ochel v'chevra* [Full stomach: another look at food and society]. Jerusalem: Keter Books, 2005.
Koenig, Leah. *The Jewish Cookbook.* London: Phaidon, 2019.
Koerner, András. *A Taste of the Past: The Daily Life and Cooking of a Nineteenth-Century Hungarian Jewish Homemaker.* Lebanon, NH: University Press of New England, 2004.
———. *Jewish Cuisine in Hungary: A Cultural History with 83 Authentic Recipes.* Budapest: Central European University/Corvina, 2018.
Kort, Miriam. *Hamitbach shel Sanu* [Sanu's Kitchen]. Rishon Letzion, Israel, 2016.
*Kosher Cuisine.* Johannesburg: Yeshiva College, 2000. (Reprinted, 2021).
Koval, Ramona. *Jewish Cooking Jewish Cooks.* Sydney: New Holland, 2001.
[Krasilnikova, Tamara], T. Ram. *Алеф бейт еврейской кухни* [The aleph bet of Jewish cooking]. Jerusalem: Shvut Ami, 1990.
———. *The Aleph-Bet of Jewish Cooking.* Jerusalem: Shvut Ami International Center for Soviet Jews, 1991.

Lamm, Norman, trans. and ed. *The Religious Thought of Hasidism: Text and Commentary.* Hoboken, NJ: Ktav, 1999.
Larkey, Sue Spertus. *Bone Soup and Flipped Bread: The Yemenite Jewish Table.* Jerusalem: Modan/Geffen, 2017.
Lederer, Therese. *Israelitische Küche: Kochbuch für Originalgerichte der israelitischen Küche* [Israelite cuisine: cookbook for original dishes of Israelite cuisine]. Budapest: Dessauer, 1876. (Reprinted Bremen: Salzwasser-Verlag, 2010).
Leonard, Leah W. *Jewish Cookery: In Accordance with the Jewish Dietary Laws.* New York: Crown, 1949.
Lessa, Viviane & Léo Steinbruch. *Cozinha Judaica da Maria* [Maria's Jewish Kitchen]. Sao Paulo: Alaúde, 2011.
Lester, Osnat. *Tavshilei hamin shel shabbat* [Hamin Sabbath stews]. Israel: Sifrei Niv, 2017.
Levenson, Alan T. ed. *The Wiley-Blackwell History of Jews and Judaism.* Chichester, West Sussex, United Kingdom, 2012.
Levine, T. Gila. *Simply Israel: A Collection of Recipes from the People of Israel.* Israel: T. Gila Levine, 2007.
Levy, Esther. *The First Jewish-American Cookbook.* n.p.: 1871. (Reprinted Mineola, NY: Dover, 2004).
Levy-Mellul, Rivka. *Habishul hamorokai* [Moroccan Cooking]. Jerusalem: Beit Hahotza'ah HaYerushalmi, 1982,
Lewando, Fania. *The Vilna Vegetarian Cookbook.* Eve Jochnowitz, trans. New York: Schocken, 2015.
Lewi, Mady-Laure. *La Cuisine Juive de Constantine: Les 70 Recettes Incontournables pour Transmettre et se Régaler* [The Jewish cuisine of Constantine: The 70 essential recipes to share and enjoy]. Paris: Vérone éditions, 2018.
Liberzon, Rotem. *Mitbach parsi* [Persian kitchen]. Israel: LunchBox, 2017.
Loeb, Laurence D. *Outcaste: Jewish Life in Southern Iran.* New York: Gordon & Breach, 1977. (Reprinted Abingdon, England: Routledge, 2011).
Lurie, Sharon. *Cooking with the Kosher Butcher's Wife.* Cape Town: Struik, 2006.
Luzon, Tziki and Rinat Mizrachi. *Mah basimah: sefer hamatkonim shel Varda Nachum* [How tasty: recipe book of Varda Nachum]. Israel, 2015.

Marcus, Ivan G. *Jewish Culture and Society in Medieval France and Germany.* Farnham, England: Ashgate, 2014.

Marcus, Jacob R. *The Jew in the Medieval World: A Source Book: 315–1791*. New York: Meridian, 1938 (Reprinted 1960).

Marks, Copeland. *The Varied Kitchens of India: Cuisines of the Anglo-Indians of Calcutta, Bengalis, Jews of Calcutta, Kashmiris, Parsis, and Tibetans of Darjeeling*. New York: M. Evans, 1986.

Marks, Gil. *Encyclopedia of Jewish Food*. Hoboken, NJ: John Wiley & Sons, 2010.

McCagg, William I., Jr. *A History of Habsburg Jews, 1670–1918*. Bloomington: Indiana University, 1989.

Meisels, Dovid. *Shabbes Secrets: The Mysteries Revealed*. Avraham Yaakov Finkel, trans. Lakewood, NJ: Israel Book Shop, 2003.

Meyer, Erna. *Eich levashel b'Eretz Yisrael* [How to cook in the Land of Israel]. Tel Aviv: WIZO, [1936?]. https://archive.org/details/b21538505/mode/2up?view=theater.

Mikdash-Shamilov, Liya, ed., *Mountain Jews: Customs and Daily Life in the Caucasus*. Jerusalem: The Israel Museum, 2002.

[Montefiore, Judith] "A Lady," ed., *The Jewish Manual or Practical Information in Jewish & Modern Cookery with a Collection of Valuable Recipes & Hints Relating to the Toilette: A Facsimile of the First Jewish Cookbook in English Published in 1846*. Introduction by Chaim Raphael. London: T. & W. Boone, 1846. (Reprinted New York: NightinGale, 1983).

Moryoussef, Viviane and Nina. *350 Recettes de Cuisine Juive Marocaine* [350 recipes of Moroccan Jewish cuisine]. Paris: Grancher, 2007.

Muḥammad b. al-Ḥasan b. Muḥammad b. al-Karīm. *A Baghdad Cookery Book: The Book of Dishes (Kitāb al-Ṭabīkh)*. Charles Perry, trans. Blackawton, England: Prospect, 2005.

Nakhimovsky, Alice. "You Are What They Ate: Russian Jews Reclaim Their Foodways," in *Shofar: An Interdisciplinary Journal of Jewish Studies*, 25, no. 1 (Fall 2006), Special Issue: "Beyond Klezmer: The Legacy of Eastern European Jewry." Sander L. Gilman and Elizabeth Loentz, eds.: 63–77.

Nasrallah, Nawal. *Annals of the Caliphs' Kitchens*. Leiden, Netherlands: Brill, 2007.

———. *Treasure Trove of Benefits and Variety at the Table*. Leiden, Netherlands: Brill, 2018.

———. *Best of Delectable Foods and Dishes from Al-andalus and Al-maghrib: a Cookbook by Thirteenth-century Andalusi Scholar Ibn Razin Al-tujibi (1227–1293)*. Leiden, Netherlands: Brill, 2024.

———. *Smorgasbords of Andalusi and Maghribi Dishes and Their Salutary Benefits: English Translation of the Thirteenth-Century Cookbook*. Anwāʿ al-Ṣaydala fī Alwān al-Aṭʿima *with Introduction and Glossary*. Leiden, Netherlands: Brill, 2025.

Nathan, Joan. *Jewish Cooking in America, Expanded Edition*. New York: Alfred A. Knopf, 1998.

———. *Quiches, Kugels, and Couscous: My Search for Jewish Cooking in France*. New York: Alfred A. Knopf, 2010.

Nathans, Benjamin. *Beyond the Pale: The Jewish Encounter with Late Imperial Russia*. Berkeley, CA: University of California, 2002.

National Library of Israel. *Historical Jewish Press*. https://www.nli.org.il/en/discover/newspapers/jpress.

Netanyahu, Benzion. *The Marranos of Spain: From the Late XIVth to the Early XVIth Century According to Contemporary Hebrew Sources*. New York: American Academy for Jewish Research, 1966.

Newhouse, Alana, ed. *The 100 Most Jewish Foods: A Highly Debatable List*. New York: Artisan, 2019.

*Nuestras Mejores Recetas de Cocina* [Our best cooking recipes]. Caracas: WIZO Aviv Kadima, 1997.

Peretz, Gay, and Nissim Krispil. *Kesem hamitbach hamorokai* [The Magic of Moroccan Cuisine]. Tel Aviv/Jerusalem: Al Hashulchan/Keter, 2005.
Perez-Rubin, Pascale. *Matamim Tripolitaniyim* [Tripolitan foods]. Ra'anana, Israel: BRGS, 2005.
Perry, Charles. "*Kitab al-Tibakhah*: A Fifteenth Century Cookbook," *Petits Propos Culinaires*, 21 (November 1985): 17–22.
———, trans. *Scents and Flavors: A Syrian Cookbook*. New York: New York University, 2020.
Persoff, Menachem, ed. *The Jews in Syria*. Jerusalem: World Zionist Organization, 1975.
Petrovsky-Shtern, Yohanan. *The Golden Age Shtetl: A New History of Jewish Life in East Europe*. Princeton: Princeton University, 2014.
Piñer, Hélène Jawhara. *Jews, Food, and Spain: The Oldest Medieval Spanish Cookbook and the Sephardic Culinary Heritage*. Boston: Academic Studies Press, 2022.
Pintar, Lorenza. *Rebelot: Authentic Sephardic and Ashkenazi Italian Recipes*. n.p.: Lorenza Pintar, 2000.
Pintel-Ginsberg, Idit. *The Angel and the Cholent: Food Representation from the Israel Folktale Archives*. Detroit: Wayne State University, 2021.
Polliack, Meira, ed. *Karaite Judaism: A Guide to its History and Literary Sources*. Leiden, Netherlands: Brill, 2003.
Polonsky, Antony. *The Jews in Poland and Russia*, Vol. 1: *1350–1881*. Portland, OR: The Littman Library of Jewish Civilization, 2010.
Pomerantz, Kay Kantor. *Come For Cholent: The Jewish Stew Cookbook*. New York: Bloch, 1991.
———. *Come For Cholent Again: Cholent Stories and More Recipes*. New York: Bloch, 1994.
Pomiane, Édouard de. *The Jews of Poland: Recollections and Recipes*. Josephine Bacon, trans. Garden Grove, CA: Pholiota, 1985.
Project Kesher. *A Woman's Place Is in the Kitchen . . . and the Kremlin: The Project Kesher Cookbook*. Evanston, IL: Project Kesher, [2008?].

Rabinowitz, Louis. *Jewish Merchant Adventurers: A Study of the Radanites*. London: Edward Goldston, 1948.
Ram, Uri. *Jews in Germany: From Roman Times to the Weimar Republic*. Tel Aviv: Beth Hatefutsoth, The Nahum Goldmann Museum of the Diaspora, 1984.
———, *The Story of the Jews in Hungary*. Tel Aviv: Beth Hatefutsoth, The Nahum Goldmann Museum of the Jewish Diaspora, 1984.
*Recipes of Mountain Jewish Cuisine*. Moscow: STMEGI, 2016.
Rejwan, Nissim. *The Jews of Iraq: 3000 Years of History and Culture*. London: Weidenfeld & Nicolson, 1985.
Riley, James. *Sufferings in Africa: An authentic narrative of the loss of the American brig Commerce, wrecked on the western coast of Africa in the month of August, 1815* (New York: T&W Mercein, 1817). https://americanliterature.com/author/james-riley/book/sufferings-in-africa/chapter-xxviii.
Robinson, Avery. "Kugel and Pudding: Tasting Jewish American Foodways," unpublished master's thesis. Ann Arbor, MI: University of Michigan, 2014.
Roden, Claudia. *The Book of Jewish Food: An Odyssey from Samarkand and Vilna to the Present Day*. London: Penguin, 1996.
Rubin, Varda. *Ha'ochel shel mama: me'hamitbach hamitzri v'od* [Mama's food: from the Egyptian kitchen and more]. Israel, 2004.

*El Sabor de la Tradicion* [The taste of tradition]. Panama City: WIZO, 1993.
Sachar, Howard M. *Farewell España: The World of the Sephardim Remembered*. New York: Alfred A. Knopf, 1994.

Sarna, Jonathan D. *American Judaism: A History, Second Edition*. New Haven: Yale University, 2019.

Sassoon, Essie, Bala Menon, and Kenny Salem. *Spice & Kosher: Exotic Cuisine of the Cochin Jews*. Toronto: Tamarind Tree, 2013.

Sax, David. *Save the Deli: In Search of Perfect Pastrami, Crusty Rye, and the Heart of Jewish Delicatessen*. Boston: Mariner, 2010.

Schama, Simon. *The Story of the Jews*, Vol. 2: *Belonging 1492–1900*. New York: HarperCollins, 2017.

Segev, Tom. *1949: The First Israelis*. New York: Free Press, 1986. (Reprinted New York: Henry Holt, 1998.

*The Shalvi/Hyman Encyclopedia of Jewish Women*. https://www.jwa.org/encyclopedia.

Shilo, Varda. *Habishul hakurdi* [Kurdistani Cooking]. Jerusalem, 1986.

Shosteck, Patti. *A Lexicon of Jewish Cooking: A Collection of Folklore, Foodlore, History, Customs, and Recipes*. Chicago: Contemporary, 1979.

Shternshis, Anna. *Soviet and Kosher: Jewish Popular Culture in the Soviet Union, 1923–1939*. Bloomington, IN: Indiana University, 2006.

Sirkis, Ruth. *Meihamitbach b'ahava* [From the Kitchen with Love]. Tel Aviv: Zmora, Bitan, Modan, 1975.

——. *Popular Food From Israel*. Ramat Gan, Israel: R. Sirkis, 1985.

Sogolow, Rosalie, ed. *Memories from a Russian Kitchen: From Shtetl to Golden Land*. Santa Barbara, CA: Fithian, 1996.

Specht, Joshua. *Red Meat Republic: A Hoof-to-Table History of How Beef Changed America*. Princeton: Princeton University, 2019.

Spengler, Robert N., III. *Fruit from the Sands: The Silk Road Origins of the Foods We Eat*. Oakland, CA: University of California, 2019.

*Spice and Spirit: The Complete Kosher Jewish Cookbook*. Brooklyn, NY: Lubavitch Women's Cookbook Publications, 1990.

Spieler, Marlena. *Best-Ever Book of Jewish Cooking*. London: Hermes House, 2008/2010.

Spitzer, Emma. *Fress: Bold Flavors From a Jewish Kitchen*. London: Mitchell Beazley, 2017.

Stavans, Ilan and Margaret E. Boyle. *Sabor Judío: The Jewish Mexican Cookbook*. Chapel Hill, NC: University of North Carolina, 2024.

Stavroulakis, Nicholas. *Cookbook of the Jews of Greece*. Greece: Lycabettus, 1986.

Stein, Siegfried and Raphael Loewe, eds. *Studies in Jewish Religious and Intellectual History Presented to Alexander Altmann on the Occasion of his Seventieth Birthday*. Alabama: University of Alabama, 1979.

Steinberg, Ellen F. & Jack H. Prost. *From the Jewish Heartland: Two Centuries of Midwest Foodways*. Urbana, IL: University of Illinois, 2011.

Stern, Sacha, ed. *Sects and Sectarianism in Jewish History*. Leiden, Netherlands: Brill, 2011.

Sternberg, Alex. *Recipes from Auschwitz: The Survival Stories of Two Hungarian Jews with Historical Insight, Kindle Edition*. Woodsburgh, NY: Alex Sternberg, 2020.

Stessel, Zahava Szász. *Wine and Thorns in Tokay Valley: Jewish Life in Hungary: The History of Abaúszántó*. Madison, NJ: Fairleigh Dickinson University, 1995.

Stillman, Norman A. *The Jews of Arab Lands: A History and Source Book*. Philadelphia: Jewish Publication Society of America, 1979.

Stutchkoff, Nahum. *Der oytser fun der Yidisher shprakh* [Dictionary of the Yiddish language]. New York, NY: YIVO, 1950.

Sussman, Adeena. *Shabbat: Recipes and Rituals from My Table to Yours*. New York: Avery, 2023.

Ṭāhā, 'Abd al-Wāḥid Dhannūn. *The Muslim Conquest and Settlement of North Africa and Spain*. London: Routledge, 1989.

Twitty, Michael W. *Koshersoul*. New York: Amistad, 2022.
Tzabar, Naomi and Shimon. *Yemenite and Sabra Cookery*. Tel Aviv: Sadan, 1963.

Vaneker, Karin. "Cooking Pom," *Petits Propos Culinaires 83* (April 2007): 31–48.
Vaturi, Rossella Tammam. *La Cucina Ebraica Tripolina* [The Tripolitan Jewish Kitchen]. Firenze: Giuntina, 2005.
Veidlinger, Jeffrey. *In the Shadow of the Shtetl: Small-Town Jewish Life in Soviet Ukraine*. Bloomington, IN: Indiana University, 2013.
Vidal, Shula. *Matamei malchut: mitbach Morokai autenti* [Royal Delicacies: Authentic Moroccan Cuisine]. Israel: Shula Vidal, 2014.
Vitali-Norsa, Giuliana Ascoli. *La Cucina Nella Tradizione Ebraica* [Cuisine in the Jewish tradition]. Padova: Edizione dell'Adei Wizo, 1979.

Waines, David, ed. *Patterns of Everyday Life (The Formation of the Classical Islamic World, Vol. 10)*. Aldershot, United Kingdom: Ashgate-Variorum, [2002?].
Weinreich, Max. *History of the Yiddish Language*. Shlomo Noble, trans. Chicago: University of Chicago, 1980.
Weintraub, P. A. *Поваренная книга для евреекъ: болѣе четырехъ сотъ блюдъ, приготовляемыхъ по обрядамъ еврейской вѣры* [Cookbook for Jewish women: more than four hundred dishes prepared according to the rituals of the Jewish faith]. Kiev, 1889. (Reprinted Vladivostok: Jewish Religious and Cultural Community Center, 2000).
Weinryb, Bernard D. *The Jews of Poland: A Social and Economic History of the Jewish Community in Poland from 1100 to 1800*. Philadelphia: Jewish Publication Society of America, 1972.
Wexler, Paul. "'The Term 'Sabbath Food': A Challenge for Jewish Interlinguistics (Yiddish čolnt, šalet = Moroccan Yahudic sxīna versus Judezmo adefina, adafina = Algerian, Tunisian Yahudic dfīna = Iraqi Yahudic t(ə)bīt = (?) Yemenite Yahudic kubânäh, gilläh)," *Journal of the American Oriental Society*, vol. 98, no. 4, 1978, pp. 461–5. JSTOR, https://www.jstor.org/stable/599759.
William, Cutter and David C. Jacobson, eds. *History and Literature: New Readings of Jewish Texts in Honor of Arnold J. Band*. Providence, RI: Brown Judaic Studies, 2020.
Wirkowski, Eugeniusz. *Cooking the Polish-Jewish Way*. Hilda Rusiecka, trans. Warsaw: Interpress, 1988.
*World Jewish Congress*. https://www.worldjewishcongress.org.

*Yad Vashem*. https://www.yadvashem.org.

Zamir, Levana. *Matamei mitzraim* [Cooking from the Nile's Land]. Tel Aviv: Hitachdut Olei Mitzraim B'Yisrael, 2004.
Zana-Murat, Andrée. *De Mére en Fille: La Cuisine Juive Tunisienne* [From mother to daughter: Tunisian Jewish cuisine]. Paris: Albin Michel, 1998.
Zeitoun, Edmond. *250 Recettes Classiques de Cuisine Tunisienne* [250 classic recipes of Tunisian cuisine]. Paris: Jacques Grancher, 1977.
Zenner, Walter P. *A Global Community: The Jews from Aleppo, Syria*. Detroit: Wayne State University, 2000.
Ziegelman, Jane. *97 Orchard: An Edible History of Five Immigrant Families in One New York Tenement*, paperback edition. New York: HarperCollins Publishers, 2011.

# General Index

# Index of Recipes and Ingredients

Entries in **bold** refer to complete recipes. Ingredient entries are given for major (including optional) items only (no salt or black pepper, for example).